Arab Nationalism
AN ANTHOLOGY

PUBLISHED UNDER THE AUSPICES OF THE NEAR EASTERN CENTER
UNIVERSITY OF CALIFORNIA, LOS ANGELES

rab Nationalism

AN ANTHOLOGY

Selected and Edited, with
an Introduction, by Sylvia G. Haim

University of California Press / Berkeley, Los Angeles, London

UNIVERSITY OF CALIFORNIA PRESS

Berkeley and Los Angeles, California

UNIVERSITY OF CALIFORNIA PRESS, LTD.

London, England

In Memory of
My Father, Gourgi Haim

Preface

IN THIS ANTHOLOGY of Arab Nationalism I have tried to give a complete picture of the literature on the subject and have therefore chosen every piece either for its historical importance or because it best represents some noteworthy current of opinion. Throughout the book the text in each instance is given in full, even at the risk of repetitiveness, in order to retain the flavor of the original. I have selected and translated all the pieces myself. The transliteration of Arabic into English has been kept as simple as possible, using the more familiar English forms where these exist, and dispensing with all but a few essential diacritical markings. No glossary has been included, but in certain cases, for greater precision, I have included the Arabic word in brackets. In the bibliography, however, I have found it more exact to give cross references to variant spellings of the names of Gamal Abdel Nasser, C. Zurayk, and N. Ziadeh, in order to make the listing of published works in Arabic more uniform. Footnotes to the introduction, of course, are entirely mine; footnotes to the various sections of the anthology are by their respective authors, unless they are followed by my initials. Because the nature of the book does not seem to call for an index, none has been provided.

I would like to thank M. Jean Vigneau of the Centre de Documentation et de Synthèse, Paris, for putting at my disposal the French text of the Constitution of the Ba'th Party, which I have not been able to obtain in the original Arabic. I also want to express my gratitude to Professor G. E. von Grunebaum, Director of the University of California's Near Eastern Center, Los Angeles, for his assistance in making the publication of this book possible.

The article by Charles Malik is reprinted here by special permission of *Foreign Affairs*, articles published in that periodical being copyrighted by the Council on Foreign Relations, Incorporated, New York.

SYLVIA G. HAIM

Contents

Introduction

Introduction

ARAB NATIONALISM as an ideology and as a factor in Middle Eastern politics is a recent development. It was hardly known before the beginning of the twentieth century, and it was only after the First World War (that is, after the setting up of Iraq, Palestine, Syria, and the Lebanon as mandated territories under British and French rule) that a comprehensive doctrine of Arab nationhood was elaborated. Thereupon, politicians in Iraq and Syria, enjoying a measure of independent action and able to exploit the rivalries of the Great Powers in the Middle East, began to attempt the creation of a state which would embrace the whole of the "Arab Nation."

Some writers, it is true, would date the beginnings of Arab Nationalism much earlier. Thus, George Antonius, in his book *The Arab Awakening* (1938), sees manifestations of Arab resurgence—in this instance ephemeral, it is true—in the Wahabi movement which originated in Nejd toward the end of the eighteenth century, and in Muhammad Ali's attempt to found a Near Eastern empire based on Egypt and the territories of the Levant. Such views, however, seem to lack historical evidence. The Wahabis were not nationalists by any acceptable definition of the term; they were purists, rather, who wished to restore Islam to what they took to be its original austere purity. Their concern was with Islam, not with the Arabs, and they directed their zeal against lax, backsliding, or heretical Muslims rather than toward the creation of an Arab national state. As for Muhammad Ali, he was a dynast and an opportunist who tried to take advantage of

3

the enfeeblement of his Ottoman masters and of Anglo-French rivalry in the Levant in order to enlarge the domain which luck, circumstance, and his own considerable ability had enabled him to seize and retain. As his methods of government in Egypt show, he would have been skeptical of the use or value of ideology as a tool of political power, and it is safe to say that had he attempted to use it in the Levant he would have found it useless, since it is generally agreed that in his times political passions in the Middle East were stirred by religion, not nationality.

Another manifestation of emergent Arab nationalism, one to which Antonius attaches greater importance, is the founding of a secret society in Beirut pledged to the eviction of the Ottomans from Syria. But such a society could not have been very important politically, since its activity—whatever it was—aroused no echo and led to no result. Further, Arab nationalism, as an ideology and a political force, was the work of men quite different in their circumstances and views from those who belonged to this society. One bit of testimony, drawn from personal experience, may be cited in support of this view. It is that of Faris Nimr Pasha (circa 1854–1951). Born and educated in the Lebanon, Faris Nimr emigrated to Cairo in 1885, and there, together with Ya'qub Sarruf and Shahin Makkarius, he founded the well-known *Muqattam* newspaper a year later. He gave his recollections to Professor Z. N. Zeine, who has recorded them in his book *Arab-Turkish Relations and the Emergence of Arab Nationalism* (Beirut, 1958). A group of young Christians, including Faris Nimr, Ibrahim al-Yaziji, Ya'qub Sarruf, and Shahin Makkarius, who were studying at the Syrian Protestant College (later the University of Beirut), fell under the influence of a Maronite, a teacher of French at the college, who advocated advanced and revolutionary views. He talked politics to his students and inculcated in them the desire to eject the Ottomans from the Lebanon and to end Muslim supremacy over the Christians. These young men took their ideas so far as to write and surreptitiously post in public places certain anti-Ottoman proclamations, many of them, as Faris Nimr has recorded, in his own handwriting. They soon decided, however, that Ottoman domination could be ended only if local Muslim support were forthcoming. Approaches to the Muslims were made, but these proved to be fruitless, and as Faris Nimr put it, the group "became convinced that between the Christians and the

4

Muslims no agreement or understanding could be reached on the expulsion of the Turks from Lebanon and therefore no united action was possible." The society was dissolved in 1882–83.[1]

Seen in the light of these facts, the poem by Ibrahim al-Yaziji exhorting the Arabs to awaken and arise (the first verse Antonius prints as an epigraph to his book) is not, as has been represented, a nationalist manifesto. Rather, it is an appeal by a Christian to Muslims to adopt certain European political ideas; these ideas, if accepted, would end the inferior position of the Christians and raise them to equality with the Muslims. Such an interpretation of the poem is confirmed by the fact that after the first line al-Yaziji exhorts the Muslims to forget religious divisions and abjure fanaticism. They ought to remember that among the Arabs there are both Christians and Muslims.[2] Another writer, the scholar Ettore Rossi, has also dated the beginning of Arab nationalism rather earlier than the facts seem to warrant. His collection of documents relating to the Arab movement is entitled *Documenti Sull'origine e gli Sviluppi della Questione Araba 1875–1944;*[3] but in choosing 1875 as his starting point, Rossi is following Antonius, for the first document in his collection is the manifesto

---

[1] Z. N. Zeine, *Arab-Turkish Relations and the Emergence of Arab Nationalism* (Beirut, 1958), pp. 56–57. See further S. G. Haim, "The Arab Awakening: A Source for the Historian?" *Die Welt des Islams*, n.s., II (1953), no. 4, pp. 238–250.

[2] One view of the circumstances in which this and a similar composition were written by al-Yaziji is suggested by Jurji Zaidan, who had been intimate with him during his last years in Cairo, when he says in his notice of him that the poems were possibly written on the order of a prominent person or at the suggestion of a group. See *Tarajim mashahir al-sharq fi'l-qarn al-tasi' ashar* (*Biographies of Celebrated Men of the East in the Nineteenth Century*) (3d ed.; Cairo, 1922), II, 115. A pamphlet published in New York in 1910 containing one of al-Yaziji's supposedly anti-Turkish poems has a preface which states that it was Midhat Pasha, when vali of Syria, who made al-Yaziji write the poem in order to frighten the Sultan into reforming the empire. See Ibrahim al-Yaziji, *al-arab wa'l-turk* (*Arabs and Turks*) (New York, 1910). It seems that Abdul Hamid was afraid that Midhat wanted to establish himself as ruler of an independent Syria; indeed, it is a fact that Midhat forcefully urged that greater authority be given to governors of provinces and that less control be exerted by Constantinople. See the *Memoirs* of Midhat Pasha, Arabic translation by Yusuf Kamal Hatata (Cairo, 1913), pp. 43–44, 118. Lady Anne Blunt, in her book A *Pilgrimage to Nejd* (London, 1881), vol. I, p. 18, writes: "Midhat's reign at Damascus lasted for twenty months and is remarkable only for the intrigues in which it was spent. The rest of his time and resources were spent in an attempt to gain for himself the rank and title of khedive, a scheme which ended in his recall."

[3] Rome, 1944.

of 1880 produced by Faris Nimr and his friends. It is noteworthy that between this and the next document in the collection there is a gap of twenty-five years.

To argue that Arab nationalism is a twentieth-century phenomenon, however, is not to say that its appearance in this century is a mere fortuitous event. On the contrary, considered as a doctrine, and divorced from the accidents of war and politics which have facilitated its prodigious spread, it is possible to see in it the outcome of the severe intellectual crisis that Islam experienced during the nineteenth century, and from which it emerged damaged, enfeebled, no longer the living faith shared by ruler and subject, but as an ideology, a political weapon against European domination or else a system of ethics which educated men, unable to believe in revelation but shrinking from atheism, were disposed to adopt as most convenient and least contentious.

The assault which Islam had to endure in the nineteenth century was twofold. It consisted, in the first place, of military attack on Muslim states or their political subjugation by different European powers, and, in the second place, of criticism of Islam as a system of beliefs and a way of life, a way of life that was belittled, ridiculed, and made to seem backward and barbaric in comparison with the achievements of Western learning, philosophy, and technical advance. The latter attack was perhaps even more dangerous and insidious than political and military subjugation, for it could penetrate the spiritual defenses of the Muslim community and of its intellectual leaders, thereby effecting a dissolution of Islam such as foreign rule, by itself, could hardly accomplish. In so parlous a situation, Islam was bound to make many attempts at its own defense, and of these attempts the most significant, and certainly the most influential, was that of Jamal al-Din al-Afghani.

Jamal al-Din al-Asadabadi (1838–1897), commonly known as al-Afghani, was the very type of revolutionary conspirator and activist so well known in Europe in modern times. It is only his remoteness from the main stream of European history, together with his clerical garb, his reputation as a religious thinker and controversialist (a reputation resting on very slender evidence), and the scant and contradictory nature of the facts of his life, that may have obscured the true character of the man and the real nature and portent of his activities. His very name and origin

6

are subject to dispute: in the Ottoman Empire, in Egypt, and in Europe, he was commonly known as al-Afghani, and it seems he himself desired to be known by the latter name. But in Persia he was known as al-Asadabadi. There now seems little doubt that he was in fact a Persian Shiite born of a family tracing its origin to the Prophet. He also called himself Jamal al-Din al-Husaini, however, thereby claiming descent from Husain, the son of Ali, the fourth caliph, and the cousin and son-in-law of the Prophet. Outside Persia he adopted the surname of al-Afghani, perhaps wishing to avoid the imputation of Shiism among Sunni Muslims, or perhaps to disavow any connection with Persia, with whose government he was usually on bad terms. Indeed, the Shah, Nasir al-Din, expelled him from Persia in 1891, and the Persian government sought his extradition from Istanbul, charging him with implication in the murder of Nasir al-Din, in 1896.[4]

Both the activities and the teaching of al-Afghani contributed to the spread of revolutionary temper and a new attitude toward politics all over the Muslim East. He was everywhere: he was deeply involved in Afghan politics and diplomacy; he lived among the Indian Muslims; his short stay in Egypt ended in expulsion because of his subversive activities. In Paris, where he lived for a time, he edited an influential newspaper, *al Urwa al-wuthqa* (*The Indissoluble Link*) and preached Muslim unity and solidarity in the face of European encroachments. From Paris he went to Persia, to Russia, then back to Persia, the country from which he was finally expelled. Exiled beyond the Persian borders, he was nevertheless instrumental in engineering a successful boycott of

---

[4] Details of the early life of Jamal al-Din are found in the book written by his nephew, Mirza Lutfallah Khan. It was published in Persian in 1926 and translated into Arabic by Sadiq Nash'at and Abd al-Nadim Hasanain, *Jamal al-Din al-Asadabadi al-ma'ruf bi'l-Afghani* (*Jamal al-Din al-Asadabadi Known as al-Afghani*) (Cairo, 1957). See also E. G. Browne, *The Persian Revolution* (Cambridge, 1910), and the article by I. Goldziher on Jamal al-Din in *The Encyclopaedia of Islam* (1st ed.). A despatch from the United States Minister to Egypt dated March 17, 1936 (no. 883.91/1) records the researches of the Secretary of Legation, J. R. Childs, while on a visit to Persia, into the mystery of al-Afghani's origin. Childs satisfied himself, on the basis of published investigations of Persian scholars and the presence of al-Afghani's relatives in Iran, that al-Afghani was a native of Iran, and that he assumed the title of Al-Afghani in order that his Shiite origin should not vitiate his influence with the Sunni world of Afghanistan, Turkey, and Egypt. I am indebted for the latter information to my husband, Elie Kedourie.

tobacco in Persia, in protest against the Shah's granting the tobacco monopoly to a foreign *concessionaire*. He then went to
London, where he produced a newspaper attacking the Shah; and
he spent the last few years of his life, busy with intrigue and
politics, as the pensioner of the Sultan, in Istanbul.

Of the political methods which he favored, a few examples
have been recorded. He spent some eight years in Egypt, from
1871 to 1879. During that time he became a leader of al-hizb
al-watani (The National Party), a secret society of some 300
young Egyptians who were discontented with the maladministra-
tion of the Khedive Ismail and with the ever-increasing hold of
Europeans over the country. He preached to them direct action
as the remedy for their ills. In a speech at Alexandria he said:
"Oh! you poor fellah! you break the heart of the earth in order
to draw sustenance from it and support your family. Why do you
not break the heart of your oppressor? Why do you not break
the heart of those who eat the fruit of your labor?" [5] He headed
a delegation of Egyptians to the French consul general to demand the deposition of Ismail.

As W. S. Blunt recounts, al-Afghani proposed to his disciple
Muhammad Abduh (1849–1905), later Mufti of Egypt, that
Ismail should be assassinated; "Sheikh Jemal ed Din proposed to
me, Mohammed Abdu," Blunt records him as saying, "that Ismail
should be assassinated some day as he passed in his carriage daily
over the Kasr-el-Nil bridge, and I strongly approved, but it was
only talk between ourselves, and we lacked a person capable of
taking lead in the affair." [6] It was al-Afghani, again, who induced
and encouraged the assassin of Nasir al-Din Shah, in 1896, to do
his deed. A Persian friend, Mirza Husain Khan Danish, recounted
many years later that a fortnight or so before this assassination
he visited al-Afghani at his house in Istanbul and found him
pacing his room, oblivious of his surroundings and shouting with
frenzy: "There is no deliverance except in killing, there is no
safety except in killing." [7] When the murderer, al-Afghani's former servant, was being interrogated concerning his accomplices

---

[5] Quoted in Ahmad Shafiq Pasha, *Mudhakkirati fi nisf qarn* (*My Memoirs during Half a Century*) (Cairo, 1936), I, 109.

[6] W. S. Blunt, *Secret History of the British Occupation of Egypt* (new ed.; 1924), p. 489.

[7] Mirza Lutfallah Khan, *op. cit.* (Arabic trans.), p. 134.

and sympathizers, he said: "Those who think like me are legion in this city and in this kingdom. I have thousands of accomplices among the ulemas, the ministers, the merchants, and you know it! When Sayyid Jamal al-Din came to this city, all, whatever their status, hastened to see him and listened to what he had to say. Everybody profited from what he heard. It was he who sowed the seeds of these high thoughts in our hearts. Then men awoke, understanding burgeoned, and now everybody thinks as I do! But I swear by God, the Creator of Sayyid Jamal al-Din, and my Creator, that nobody except myself and him knew of my plan." The assassin further gloried in the fact that he had struck the Shah down on the very spot where al-Afghani had been seized to be deported from Persia.[8]

Al-Afghani justified his political activity by a simple theory. The Islamic peoples of the world were in a deplorable situation; the states which ought to protect them and procure for them a good life were weak, misgoverned, and the prey of European ambitions. To remedy this state of affairs, the Muslims had to take matters into their own hands; they had to force, even terrorize, their rulers into governing efficiently, and they had to band together in order to present a powerful and united front to the encroaching European. In this enterprise Islam was the essential factor. It was the only bond of union between the Muslims, and if this bond could be strengthened, if it were to become the spring of their lives and the focus of their loyalty, then prodigious forces of solidarity would be engendered to make possible the creation and maintenance of a strong and stable state. Al-Afghani's political projects centered, therefore, on Pan-Islamism, or a union of Muslim states, and it was this which perhaps made Abdul Hamid, who was himself interested in Pan-Islamism, welcome him to Istanbul.

But it is clear that such a view of the role of Islam in the life of the Muslims is very different from the traditional one. The traditional and orthodox view is that the Muslims are Muslims because they believe in the revelation of God to Muhammad, and because they order their lives according to divine law. They are not Muslims because Islam constitutes a powerful political force

---

[8] A.-M. Goichon, p. 17 of the introduction to her translation of al-Afghani's treatise, *Réfutation des Matérialistes* (Paris, 1942), quoting *Revue du Monde Musulman*, XII, 612–614.

which enables men to band together in a strong state and successfully withstand their enemies. Al-Afghani, it can be said, transformed Islam into an ideology which the shrewd statesman can utilize to effect his ends. He was a remarkable man, and we may suspect that he did not advance such views inadvertently or, as it were, unawares. In matters of religion, it would seem, he was a skeptic. He was also, it must be remembered, a Shiite who had studied theology in his youth under the Persian divines, and Shiism, as is well known, may easily tend to Sufi esotericism, or to that *falsafa* which transforms the Allah of the Koran into an impersonal Principle, First Cause, or some other rationalist concept.

What is clear is that in both Egypt and Constantinople his public teaching aroused great suspicion among the orthodox theologians. In 1870, he gave an address in Constantinople on arts and crafts and their place within the body politic. He likened human society to the human body, in which every organ had to perform its appointed function if the happiness of the whole was to be attained. This happiness, however, depended not only on the mundane activities of the organs, but also on the activity of the soul; in the body politic the soul was either philosophy or prophecy. The Sheikh al-Islam took great exception to this view, and accused al-Afghani of debasing Muhammad's prophetic office to the level of a craft, and, as A.-M. Goichon rightly points out,[9] he was somewhat justified, since the tendency of al-Afghani's argument was to emphasize, in a manner contrary to orthodox teaching, the social or utilitarian function of prophecy. His skepticism concerning Islam as a religion comes out very clearly in the well-known rejoinder he made to Ernest Renan in the *Journal des Débats* in 1883.[10] Renan had given an address on Islam and science in which he had argued that Islam was, in its essence, opposed to science, and that the Arabs were by nature indifferent to metaphysics and philosophy. Al-Afghani sought to rebut Renan's views and pointed out that it was the Muslims who had transmitted Aristotle to the West. Significantly enough, however, he agreed with Renan that Islam had sought to arrest scientific activity. But in this, he said, Islam's attitude was similar to that of the Christian Church; the conclusion he was driving at was

---

[9] *Ibid.*, p. 41, n. 2.
[10] A.-M. Goichon reprints al-Afghani's answer to Renan, *ibid.*, pp. 174–185.

that every religion could be obscurantist, and that it was not right to conclude that Muslims would remain forever ignorant and backward. "Every time that religion has the upper hand," he concluded, "it will eliminate philosophy; and the contrary happens when philosophy rules as a sovereign mistress. So long as humanity exists, the struggle between dogma and free enquiry, between religion and philosophy will not cease, a bitter struggle in which the victory will not, I fear, lie with free thought, because reason does not attract the masses, and its teachings are understood only by a few choice spirits, and also because science, however beautiful it is, does not wholly satisfy humanity, which is athirst for an ideal which it likes to place in obscure and distant regions which philosophers and men of science can neither discern nor explore."

In this passage, which it must be remembered was not destined for a Muslim audience, al-Afghani's religious skepticism is fully manifest, as is also the sharp distinction—perhaps one of the fundamental features of his thought, surely derived from the tradition of heterodox esotericism and *falsafa* in Islam—between the vulgar mass lost in illusions and the clear knowledge, unclouded by prejudices or sentimental yearnings, reserved for the elect few. The vulgar mass needs religion, its gaze is too weak to behold the truth without intermediaries and without the help of myths or "ideals."

Another facet of his utilitarian, skeptical, and activist bent remains to be mentioned. His Persian friend, Mirza Husain Khan Danish, recounts that he heard al-Afghani say on different occasions: "There are two kinds of philosophy in the world. One of them is to the effect that there is nothing in the world which is ours, so we must remain content with a rag and a mouthful of food. The other is to the effect that everything in the world is beautiful and desirable, that it does and ought to belong to us. It is the second which should be our ideal, to be adopted as our motto. As for the first, it is worthless, and we must pay no attention to it." [11]

If the good things of the world can and should be ours, and if, also, the vulgar mass has need of religion, then the proper political strategy consists in making use of this need to attain

---

[11] Mirza Lutfallah Khan, *op. cit.* (Arabic trans.), p. 135.

the desired aim. Politics is a secular activity; its end is earthly
happiness, and its tools are human wills and human loyalties.
These considerations, then, govern the political teaching addressed to the mass. An essay published in *al-Urwa al-wuthqa*,
entitled "The Causes of the Preservation of Rule," begins by
saying that a people does not meet with catastrophe except
through its own fault. Natural factors and supernatural prescriptions of course have a share in determining the fate of humanity,
and these are beyond men's power, may even be hidden from the
understanding, but the effect of men's behavior on their social
institutions is easily discerned by any man of intelligence. The
first requirement of good social institutions is that men should
seek consensus in common matters, and unite by the tie of so-
ciability one to another; this is the foundation of power and com-
modious life on this earth, and of happiness hereafter. This is
why—and al-Afghani's utilitarian interpretation of religion is here
characteristic—God has exhorted men in the Koran to avoid dissension and to be united in clinging to His power and protection.
Dissension, arbitrariness, estrangement between ruler and ruled,
preference of individual interests over the common interest are
so many causes of political ruin. Every man must do the work
peculiar to his station, and must not sink into luxury and self-
indulgence. The best safeguard of private interests is the advancement of the public interest. This maxim is incumbent on
the ruler even more than on the subject. And here al-Afghani
embarks on a philippic against rulers who consider their own interests first, and who are negligent of the public interest and
fail to defend it against foreign cupidity.

If we consider the history of Islamic states, al-Afghani goes on
to say, we shall see that precisely these are the causes of their
ruin: they have indulged in dissension, they have given their confidence to men of doubtful loyalty, they have failed to consider
the public interest and have been negligent in its defense.[12] The
Muslims had once followed their religion devoutly, and their state
was strong, so that the foreigner had no hold over them because
the religion preserved their unity and imbued them with soli-

[12] "Asbab hifd al-mulk," in *al-Urwa al-wuthqa* (Beirut ed.; 1933), pp.
228–237.

Introduction

darity. Solidarity (*asabiyya*)[13] is indeed the concept which, for al-Afghani, sums up all the desirable features of a polity, which make it strong and able to look after the welfare of its members. It was the Islamic religion, as he explained, which earlier endowed the disunited Arab tribes with a strong enough solidarity and *esprit de corps* to enable them to conquer and maintain a powerful empire in less than eighty years. This empire declined and disappeared, in due course, but the reason was not that the Muslims had become fewer in numbers; on the contrary, their numbers were never greater than when they lost their power. Rather, the decline in power was to be attributed to the weakening of the influence of religion in the soul of the Arabs, a religion which had been able, better than any feeling of race and kinship, to unify them and make them into a great conquering force.[14]

Solidarity, or *asabiyya*, is, then, the primary requirement in human society, and religion may be said to be an efficient machine for the production of solidarity. That this is not an exaggeration of al-Afghani's attitude becomes clear when we consider his comparison of the efficacy of the bonds of nationality (*jinsiyya*) and of religion respectively. Men, he explains, are naturally found in groups which are in conflict with one another over subsistence, security, and riches. This conflict forces the different groups to unite according to the bonds of kinship, and to form nations such as the Hindu, the English, the Russian. Thus, national solidarity is called forth and subsists by the power of necessity; and should the necessity disappear, it, too, will disappear. In the case of the Muslims, a revealed religion came to create a higher solidarity transcending different national solidarities which the Muslims have therefore abandoned.[15]

Al-Afghani himself believed that true Islamic solidarity was far more effective than national solidarity. But if efficacy be the criterion, and if Islamic solidarity be shown to be less efficacious

---

[13] On the origin and derivation of '*asabiyya* see no. 1 in the anthology: Rashid Rida, "Islam and the National Idea."

[14] Muhammad al-Makhzumi, *Khatirat Jamal al-Din al-Afghani* (*The Opinions of Jamal al-Din al-Afghani*) (Beirut, 1931), p. 257. This book is a record of the conversations which al-Afghani held with its author during his last years in Istanbul. The similarity of al-Afghani's views on solidarity with those of Ibn Khaldun is to be noted.

[15] *Ibid.*, pp. 421–425.

than some other kind, then it is fair to infer that al-Afghani would prefer the more to the less efficacious. Nor is evidence for such an inference lacking, for he warned the Muslims that the Western assault on them was not merely military or political, but cultural as well. To adopt a Western language in preference to an Eastern was, for the Muslims, an insidious and most perilous trap, for, he said, "a people without unity, and a people without literature is a people without language. A people without history is a people without glory, and a people will lack history if authorities do not rise among them, to protect and revivify the memory of their historical heroes so that they may follow and emulate. All this depends on a national (*watani*) education which begins with "the homeland" (*watan*), the environment of which is "the homeland," and the end of which is "the homeland"! [16] In calling for this kind of national solidarity, al-Afghani, in this passage, was not necessarily opposing it to Islamic solidarity. Indeed, since his purpose was to mobilize the Muslims against Europe, "national" and Islamic solidarity may, in his thinking, have been designed to reinforce each other. But he could and did go further, and in one article he actually showed his preference for "national" solidarity as more efficacious than any other in gaining and establishing political power. In this article, written in Persian, al-Afghani actually argued that a "national" unity based on a common language was both more powerful and more durable than one based on a common religion. Men may easily change their religion, he argued, but not so easily their language.[17] Sati' al-Husri mentions that al-Afghani had prefaced the article with a few lines in Arabic which read: "There is no happiness except through nationality (*al-jinsiyya*) and no nationality except through language. There is no language except it contains all that may be necessary to the needs of the professions and the crafts in the way of usefulness and self-improvement."

These opinions of al-Afghani have been mentioned not to establish that he was a precursor of Arab nationalism—for this, in the strict sense, he never was—but to show how radically he

---

[16] *Ibid.*, p. 140.

[17] The article is partially translated from the Persian by Mehdi Hendessi, "Pages peu connues de Djamal al-Din al-Afghani," in *Orient*, no. 6 (1958), 123–128; see also *Sati' al-Husri, Ma hiya al-qaumiyya?* (*What Is Nationalism?*) (Beirut, 1959), p. 225.

transformed the significance which Islam ought to hold in the life of the Muslim. Ultimately, he was prepared to equate national solidarity to religious solidarity, and to prefer the former should it prove more effective than the latter. But his ideas on national solidarity could not have been widely known in Arabic-speaking lands: the *Khatirat* were not published until 1931, and his Persian works still remain untranslated.[18] What al-Afghani did was to make Islam into the mainspring of solidarity, and thus he placed it on the same footing as other solidarity-producing beliefs. His political activity and teaching combined to spread among the intellectual and official classes of Middle Eastern Islam a secularist, meliorist, and activist attitude toward politics, an attitude the presence of which was essential, before ideologies such as Arab nationalism could be accepted in any degree. It is this which makes al-Afghani so important a figure in modern Islamic politics.

The man and his teaching exercised this prodigious influence not only because they were remarkable in their own right, but also because they found an answering chord in the predicament of Muslim society. If al-Afghani had not voiced such sentiments and views it is likely that somebody else would have done so.

ISLAM, WESTERN CIVILIZATION, AND THE YOUNG TURKS

The same emphasis on solidarity, the same search for the secret of European power, the same exhortatory fervor, characterizes the writings of another Muslim whose reputation, it is true, was local and circumscribed. Abdullah al-Nadim (1843–1896) was a radical Egyptian journalist and orator who played a prominent role in rousing the populace at the time of Urabi's rebellion; it is significant, also, that he had been one of al-Afghani's circle during his Egyptian years in the 1870's. In one of his articles, al-Nadim discusses the reasons for the backwardness of the East and for the success of Europe. He dismisses the reason usually offered by Europeans, namely the nature of Islam; he points out that the Eastern adherents of other religions are even more back-

---

[18] The article on national unity and its linguistic basis, translated into French by M. Hendessi, is said by Sati' al-Husri, *op. cit.*, to have been translated and published in a Turkish periodical in 1913.

ward than the Muslims. The success of the Europeans is not
bound up with the nature of their religion, but with certain political practices. European states have unified the language of
their subjects, while oriental rulers have allowed their subjects to
retain their own different languages; in European states the race
(*jins*) too has been gradually unified, and religious uniformity
imposed. It is characteristic that al-Nadim should find one other
principal reason for the success of Europe, namely the unity
which European rulers have maintained among themselves in
order to fight the East. This, of course, relates not to any feature
of European history, but to al-Nadim's belief that such unity was
desirable among Muslims, had existed in the past, and had now
disappeared, to their detriment.[19] He exhorts the Muslims to restore and preserve Muslim solidarity (*asabiyya*), and also to combine with the Copt and the Jew in support of national union (*al-
Jami'a al-wataniyya*) "and let the whole be as one man, seeking
only one thing, namely to preserve Egypt for the Egyptians." [20]

This passage again illustrates the point that if religion is prized
for its political virtues alone, then it is easy to attach it to systems with which it had been held incompatible: for to an orthodox Muslim, religious solidarity would have ruled out any thought
of solidarity with Copts and Jews, who under Islamic law could
not be full members of the body politic. But al-Nadim, preoccupied with power, sees no incompatibility between Islamic and
national solidarity, provided they serve the purpose for which
they are required. The irony and paradox of views such as those
of al-Afghani and al-Nadim is that by seeking to preserve Islamic
society against European encroachments they advocated methods
which could only increase skepticism concerning Islam and the
efficacity of Islamic institutions and Islamic solidarity. But these
were distant consequences which, most probably, were not apparent to al-Afghani or al-Nadim.

Another modern Islamic figure has contributed by his teaching
and example, albeit in a different manner, to increase the skepticism of the literate classes concerning traditional Islam. This was
Muhammad Abduh who was, himself, closely connected with al-
Afghani for nearly fifteen years, from the 1870's when al-Afghani

---

[19] Abdullah al-Nadim, *Sulafat al-Nadim* (A Collection of Articles by al-
Nadim) (Cairo, 1901), I, 99–120.
[20] *Ibid.*, II, 78.

was in Egypt until the newspaper *al-Urwa al-wuthqa* ceased publication in 1884, when they seem to have parted in some estrangement. But this long and close connection should not lead one to minimize the great difference in character between the two men. Though Muhammad Abduh fell, for a time, under al-Afghani's spell and was even ready to entertain thoughts of political assassination, yet he was not an activist, and did not have al-Afghani's utilitarian view of Islam. In youth, while he was associated with al-Afghani, he was an advocate of political reform and of constitutional government. The political situation of Egypt under Ismail must have gradually inclined him to political radicalism; he became involved in Urabi's rebellion, as a sympathizer but by no means as an uncompromising partisan, and for this he was sentenced to exile outside Egypt. But when he parted from al-Afghani, in 1885, he seems to have decided to eschew grandiose political action (and this, it seems, was the reason for his estrangement from al-Afghani[21]) and to have decided to make his peace with the authorities. Cromer had a high regard for him, and it was owing to his support that he advanced steadily in official positions and ended his life as Mufti of Egypt.

The teaching that is particularly associated with him concerns the compatibility and congruence of Islam and modernity, as well as the necessity for Muslims to abjure outdated superstitions and to strive to acquire the blessings of Western civilization. In theological and apologetic writings, in his commentary on the Koran, and in his official pronouncements as a religious-legal dignitary, he tried always to show that the evidence of Islam and its prescriptions were fully rational and consonant with the conclusions of modern science and philosophy. But in order to prove his point, Muhammad Abduh had necessarily to jettison large parts of recorded Islamic history as being either superstitious or out of line with the presumed original teaching of the Prophet, and he had always to be seeking that kernel of timeless truth which would make Islam acceptable to modern science and philosophy. The logical end of such an attitude is that in the truth which they seek and affirm all religions are at one among themselves, and at one also with philosophy. But this attempt to make

---

[21] See Muhammad Rashid Rida, *Tarikh al-ustadh al-imam* (*Biography of Muhammad Abduh*) (Cairo, 1931), I, 894–897, for Abduh's account of this estrangement.

Islam fully rational, to forswear all dogma, as well as all the positive features which actually distinguish one religion from another, was certain to discredit traditional orthodoxy and effect a radical break with an immemorial way of life. It is interesting, in this connection, to note that while Abduh was in Beirut, before returning from his exile to Egypt, he was suspected of having founded a secret society to effect a *rapprochement* between Islam, Christianity, and Judaism;[22] and again, it is not an accident that Cromer suspected that "my friend Abduh, although he would have resented the appellation being applied to him, was in reality an agnostic." [23] Another consequence of this view is that religion ceases to be properly religion and is transformed into a system of ethics or rules for successful conduct in this life, rather than a discipline preparatory of the last judgment and life hereafter. His diagnosis of the present state of Islam can be summed in one word, stagnation *(jumud)*. This stagnation is not inherent in Islam as such, but is the result of despotic rule and obscurantist theology. Once these are removed—and they can be removed— science and religion, he was firmly convinced, would walk side by side in fraternity, as the Koran envisaged.[24]

In all of this there is, of course, no nationalism. The relevance of Muhammad Abduh to the study of Arab nationalism lies in the fact that he exemplified and made popular a hopeful attitude toward politics, a belief that human action, based on rational and scientific principles, could ameliorate the human condition. He felt that the intellectual, by denouncing superstitions and propagating science and philosophy, held the key to political and social progress. Needless to say, such an attitude is a radical departure from the attitude of the traditional intellectual leaders of Islam, whether they were in the mainstream of orthodoxy or were philosophers transmitting a corpus of esoteric knowledge deeply suspect to orthodoxy. In the first category, al-Ghazali, with his political pessimism and his clinging to the sheet-anchor of Revelation, and in the second, Ibn Bajja, who looked on the philosopher as a solitary shunning the wicked and vulgar world of men,

[22] *Ibid.*, I, 819.
[23] Lord Cromer, *Modern Egypt* (London, 1908), II, 180.
[24] Muhammad Abduh, *al-Islam wa'l-nasraniyya* (*Islam and Christianity*), first published in 1902 (5th ed.; Cairo, 1938), p. 139, and the chapter entitled "al-jumud 'illa tazul" ("Stagnation Is a Passing Illness"), pp. 132–140.

are rather the typical thinkers of Islam. Both men would have looked with contempt and hostility on the worldly optimism and progressive hopefulness of Muhammad Abduh.[25] If both al-Afghani and Muhammad Abduh are essential to the understanding of a phenomenon such as Arab nationalism, it is as well to emphasize that they nevertheless cannot be considered as its initiators. To do so would be to run the risk of confusion by dissolving the lineaments of a clear-cut ideology and a specific history into amorphous speculation and loose generalization.[26]

While Muhammad Abduh is himself entirely unconnected with Arab nationalism, it is with some writings of the best-known of his disciples, Muhammad Rashid Rida (1865–1935) that we may date the beginning of the movement. Rashid Rida was born in al-Qalamun, near Tripoli in Syria, and came to Egypt in 1897, where he remained for the rest of his life editing the well-known monthly periodical *al-Manar*.[27] From his autobiography,[28] we gain the picture of a young man with religious zeal and attainments, growing steadily dissatisfied with the social and political situation of Islam. He resolved to get in touch with al-Afghani in order to learn at first hand how best to remedy this situation, and he wrote to him in these terms. But he soon heard of al-

---

[25] Sulaiman Dunia, *al-Shaikh Muhammad Abduh bain al-falasifa wa'l-kalamiyyin* (2 vols.; Cairo, 1958), contains (what is a rarity) a reasoned criticism of Abduh's view, from an orthodox Muslim point of view. The work is an edition of a treatise, *al-aqa'id al-addiyya*, by Jamal al-Din al-Iji, with a marginal commentary by Jalal al-Din al-Dawani and Muhammad Abduh. In his preface, Vol. I, pp. 3–64, the editor takes Abduh to task for indulging in *falsafa* and preferring its conclusions to those of Muslim dogma, also for his indifference as between heresy and orthodoxy, a thing which would tend to encourage disunity in the *umma*.

[26] H. Z. Nuseibeh, *The Ideas of Arab Nationalism* (Ithaca, 1956), which attempts, among other things, "to explore the genesis" of Arab nationalism, seems to suffer from this failing. For in this genesis are included (chap. 7) writers who exemplify in different ways the impact of European thought and civilization on Middle Eastern minds, Tahtawi, Marrash, Shibli al-Shumayyil, Shakir al-Khuri, but hardly the development of Arab nationalist thought. Some of these writers would indeed have been hard put to it to know what Arab nationalism could mean; others, notably Mustafa Kamil, so far as they knew it, disapproved strongly of it.

[27] On Rashid Rida see Henri Laoust, *Essai sur les Doctrines sociales et politiques de . . . ibn Taymiya* (Cairo, 1939), pp. 547–563, and his *Le Califat dans la Doctrine de Rachid Rida* (Beirut, 1938).

[28] First published as articles, and later reprinted by Shakib Arslan in his *al-Sayyid Rashid Rida au akha' arba'in sana* (*Sayyid Rashid Rida, or a Brotherhood of Forty Years*) (Damascus, 1937).

Afghani's death and of the rumors then current that the Sultan Abdul Hamid had done away with him, and he resolved to go to Egypt, where he could write and work in freedom. His strongest motive, however, as he tells us, was "to gather what al-Shaikh Muhammad Abduh had derived in the ways of wisdom, experience, and reforming plans from the company of Sayyid Jamal al-Din." [29] From this account it appears that Rashid Rida, judging, no doubt, by the past reputation and history of the two men, was attracted to Muhammad Abduh because he considered him a disciple of al-Afghani; but this, as has been seen, was by then no longer the case. The incident nonetheless indicates a certain radicalism of temper which seemed to have affected widely the younger generation in the last decades of the nineteenth century, making them discontented with their lot and eager to experiment with the most novel and untried remedies. This is as true of the young Christian conspirators of Beirut who have been mentioned earlier and of the young Muhammad Abduh and his Egyptian circle as of the studious young Rashid Rida in his little Syrian town.

If Rashid Rida came to Cairo and to Muhammad Abduh somewhat under a misapprehension, the misapprehension was not complete. Two things that he had in common with both Muhammad Abduh and al-Afghani were a discontent with the state of Islam and a deep desire for reform. Al-Afghani and his disciple, when they started publishing *al-Urwa al-wuthqa* in Paris, adopted as their motto the return to the ways of the ancestors (*salaf*).[30] They may therefore be said to have inaugurated that modern movement of Islamic reform known as the *salafiyya*, which subsequently took many forms, and of which Rashid Rida himself became later the undoubted intellectual leader. It is also true that for al-Afghani this return to the ways of the ancestors had a distinctly utilitarian form: its chief purpose was to renovate the solidarity of the Muslims and make them into a world power feared and respected. For Muhammad Abduh it meant the return to a presumed rationalist Islam cleansed of superstitions and tyranny. For Rashid Rida it came to mean a puritanical revival of

---

[29] *Ibid.*, pp. 127–128.
[30] H. Laoust, "Le Réformisme Orthodoxe des 'Salafiya,'" *Revue des Etudes Islamiques* (1932), p. 175. Laoust is here no doubt referring to the third article of the society of *al-urwa al-wuthqa*, which enjoined emulation of the *salaf*. See Muhammad Rashid Rida, *Tarikh al-ustadh al-imam*, I, 284.

strict Islamic practices and religious fervor; it was for this reason that he was a Hanbalite, following the strictest of the four schools of Islamic laws, and that he later cast his lot with the Saudis and the Wahabi revival. It may be said that of the three men, he was the only *salafi* in a strictly orthodox manner, the only one whose call to a return to the ways of the ancestors was genuine, rather than a spurious construct of his own imagination. It remains true, nonetheless, that *salafiyya* constituted the intellectual bond which drew together Muhammad Abduh and Rashid Rida.

Indeed, it is in the arguments of the *salafiyya* that we may trace the first intellectual burgeoning of Arab nationalism. The word indicates, of course, a return to the ways of the Prophet, his Companions, and the Muslims of the early centuries, when Islam was in its pure state and the Arab caliphate in the heyday of its glory. It is to this period that al-Afghani returns to explain the proper significance of *asabiyya* and the benefits to be derived from it.[31] Again it is to this period that Muhammad Abduh returns to show that Islam was not always superstitious and degraded and did not always encourage political tyranny. In a passage of *al-Islam wa'l-nasraniyya*, Muhammad Abduh dates the decline of Islam to the day of the caliph (al-Mu'tasim, according to Rashid Rida), who, suspecting the loyalty of the Arab troops of his household, made use of Turkish and Dailamite mercenaries, who soon came to act as a pretorian guard and inaugurated a military despotism. Under the influence of these barbarians, Muhammad Abduh explains, the intellectual civilization of Islam withered and wilted, for these barbarians "wore Islam on their bodies, but nothing of it penetrated their soul." [32] Thus, implicit in the arguments of the *salafiyya* is a glorification of Arab Islam and a depreciation of Ottoman Islam; and to these arguments may be traced the fashionable "periodization" of Islamic history, in contemporary Arab historiography, which sees in the times of the Prophet the glorious dawn, in the Umayyad period the promise of the forenoon, in the Abbassid period the splendor of noon, and in all that followed the sad decline and the shades of night slowly closing in. These arguments were themselves reinforced by some European orientalists, professionals such as L. Sédillot, or

---

[31] Muhammad al-Makhzumi, *op. cit.*, p. 257.
[32] *Ibid.*, pp. 112–113.

amateurs such as G. Lebon, who looked on Islamic history in
the same manner and whose writings, especially those of Lebon,
met with prodigious popularity when translated into Arabic.

But this partiality to Arab Islam, in the case of al-Afghani and
of Muhammad Abduh, did not betoken an interest in or an encouragement of Arab nationalism. It was otherwise with Rashid
Rida.[33] A good example of the divergence between his views and
those of Muhammad Abduh occurs in a footnote he added to
the passage in *al-Islam wa'l-nasraniyya* mentioned above, in
which Muhammad Abduh discusses the causes of the stagnation
of Islam. The caliph who was responsible for introducing the
Turks as mercenaries, says the footnote, was al-Mu'tasim, and,
it adds, "how miserable was his helping (blameworthy) innovation to triumph over the sunna,[34] and how miserable was his action in enabling the Turks to spoil the *umma*." The footnote
is noteworthy not only because it makes explicit and exaggerates
a possible tendency of Muhammad Abduh's argument, but also
for the implicit change it introduces into the concept of *umma*.
Traditionally, the word meant the body of all the Muslims, and
made no distinction based on race, language, or habitation. But
Rashid Rida seems here to be saying that the Turks, Muslims
as they were, were not really part of the *umma*, that the *umma*
consisted only of Arab Muslims. This remains an ambiguous hint,
however, and is not made explicit. In articles in the early volumes
of *al-Manar*, Rashid Rida takes up the cause of the Arabs against
the Turks, in evaluating the contribution of both to Islam. "The
Turks are a warlike nation," he said in an article of 1900, "but
they are not of greater moment than the Arabs; how can their
conquests be compared to those of the Arabs, although their state
lasted longer than all the states of the Arabs together? It is in
the countries which were conquered by the Arabs that Islam
spread, became firmly established and prospered. Most of the
lands which the Turks conquered were a burden on Islam and
the Muslims, and are still a warning of clear catastrophe. I am
not saying that those conquests are things for which the Turks
must be blamed or criticized, but I want to say that the greatest

---

[33] He himself states that Muhammad Abduh approved all that he wrote in
al-Manar, except what concerned the Ottoman Empire. See Muhammad
Rashid Rida, *Tarikh al-ustadh al-imam*, I, 995.
[34] The law and practice of orthodox Islam.

glory in the Muslim conquests goes to the Arabs, and that religion grew, and became great through them; their foundation is the strongest, their light is the brightest, and they are indeed the best *umma*[35] brought forth to the world. I do not deny that the Turks have virtue, intelligence, and nobility, and I do not like to continue the comparison of the conquests of the Arabs and of the Turks, and the greater import to Islam of the Arab contribution. A little knowledge of past and present history shows that most of the countries where Islam was established were conquered by the Arabs who were the active agents of the propagation of Islam." [36]

This passage shows clearly Rashid Rida's partiality to the Arabs, but it shows as clearly that this partiality was based on a regard for Islam and on a zeal in its defense which, so Rashid Rida thought, had been best insured by the Arabs. Another passage of the same year emphasizes his point of view. "To care for the history of the Arabs and to strive to revive their glory," he wrote in an article entitled "The Civilization of the Arabs," "is the same as to work for the Muslim union which only obtained in past centuries thanks to the Arabs, and will not return in this century except through them, united and in agreement with all the races. The basis of this union is Islam itself, and Islam is none other than the book of God Almighty, and the Sunna of his prophet—prayer and peace be on Him. Both are in Arabic. No one can understand them properly unless he understands their noble language. . . ." [37] An indication again of his sympathies is the fact that it was in *al-Manar* that Abd al-Rahman al-Kawakibi first published, serially, his book *Umm al-qura*, a sustained diatribe against the Ottomans and a plea in favor of an Arab caliphate. It is therefore not surprising that *al-Manar* was banned in Ottoman dominions, soon after its appearance.

Rashid Rida's pro-Arab sympathies do not necessarily mean that, at the beginning of the century and before the Young Turk Revolution, he would have condoned or supported an Arab separatist movement in the Ottoman Empire. After all, he was, and

---

[35] Here the term is used in its general sense, as a body of people.
[36] "Al-turk wa'l-arab" ("The Turks and the Arabs"), *al-Manar*, III (Cairo. 1900), 172.
[37] *Al-Manar*, III, 290–291.

all his life remained, a stanch Muslim, and while the Ottoman Empire represented the cause of Islam in the world and the caliph remained the head of the state, he would have shrunk from actively contributing to dissension among different Muslim groups in the empire. It was only after the Young Turks had deposed Abdul Hamid, and still more when they manifested indifference to Islam and permitted irreligion, that Rashid Rida felt able wholeheartedly to support Arab nationalism. Of him it is true to say, as H. Laoust has remarked of the *salafiyya*,[38] that he was more an Arab *Muslim* than a Muslim *Arab*. The cast of his thought remained traditional, and the extract from his writings, given in the anthology below, is typical. On the whole, it represents the settled convictions of a man who, in nearly forty years of controversial and apologetic writings, had to cope with various circumstances and problems.

The distinction between what he wrote and the action he was prepared to take is reinforced by his political record during his early years in Egypt, before the Young Turk Revolution. He came to Egypt as a radical, discontented with the situation of the Ottoman Empire and anxious for reform. And there, significantly enough, Rashid Rida joined the party of the Young Turks. "The first political association which we founded in Egypt," he wrote in 1926, "was the *jam'iyat al-shura al-uthmaniyya* (the Ottoman Party of the Constitution), and men drawn from the main Ottoman peoples, with the Turks, the Circassians, and the Armenians in the forefront, collaborated with us in its foundation. One of its founding members was the officer Sa'ib Bey who was aide-de-camp to His Excellency the Ghazi Ahmad Mukhtar Pasha, and delegate of the Committee of Union and Progress in Egypt. . . . Among the members were also the famous Abdullah Jevdet[39] who was its Turkish secretary and [Rafiq al-Azm] its treasurer and his cousin Haqqi Bey its Arabic secretary, and the writer of these lines the head of its administrative council." [40]

It was after the Young Turk Revolution, and indeed after the Balkan Wars, that Rashid Rida joined others in forming the

[38] Laoust, "Le Réformisme Orthodoxe des 'Salafiya,'" p. 204.

[39] Concerning Abdullah Jevdet see E. E. Ramsaur, Jr., *The Young Turks* (Princeton, 1957), *passim*.

[40] Muhammad Rashid Rida, preface to Rafiq al-Azm, *Majmu'at athar Rafiq al-Azm* (*Literary Remains of Rafiq al-Azm*) (Cairo, 1926), I, v.

Introduction

Decentralization Party, the necessity for which appeared, he says, when the Young Turks showed themselves bent on a centralizing policy detrimental both to the Arabs and to the empire.[41] By then, he was prepared to go even further. He joined another society, a secret one unlike the Decentralization Party, the aim of the new society being to create concord among the potentates of the Arabian Peninsula, in order to bring strong pressure on the Turks on behalf of the Arabs and to provide for the defense of the Arabs against foreign ambitions, should the Ottoman Empire fall to pieces. The latter seemed likely, after Ottoman defeats in Tripoli and during the Balkan Wars.[42] These discreet indications may perhaps hide even more extensive activities than Rashid Rida thought it wise to reveal; for Shakib Arslan has recorded that after the Tripoli and the Balkan wars the Decentralization Party in Cairo was openly intriguing against the Ottoman government and was looking to the British for help to found an independent Arab state.[43]

The case of the Arabs against the Turks was put in a much more resounding manner by Rashid Rida's fellow Syrian, Abd al-Rahman al-Kawakibi (1849–1902), who left his native Aleppo for Egypt in 1898 in obscure circumstances and there published two books before his early death, *Tabai' al-istibdad* (*The Characteristics of Tyranny*), which was a virtual, though unacknowledged crib of the Italian writer Alfieri's *Della Tirannide*,[44] and *Umm al-qura* (a name by which Mecca is also known), which seems to have been adapted from a book by W. S. Blunt called *The Future of Islam*, published in 1881.[45] In Cairo, al-Kawakibi

---

[41] *Ibid.*, p. vii.

[42] *Ibid.*, p. vi.

[43] Shakib Arslan, *op. cit.*, pp. 152–153.

[44] See S. G. Haim, "Alfieri and al-Kawakibi," *Oriente Moderno*, XXXIV (1954), 321–334.

[45] See S. G. Haim, "Blunt and al-Kawakibi," *Oriente Moderno*, XXXV (1955), 132–143. A pointer to the currency of Blunt's ideas is a passage by Abd al-Muta'l al-Sa'idi, an Azharite without tincture of European learning, in which he mentions Rashid Rida's favorable response to Fuad's ambition concerning the caliphate, in spite of the fact that Fuad did not have the necessary qualifications for the Islamic caliphate and that his caliphate would have been as fictitious as that of the Ottomans. Moreover, it would have had the disadvantage of being in a land in whose affairs the British interfered, and they would have approved of it only insofar as it would support their policy and steer the Muslims toward such support. The author goes on to remark that this was no doubt the sort of caliphate that Mr. Blunt, a

25

belonged to Rashid Rida's circle and was imbued with the same radical views concerning the Ottoman Empire and the unsatisfactory position of Islam. A contemporary who knew him in Egypt says that he was "in truth a revolutionary in spirit and inclination" and that he often used to say: "If I had an army, I would have overthrown the government of Abdul Hamid in twenty-four hours." [46] This estimate is confirmed by *The Characteristics of Tyranny*. In this book, al-Kawakibi attacks political and religious tyranny and its nefarious effects on science, morality, and progress. True Islam, he argues, is incompatible with tyranny, and it must lead to the just state in which the individual lives happily, at one with his nation, completely free, yet completely owned by it. It is only a just political order, he says, that makes possible science, morality, and progress. In this book, which was and still remains very popular, al-Kawakibi gave currency to a secular view of politics which holds that the only just government is government according to the will of the people, that any other government is tyrannical and can be removed by the governed.

The ideas that he expressed in his other book, *Umm al-qura*, were even more revolutionary. This book attempts to explain the stagnation of Islam and to provide a remedy for it. The Muslims, he says, are now a dead people with no corporate being or feelings. Their stagnation is the result of tyranny, of the decline of Islamic culture, and of the absence of racial and linguistic bonds among Muslims, and partly for this reason the Ottoman Empire is not fit to preserve Islam. The Muslim kingdom is made up of different countries professing different religions and divided into numerous sects, and their ministers are drawn from different nationalities. Thus the Ottoman Empire cannot effect the regeneration of Islam. Regeneration should be the work of the Arabs who would supply a caliph, residing in Mecca, and acting as the spiritual head of an Islamic union. Such a caliph, contrary to traditional notions, would exercise no political power. He would be merely a religious authority, a kind of Islamic pope, an ultimate authority in matters of religion,

---

friend of both Muhammad Abduh and Rashid Rida, was striving for. See *al-Mujaddidun fi'l-Islam min'al-qarn al-awwal ila'l-rabi' ashar* (Cairo, 1952[?]), pp. 542–543.

[46] Ibrahim Salim al-Najjar, quoted in Sami al-Dahhan, *Abd al-Rahman al-Kawakibi* (Cairo, 1955), p. 37.

and a symbol of Islamic unity. Al-Kawakibi also provides a list of twenty-six different reasons to prove the superiority of the Arabs and why the caliphate should devolve upon them.[47] Among these reasons are the following: the Arabs of the Arabian Peninsula are free of racial, religious, and sectarian divisions; the peninsula is a land of free men; it is the birthplace of Islam; the Arabs of the peninsula are the most zealous in preserving religion; they have a powerful solidarity, are able to bear hardships, and have not succumbed to luxury; they do not know political tyranny, they practice consultation in public affairs and follow the principles of socialist living; they are, as he concluded, "of all nations the most suitable to be an authority in religion and an example to the Muslims; the other nations have followed their guidance at the start and will not refuse to follow them now."

Al-Kawakibi, then, may be considered as the first true intellectual precursor of modern secular Pan-Arabism. He deserves the title on two counts. He was the first to declare himself, without ambiguity, as the champion of the Arabs against the Turks. Moreover, in his praise and condemnation there were no half tones, no reticences: the Arabs were better people than the Turks and ought to have the primacy. And by launching, in Arabic, the idea of a merely spiritual caliphate he took the first step toward a purely secular politics. Traditionally, the well-known European distinction between the spiritual and the temporal has no place in Islam, and those who wanted to reform Islam, toward the end of the nineteenth century, were never really prepared to envisage a political system in which the temporal would be divorced from the spiritual. For all his preoccupation with the state of Islam, al-Kawakibi, once he introduced the idea of a spiritual caliph, was led to consider politics as an autonomous activity divorced from divine prescription, and fully subject to the will of men. Such an idea is an essential prerequisite of nationalism.

The mode of al-Kawakibi's attack on the Turks remains puzzling. He was an entirely derivative thinker, and his analysis of the stagnation of Islam is found in other writers; but he was alone among Muslims in advocating that a spiritual caliph should be chosen from among the Arabs. This idea, too, he seems to have taken from someone else, probably W. S. Blunt, but the

---

[47] See extract from *Umm al-qura*, no. 2 in the anthology.

question remains why he adopted this particular idea, so little consonant with Islamic traditions and so startlingly novel for a Muslim. Was it love of extreme innovation, in keeping with his radical temper, or were other considerations involved? After coming to Egypt, he went for a mysterious journey around the coasts of Arabia, eventually reaching Karachi. There is a story that he undertook this journey in order to further the ambitions of the Khedive Abbas Hilmi, who is said to have aspired to the caliphate; it is even said that the Khedive paid him a salary of £50 a month.[48] Such a story would tally with an observation which Marmaduke Pickthall reported in 1914: "In the years 1894–1896, I was in Syria," he wrote, " 'living native,' as the English call it. I can remember hearing Muslim Arabs talking more than once of what would happen on the downfall of the Turks. They looked to Egypt, remembering the conquests of Mehmet Ali, and the gospel of an Arab empire under the Lord of Egypt which Ibrahim Pasha preached in Palestine and Syria. That gospel, I gathered, was still being preached in secret by missionaries from Egypt. . . . I gathered then and subsequently that the Sherif of Mecca was to be the spiritual head of the re-constituted realm of El Islam, the Khedive of Egypt the temporal head. . . ."[49]

It is significant that when *Umm al-qura* was serialized in *al-Manar*, Rashid Rida added a footnote at the end of the series —by that time al-Kawakibi was dead—to say that he had omitted one sentence from the work in which the writer had called on the Khedive of Egypt to extend his aid for the realization of the plan. Was *Umm al-qura* then a piece of Khedivial propaganda? The possibility is not to be dismissed; it is, on the contrary, strengthened by another piece of evidence. Rafiq al-Azm, writing

---

[48] *Al-fusul* (Cairo, August, 1952), p. 39. On the Khedive's ambition to assume the caliphate see Muhammad Rashid Rida, *Tarikh al-ustadh al-imam*, I, 560. In a letter of February 20, 1901, to Abu'l-Huda al-Sayyadi in Constantinople, the Egyptian journalist Ibrahim al-Muwailihi alleged that the Khedive was paying allowances to many refugees in Cairo who were on bad terms with the Ottoman sultan, among others, al-Kaukabi [*sic*]; the letter is quoted in Ahmad Shafiq Pasha, *op. cit.*, Vol. II, Part 1, pp. 351–352. The same writer records that he saw in Constantinople, in October, 1901, a manifesto purportedly signed by the Khedive exhorting Muslims to rebel against the sultan and to assume the caliphate himself. The manifesto is said to have been captured from anti-Ottoman dissidents in the Yemen. See *ibid.*, p. 367.

[49] *The New Age* (London, Nov. 5, 1914), p. 9.

before 1914 and seeking to explain the estrangement between Arabs and Turks, asserted that when one of the Young Turk leaders, Murad Bey al Daghistani,[50] escaped from Constantinople to Egypt in 1894, he, together with other Young Turks, "arranged a plot with some high quarters in order to terrorize [the Sultan] so that he might restore the Constitution and acquiesce in constitutional government. The plot consisted in imagining an Arab caliphate and persuading the Sultan that it existed in reality." Rafiq al-Azm went on to say that this disquietened the Sultan and created a bad impression among the Turks which persisted after 1908, making the Young Turks mistrust the Arabs.[51] It is known that the Khedive was in touch with the Young Turks, both in Egypt and in Europe, and that he alternately wooed and repulsed them.[52] It is also known that Abbas Hilmi was friendly with Blunt and probably knew Blunt's ideas on the caliphate. It may well be, then, that the idea of a spiritual Arab caliphate found currency in this twilight zone of intrigue and plot, that its origin in the 1890's is to be traced to the ambitions and encouragement of Abbas Hilmi, that the Young Turks, whether Turk or Arab, found in it a useful weapon against Abd al-Hamid, and that in the minds of some of the Arabs it was not to be connected with an actual secession by the Arabs from the Ottoman Empire. All this would put *Umm al-qura* in a new light, but would not, of course, alter the fact that this book openly praised the Arabs at the expense of the Turks and openly demanded that the caliphate should devolve on an Arab. It is this which makes it a milestone in the history of Arab nationalism.

The ideas of al-Kawakibi were, a few years later, taken up and given even more precision by another writer. This was Negib Azoury (d. 1916) who in 1905 published in Paris a book entitled *Le Réveil de la Nation Arabe*. He was an Ottoman Christian who had studied in Paris and then become an official in the provincial government of Jerusalem. He left his post in suspicious circumstances; apparently he was condemned to death *in absentia*, in 1904, for treasonable activities in Paris. He founded in Paris

---

[50] See Ramsaur, *op. cit.*, p. 27 and *passim*.
[51] Rafiq al-Azm, *op. cit.*, I, 122.
[52] Evidence for Abbas Hilmi's relations with the Young Turks is found in Ahmad Shafiq Pasha, *op. cit.*, II, and in Ramsaur, *op. cit.*, *passim*.

the Ligue de la Patrie Arabe and published a monthly periodical, of which eighteen numbers came out, entitled *L'Indépendance Arabe*.[53] The Ligue de la Patrie Arabe was probably a one-man business, since no Arab, so far as it is known, was associated with it, and Azoury seems to have been a shady character who may have been a French agent actually taking money from French sources. At any rate, it is certain that he went so far as to ask for it.[54] *Le Réveil de la Nation Arabe* adopts al-Kawakibi's idea of a spiritual Arab caliphate. The separation of civil and religious powers, Azoury explains, is in the interest of both Islam and the Arab "nation." Azoury also had another proposal which went further than al-Kawakibi's plans. He desired to have an Arab empire set up; its "natural" frontiers would be the valley of the Euphrates and the Tigris, the Suez Canal, the Mediterranean, and the Indian Ocean. And the throne of this empire would be filled, so Azoury explained, by a prince of the Khedivial family, who would openly proclaim himself to be in favor of this program![55]

Azoury's program thus constitutes the first open demand for the secession of the Arab lands from the Ottoman Empire. It is especially significant that the demand was made by a Christian, for Muslims were chary of any move that might disrupt the Ottoman Empire, the only great Muslim power in the world. Al-Kawakibi had gone so far as to demand an Arab caliphate, though not an Arab empire; but Rashid Rida had confined himself to praising the Arabs and depreciating the Turks. As has been seen, Arab Muslim radicals sought an outlet for their discontents by joining the Young Turk societies. This was the case with Rashid Rida, with Rafiq al-Azm, with his cousin Haqqi al-Azm, with Abd al-Hamid al-Zahrawi, who was later to be executed as a nationalist in Syria in 1915,[56] and many an army officer who would later desert to the Allied side, in the First World War, in the name of Arab nationalism.

---

[53] E. Jung, *La révolte Arabe* (1906–1924) (2 vols.; Paris, 1924), gives details of Negib Azoury's activities; Jung was his collaborator.

[54] See *ibid.*, I, 47.

[55] Negib Azoury, *Le Réveil de la Nation Arabe dans l'Asie Turque . . .*, pp. i–iii, 245–248. See no. 3 in the anthology for Azoury's program.

[56] Abd al Hamid al-Zahrawi had established a secret paper in Homs to support the Young Turks; *al-Manar*, XIX, 169.

But the situation changed radically with the Young Turk Revolution and the deposition of Abdul Hamid. At the revolution, the floodgates were opened. Once change was initiated, in a violent and abrupt manner by a *coup d'état* of the Young Turks, change became attractive to the official and intellectual classes of the Ottoman Empire. The effervescence was increased by the sudden restoration of parliamentary institutions; if deputies were elected, then they had to talk, expound policies, and make their views known.

Such was the background against which Arab opposition to the Young Turks in the last years of peace was organized and became vocal. The Young Turk Revolution itself created some causes of estrangement between the Arabs and the government. There was, as has been seen, the suspicion that some Arab leaders wanted an Arab caliphate; Rafiq al-Azm, who had joined the Committee of Union and Progress after the outbreak of the revolution,[57] was persuaded of this. Another factor was that Abdul Hamid had surrounded himself with Arab counselors such as Abu'l-Huda al-Sayyadi, Izzat Pasha al-Abid, and Salim Malhama; and with the fall of Abdul Hamid, these officials were removed from their positions. It was not only that in denouncing them the Young Turks may have denounced Arabs in general, as reactionary tools of Abdul Hamid;[58] but the Arab official classes suddenly found themselves without the powerful patrons and protectors which Abdul Hamid's counselors must have been. Also, in the immediate aftermath of the revolution, the reaction of the Young Turks against Abdul Hamid's men may have given scope to the expression of private rivalries and enmities. Thus Shafiq al-Azm, a high official in the Caisse de la Dette, was dismissed from his post and became deputy for Damascus and president of the Arab Brotherhood Society in Constantinople, an antigovernment grouping; not unnaturally, he was at odds with the Committee of Union and Progress, and once he nearly came to blows with Tal'at in the Ottoman Chamber. The Society

---

[57] Rashid Rida, in Rafiq al-Azm, *op. cit.*, I, vi.

[58] This is what happened, according to *ibid.*, I, 120. See also Ahmad Qadri, *Mudhakkirati an al-thaura al-arabiyya al-kubra* (*My Memoirs of the Great Arab Revolt*) (Damascus, 1956), where Turkish attacks on Arabs in general are mentioned.

was eventually forced to disband, which no doubt further en-
venomed matters.[59] Again, it is well known that Sayyid Talib of
Basra organized opposition to the Young Turks in Mesopotamia;
is it only a coincidence, then, that he happened to be related
by marriage to the family of Abu'l-Huda al-Sayyadi? [60]

In the last few years before the outbreak of the First World
War, Arab agitation against the Young Turk government, now
firmly in power, became manifest. Sayyid Talib was organizing
opposition in Mesopotamia; the Decentralization Party in Cairo
openly came out with demands for the autonomy of the Arab
provinces in the empire; in Istanbul itself young officers led by
Aziz Ali al-Misri, together with students, organized themselves
into secret societies the aims of which, imprecise enough in the
circumstances, were more or less extreme;[61] and in Beirut, a committee of notables calling themselves the Committee of Reform
and Defense of Syrian Rights,[62] called for Syrian autonomy.
The aims of this committee were overtly the same as those of
the Decentralization Party, but it is possible to discern, nonetheless, some important differences in approach and emphasis. In a
circular which they sent to the Great Powers in August, 1913,[63]
they spoke of the unsettled conditions of Syria in the nineteenth
century, with sectarian divisions poisoned by the Ottoman government and resulting in the events of 1860. This reference
would show that the Maronites and other Christians of the
Lebanon had some voice in the committee. But while the
Lebanese Christians were certainly anti-Ottoman, they were not
Arab nationalists; for they were prepared to accept the protectorate of a Christian power, if this would rid them of the Otto-

---

[59] Abd al-Fattah abu'l-Nasr al-Yafi, *Mudhakkirat qa'id arabi . . . (Memoirs of an Arab Commander . . .)* (n.p. [Beirut?], n.d. [before 1935]), pp.
55–57; see also Rafiq al-Azm, *op. cit.,* I, 130.

[60] Abd al-Fattah abu'l-Nasr al-Yafi, *op. cit.,* p. 200; on Sayyid Talib see E.
Kedourie, *England and the Middle East* (London, 1956), pp. 204–205. See
also Sulaiman Faidi, *Fi ghamrat al-nidal (In the Midst of the Struggle)*
(Baghdad, 1952), for his antigovernment operations in Mesopotamia.

[61] On the activities of the officers in Istanbul see a letter from Abd al-Hamid
al-Zahrawi to Rashid Rida in Kedourie, *op. cit.,* pp. 61–62.

[62] On this committee, see Zeine, *op. cit.*

[63] Reproduced in E. Rossi, *Documenti sull'origine e gli Sviluppi della
Questioni araba 1875–1944* (Rome, 1944), doc. no. 9.

mans,[64] whereas Rashid Rida and his friends in Cairo, or Aziz Ali al-Misri and his friends in Istanbul, were not prepared to entertain such a notion.

The divergence appeared clearly at the congress called together in Paris in 1913, which was organized by the Decentralization Party, and in which the Christian notables of Beirut also appeared.[65] In his letter to Rashid Rida, mentioned above, al-Zahrawi reported on the maneuvers inside the congress. "I have already described to you in detail how, when I went to Paris, I found the affairs of the congress in chaos, and what pains we took to cover up the matter and to make, with the help of God, the congress more presentable than could be expected. At the close of the meetings, the gathering, which had been artificially brought together, dispersed. A short while later, the patience of the Beirutis was exhausted and they left for their country; so I remained all alone to represent the ideal. Khalil Zainiyya and Ayyub Thabit also stayed behind, but they had not once sipped from the fountain of Arab unity, no, nor from that of Syrian unity; their only interest was in Beirut and in Beirut alone. Because they are educated, they got on with me and I with them, and we became good friends, until I left; and there was none of this friendship, nor its quarter, between them and their other Beiruti companions, the Muslims." [66]

The Syrian Reform Committee and the Decentralization Party alike demanded administrative decentralization in the Arab provinces of the empire, the recognition of Arabic as an official language, an increase in official posts for the natives of the Arab areas, and in general better financial and judicial administration. Rafiq al-Azm lists grievances which do not seem to have been felt by the Syrian Reform Committee, and which indeed were more likely to be felt by Muslim Arab officials. He complains that Arab officials were not sent to study abroad, and that none of them was elected to executive office in the Committee of Union and Progress, in spite of the fact that they played their

---

[64] On the contracts of the Maronites with the French, prior to the First World War, see the documents published in the official Ottoman report, *La Vérité sur la Question Syrienne* (Istanbul, 1916).

[65] The resolutions of this congress are printed in Rossi, *op. cit.*, doc. no. 8.

[66] Quoted in S. G. Haim, "The Arab Awakening," p. 241.

part in the revolution. He also complains that Arab officials were dismissed unfairly, that the Young Turk regime had appointed a non-Arab as Minister of Pious Foundations, that the government held the Arab language in contempt, though Islam is the official religion of the state, and "the language of this religion is Arabic." [67]

Such were the avowed grievances and demands, but there may well have been other unavowed aims held by members of the Decentralization Party, and contacts, perhaps even intrigues, with British officials in Cairo. They were, for instance, capable of composing and distributing in Syria tracts such as the anonymous "Announcement to the Arabs, Sons of Qahtan," reprinted in the present volume,[68] full of violent abuse of the Turks and incitement against them, and of sending agents into the Ottoman Empire on the outbreak of war to seek support for the British, even of attempting to gather military information, obviously for the use of a foreign power.[69]

THE STIMULUS OF WORLD WAR I TO THE ARAB CAUSE

The outbreak of war put the Decentralization Party and the Syrian Reform Committee in the shade. The British, seeking allies against the Ottomans, tempted Husain, the Sherif of Mecca, to join their side. This man, the nominee of the Young Turks, conceived the ambition of ruling an extensive empire, and even of becoming caliph.[70] The limits of the empire he envisaged were set out in his letter of July 14, 1915, to the British High Commission in Egypt. When he rose, however, he did not justify his rebellion by an appeal to Arab nationalism; he appealed, rather, to traditionalist sentiments, calling the Young Turks impious innovators who had put Islam in danger, and representing himself as rising against them in the interests of the Faith.[71] His manifesto touched on no specific Arab grievance,

---

[67] Rafiq al-Azm, *op. cit.*, I, 130 ff.

[68] No. 4 in the anthology.

[69] Kedourie, *op. cit.*, p. 62.

[70] On the views of Husain and his negotiations with the British, see *ibid.*, chap. ii.

[71] The manifesto is reproduced in French in *Revue du Monde Musulman*, XLVI (1921), 4–10; see also Kedourie, *op. cit.*, pp. 54–55.

and even where it did, there could be doubt whether the reference was due to Husain rather than to some other.[72] Only two years later, in a document addressed to a Western government which was in all probability well calculated to appeal to that Power, the Sherif officially spoke as the representative of the Arabs and dwelt on his efforts "to rescue a race worthy of respect owing to its glorious history, and to its beneficent influence on European civilization." [73]

The absence of a specific ideology of Arab nationalism until the end of the First World War is indeed noteworthy. It was not until the 1930's that a serious attempt was made to define the meaning of Arab nationalism and what constitutes the Arab Nation. These attempts became more frequent in the 1940's, and in the period since then they have become a flood; hardly a month passes which does not see the publication of one or more books on this subject, mostly repetitive, it is true. The end of the First World War saw Faisal and his followers installed in Damascus for a brief three years before being expelled by the French.[74] During his brief period in Syria, Faisal expressed a rudimentary theory of Arab nationalism. In a speech of May, 1919, he rebutted the idea, which he attributed to Europeans, that the Arabs of the desert and those of the towns were two distinct groups. "We are one people," he said, "living in the region which is bounded by the sea to the east, the south, and the west, and by the Taurus mountains to the north." [75] Another of his recurrent themes was that he was an Arab first and a Muslim second. "We are Arabs," he used to say, "before being Muslims, and Muhammad is an Arab before being a prophet." [76] He also said, in a speech in Aleppo in June, 1919: ". . . there is neither minority nor majority among us, nothing to divide us. We are one body, we were Arabs even before the time of Moses, Muhammad, Jesus, and Abraham." [77]

---

[72] See C. E. Dawn, "Ideological Influences in the Arab Revolt," in *The World of Islam: Essays Presented to Philip K. Hitti* (New York, 1959).

[73] The Arab government of the Hijaz to the Secretary of State, U.S.A., 1917; see no. 6 in the anthology.

[74] On Faisal's Damascus years see Kedourie, *op. cit.*, chap. vi.

[75] Speech reproduced in Sati' al-Husri, *Yaum Maisalun* (*The Battle of Maisalun*) (Beirut, 1948), p. 207.

[76] Quoted in *Faisal ibn al-Husain fi aqwalihi wa khitabihi* (*Faisal ibn al-Husain in His Sayings and Speeches*) (Baghdad, 1945), p. 175.

[77] Quoted in Sati' al-Husri, *op. cit.*, p. 215.

This idea that the Arabs, as such, are the primary political entity, that the Arabs are a nation and must therefore become a state, was the first to be explored and deepened by Arab nationalist writers. There are traces of it in the manifesto written by members of the Decentralization Party,[78] when they appeal to non-Muslims to make common cause with the Muslim Arabs against the Turks. It is also the idea which occurs most frequently in the rhetoric of the older nationalists. Thus the writer Amin al-Rihani in a speech of 1938: "The Arabs existed before Islam and before Christianity. The Arabs will remain after Islam and after Christianity. Let the Christians realize this, and let the Muslims realize it. Arabism before and above everything." [79] Thus, again, Sami Shawkat, Iraqi Director-General of Education, in a speech of 1939: "We have up to now neglected a most vital aspect of our glorious history; we have made it start at the prophetic message, and this is a period of less than fourteen centuries. In reality, however, the history of our illustrious Arab nation extends over thousands of years, and goes back to the time when the peoples of Europe lived in forests and over marshes, in caves and in the interstices of the rock; at that time our own ancestors used to set up banks, sculpt statues, and lay down canons and codes of law; they invented then the first principles of medicine, geometry, astronomy, the alphabet, and the numerals. On the stele of Hammurabi in the Louvre, we find inscribed the basic law given by one of our ancestors, Hammurabi; one of its clauses concerns the legal punishment of an eye for an eye and a tooth for a tooth; this took place before the Torah, the Gospels, or the Koran. In the same way we find that everything makes us lift our heads high when we consider the histories of the Semitic empires formed in the Fertile Crescent—the Chaldean, the Assyrian, the African, the Pharaonic, or the Carthaginian. All these things must persuade us that the civilizations of the world at the present time are based on foundations laid by our ancestors. These empires and their dependencies are all our property; they are of us and for us; we have the right to glory in them and to honor their exploits, just as we have the right to cherish and exalt the glories of Nebuchad-

[78] No. 4 in the anthology.
[79] Amin al-Rihani, *al-Qaumiyyat* (*Essays on National Questions*) (Beirut, 1956), II, 160.

nezzar, Hammurabi, Sargon, Rameses, Tutankhamen, in the same way that we glory and take pride in Abd al-Rahman al-Dakhil, Abd al-Malik b. Marwan, Harun al-Rashid, and al-Ma'mun."[80]

But the idea that the Arabs by themselves constitute a true political entity could not be a familiar one in the Middle East. Hitherto, Muslim historiography had been based on and had taken its bearings from the fact of the Revelation given to Muhammad and the prodigious consequences which followed it. It had not previously occurred to a writer to claim historical continuity with pagans and idolaters, to seek glorification in their exploits, or to put on a par Hammurabi and Harun al-Rashid, Sargon and al-Ma'mun, Christians and Jews with Muslims, on the score that all these constituted original manifestations of the same original Arab genius. Yet such a revolutionary theory was necessary if the Arab nation were to be defined and endowed with an ancestry and an entity. For it would not do to identify Arabs and Islam completely, since Islam comprised many more people than the Arabs, and since it would also make nonsense of the claim that the Arabs were different from the Turks and therefore had the right to secede from them.

The resources of Western historiography and anthropology had then to be used in order to prove the continuity of the race and of its occupation of the lands which were now considered to belong to the Arab nation. A full-dress discussion of the origins of the Arabs, their history, and the consequent inevitability of their union and sovereignty today, using the results, sometimes outmoded, of Western scholarship, is the study, in French, published by Edmond Rabbath of Aleppo, in 1937, *Unité Syrienne et Devenir Arabe.*[81] The Arabs, Rabbath argues, have always formed a distinct racial stock which has spread, by means of invasions and migrations, from the Arabian Peninsula into the area commonly known as the Fertile Crescent. The history of this region has been labeled, during different periods of its history, as Babylonian, Assyrian, or Phoenician. "In truth," he said, "they were Arab, Arab in the spirit which conceived them, Arab in the hands which set them up." In fact, to be Arab

---

[80] Quoted by S. G. Haim, "Islam and the Theory of Arab Nationalism," in W. Z. Laqueur, ed., *The Middle East in Transition* (London, 1958), p. 281.

[81] See no. 9 in the anthology.

and a Semite, he argued, was one and the same thing. But it is not only blood kinship which unites the Arabs; there is also a common civilization: Arab civilization. "The astonishing history of the Arabs, wrongly called Islamic," he calmly asserts, "is known." To him, Islam is in fact the Arab national religion, which has served to make the Arabs into a cohesive group. Language also has played its part in bringing the Arabs together. But it is not only these human factors which indicate the existence of an Arab nation; the geographical area where they live, Rabbath argues, is itself all of a piece and constitutes a natural homeland, bounded by natural frontiers within which commerce is easy, indeed itself a factor of unity. Rabbath's kind of political argument, presented in a scholarly dress, was obviously important as a substitute for the traditional view, which is either no longer desirable or no longer convincing, and a host of writers have resorted to it with varying degrees of success.

A good example of the technique, as applied to the relations between Zionists and Arabs in modern Palestine, is the argument (again based on historical sources) which the Lebanese Muhammad Jamil Baihum uses to prove that the Jews have always been a disruptive and treacherous element in Middle Eastern society, and, more important, that the Arabs had lived in Palestine from prehistoric times and had even bestowed on the Jews their religion and literature: Moses married an Arab woman who taught her husband the worship of Jehovah; Job was not a Hebrew but an Arab; the Shulamite was a beautiful Arab maiden.[82] Such arguments, it must be emphasized, are nothing exceptional, but rather, are typical of a whole literature of reassurance and self-glorification, which draws on history and other scientific disciplines for its matter and which seems inseparable from the spread of nationalism. The arguments may seem crude, absurd, drawing on outmoded science and history; but this is really beside the point, since they are necessary in order to perform an important role in a society which has lost the stable and familiar image it once had of itself, and which is groping for a substitute.[83]

---

[82] See no. 11 in the anthology.

[83] On this point see W. Cantwell Smith, *Islam in Modern History* (Princeton, 1957), pp. 115–121. Professor Smith observes: "The Arab writing of history has been functioning, then, less as a genuine inquiry than as a psychological defense."

The definition of Arab nationalism is, then, the central pre-occupation of the nationalist writers. And the question is not merely what the Arab nation is, but what meaning nationalism itself has. And here a number of questions arose, after the First World War, which reflected the political condition of the Arab East. This region was divided into a number of states with governments either fully independent or aspiring to independence and having their own administrative machinery and vested interests. None of these states, however, could be called an Arab state in the sense that it embraced the whole Arab nation, as defined by the nationalists. In the eyes of these, none of the states was destined to permanence; sooner or later they would have to merge to form a united Arab state. This is the aspiration known as Pan-Arabism.

The reality was, of course, different; these states went on existing, and they even seemed to inspire a loyalty which clashed with that which ought to be felt toward the Arab nation. Hence a new vocabulary sprang up, a vocabulary that took into account, and that would be helpful in coping with, the divergence between the ideal and the reality. Thus, the term *iqlimiyya* (regionalism) came to denote a reprehensible feeling of loyalty toward a part rather than toward the whole; for an Iraqi to put the interests of Iraq before those of Arabism was to be guilty of *iqlimiyya*. Again, a feeling of loyalty toward the specific country of one's birth, for some writers, came to be known as *wataniyya*, to denote attachment to the *watan*, the fatherland, in contradistinction to *qaumiyya*, or a feeling of loyalty toward the whole Arab nation. The word *umma*, again, which as has been seen traditionally denoted the whole politico-religious community of Islam, became entirely secular in meaning and was now used to denote the whole of the Arab nation.[84] The labor of defining and redefining constantly made by Arab writers in an effort to tighten the meanings of these key words and to prevent confusion is well illustrated by an elegantly concise passage by the Lebanese Muslim Abd al-Latif Sharara.[85] "There are four words," he writes, "which people confuse prodigiously when they talk of nationalities. These are: nation (*umma*), fatherland (*watan*),

[84] For a detailed analysis of these terms see Haim, "Islam and the Theory of Arab Nationalism," pp. 287–298.
[85] See no. 17 in the anthology.

people (*sha'b*), and state (*daula*). They frequently use the word "state" when they mean "nation," and talk of "fatherland" to signify "people" or speak of "people" when they intend the "nation," without distinction between the meaning of these vocables, or precise realization of what they denote, or a firm grounding in the differences among the respective concepts." The haziness or confusion of which this writer complains is of course symptomatic: it denotes the disordered nature of political notions and indicates how unfamiliar and perplexing the idea of an Arab nation was, and still is, to a society accustomed to think of politics in terms of religious divisions.

Rabbath published his book in French. The next notable treatise on Arab nationalism appeared in Arabic in Beirut, in 1941. It was *Dustur al-Arab al-Qaumi* (*The National Constitution of the Arabs*) by Abdullah al-Alayili, a Muslim from the Lebanon. It offered a theoretical treatment of the concept of nationalism, together with its constituent factors, an analysis of Arab history proving the existence of an Arab nation, and in addition a discussion of the place of religion in the state and a political program for the realization of the aims of Arab nationalism. Al-Alayili saw in language "the essential pillar on which a stable national edifice is erected," because "the society in which only one language is prevalent must, of necessity, be stamped with its peculiar imprint, and its members must be refined anew in its crucible." He next mentions geographical environment. Climate tends to create a common temperament, he says, and natural frontiers define the area in which a nation lives. He seems to think that large countries like Russia, Brazil, and the United States, with their far-flung areas and contrasting climates, tend to create estrangement among the different groups inhabiting them. Ancestry comes next, for ties of blood are a great cohesive force. However, where the races are mixed the most important race predominates, and ought indeed to predominate. In the Arab fatherland, for instance, the Arab race has in fact succeeded in imposing its customs, mentality, and language on the other races, who now have only historical importance. Furthermore, "we must make [the Arab race] a foundation of the state and glory in it."

The factor of history is also important. History is the register of a group's past, and "when a group go back to their history,

40

their feelings and ideas go back to certain fixed points," and thus they gain in cohesion. Lastly, customs shared in common are the hallmark of a nation, and they are the focal point, so to speak, of all the other factors which make for unity.[86] All these factors are present in the Arab nation, and nationalism is therefore a natural and an existing movement among the Arabs.

It is noteworthy that in all this there is not a word about religion. Al-Alayili concentrates on environment, history, language, common customs, and common feelings. But when he comes to discuss religion we see that to him religion too is a manifestation of the nation. Religion, he writes, is the sum of spiritual and intellectual characteristics which are based on "an organic response" to a particular environment. Yet not every religion is suitable to every environment, and if a religion moves from one environment to another it must adapt itself to the change; and this has been the case with Islam. That is as far as the nature of religion can bear upon nationalism. As for its function, al-Alayili shows himself quite hostile to the established institutions of Islam. Muslim men of religion have proved a divisive force in society, and he has nothing but praise for Turkey and Persia, which have known how to curb their power. Religion indeed has a place in nationalism, the highest place, but it must be a natural religion. Natural religion is the belief in a worthy, wise, all-knowing, eternal power, the reality of which no human mind can appreciate. Such religion teaches how to live in heaven, hence it cannot conflict with nationalism, which teaches how to live on earth.

Such a view of the place of religion in society is profoundly secular, utilitarian, and totalitarian, but it is perhaps the logical culmination of both al-Afghani's and Muhammad Abduh's views. For al-Afghani judged religion according to its political value, and Muhammad Abduh made it into a system of ethics and well-nigh divorced it of dogmas. It is also strangely similar to Rousseau's view, which was that religion must be a simple belief in a benevolent deity; the analogy is a close one, for Rousseau's "civic religion" enjoining loyalty to the general will, that every citizen must profess, corresponds to al-Alayili's nationalism, which performs the same function in the body politic. The to-

---

[86] See no. 10 in the anthology.

talitarian nature of al-Alayili's thought appears also in the pages
he devotes to explaining the need for, and the importance of, a
leader to bring to realization the aims of Arab nationalism. The
mind of the mass, he says, is very much like that of a child, preoccupied with frivolous things, and easily swayed by emotions.

Such a lack of a critical faculty makes necessary the existence
of "a powerful and violent" leader, who can arouse the mass of
people by appealing to their emotions, controlling and directing
them. Thus, the leader must equip himself according to the intellectual condition of his people, in order to be spiritually
united to them; he must set himself up as an example to his
people because the mass requires its leader to be a living and
acting ideal, and not an immobile statue or a talking machine.
He must have confidence in himself, and he must also have an
attractive, penetrating personality, able to influence and control
men's thoughts. In addition, he must be ascetic in his habits,
because asceticism and sanctity go together, and he must have
suffered in a way which has left a positive mark on him, because
suffering is strength. Another totalitarian trait in the thinking of
this writer appears when he deals with foreign "minorities"
within a nation. Since a nation is the outcome of a long history,
and of an environment slowly molding a society, foreigners cannot readily be absorbed in a nation. They must not be granted
naturalization for a century, or at least three generations; otherwise they will not be able to conform to the soul of the nation or share in its common feelings and interests and beliefs.
Foreigners must also not be allowed to own landed property,
which ought to be reserved for the members of the whole nation.
It follows that national being is not possible if foreign groups
such as the Jews of Palestine or the Alawites of Syria are em-
bedded in the nation. They must either be expelled, as the Jews
were from Germany and the Assyrians from Iraq, or else ex-
changed against populations belonging to the nation and living
outside its boundaries.

Al-Alayili's work is most remarkable, yet it must have had, of
necessity, a limited audience. It is a difficult book, dealing
with unfamiliar subjects in an unfamiliar way, and written in an
involved and sometimes obscure manner. Moreover, its author
was not, and would never become, well known. The man who
did most to popularize the idea of nationalism among the literate

classes of the Arab Middle East was the writer Sati' al-Husri whose large output[87] began in the 1940's and still continues. Al-Husri was a native of Aleppo, and before the First World War he had been an Ottoman official of some standing in the Ministry of Education. Thus his culture, it would seem, was mainly Turkish, and according to those who know him he still retains a Turkish accent in Arabic.[88] When Faisal ruled in Damascus at the end of the war, al-Husri joined his movement and became Minister of Education; he followed Faisal to his exile from Syria, and then he went to Iraq, where he became, and remained for many years, the Director General of Education.

After the collapse of Rashid Ali's movement, al-Husri was banished from Iraq and was deprived of his Iraqi nationality. He then joined the cultural department of the Arab League and became its head, retiring from this post a few years ago. While he was an official in Iraq he did not publish much, but his influence among the young was extensive; he accomplished much by his direction of educational affairs and by his addresses to students, to teachers, and to nationalist clubs, for he provided both a reasoned exposition of the bases of Arab nationalism and some attractive arguments to meet traditionalist as well as modernist objections. It was only after his departure from Iraq that a flow of books under his name began to appear. It may be true that his thought is rarely original, but the ease and clarity with which he wrote, the sophisticated, (not to say sophistical) elegance of his arguments, and his pertinacity in spreading his views make him, without any doubt, the most important of the ideologists of Arab nationalism. His theory of what constitutes the Arab nation is, in spite of certain minor differences as to views, very much like those of al-Alayili, Rabbath, and a host of other writers who have tried their hand at the subject. Where the others put the main emphasis on environment, as al-Alayili did, or on race, as Rabbath did, al-Husri would stress the unity of language and history. Unity in these two respects, he says, leads to unity of feelings and inclinations, to the sharing of sufferings and hopes, and to the unity of culture; and all this makes people

---

[87] See the list of Sati' al-Husri's works dealing with nationalism in the bibliography.

[88] See, for instance, Amin al-Rihani, *Qalb al-Iraq* (*The Heart of Iraq*), first published in 1939 (Beirut, 1957), p. 221.

aware that they are the members of one nation to be distinguished from other nations.[89]

Al-Husri has concentrated his energy on making and driving home three main points: the first is that there is no freedom for the individual outside the nation, the second is that Egypt is part of the Arab nation, and the third is that Pan-Arabism neither contradicts nor is inimical to Islam. In an address to Nadi al-Muthanna, an extreme nationalist club in Baghdad, he said in 1940: "I wish it realized that freedom is not an end in itself but a means toward a higher life. . . . The national interests which may sometimes require a man to sacrifice his life, must perforce entail in some cases the sacrifice of his freedom. . . . He who does not sacrifice his personal freedom for the sake of his nation's freedom, when necessity requires, may lose his own freedom along with the freedom of his people and of his country. . . . And he who refuses to 'lose' himself in the nation to which he belongs, may, in some cases, find himself lost within an alien nation which may one day conquer his fatherland. This is why I say continuously and without hesitation: Patriotism and nationalism before and above all . . . even above and before freedom. . . ." [90]

In speaking of a man having to "lose" (*yufni*) himself in his nation, al-Husri is here speaking the genuine metaphysic of nationalism, which invests the relation between the individual and his political group with religious significance; indeed the term *yufni* (infinitive: *fana'*) had been used hitherto in the literature of the Islamic mystics to denote the union of the worshiper with the Godhead. To use such a religious term in a purely secular context is a daring innovation, and represents a momentous departure from the traditional political thought of Islam. The traditional view holds that the relation of ruler and subject is a contractual one based on the requirements of the religious law; it is also a profoundly skeptical and highly pessimistic view as to what might be expected of politics here on earth. Innovation though it is, al-Husri's argument manages to capture some echoes of tradition. The practical consequence of his doctrine is that the citizen must practice complete solidarity with, and implicit

---

[89] Sati‘ al-Husri, *Ma hiya al-qaumiyya* (*What Is Nationalism?*) (Beirut, 1959), pp. 251–252.

[90] Quoted in Haim, "Islam and the Theory of Arab Nationalism," p. 283.

obedience to, the state; and this practical consequence is the very same as that which traditional Islamic writers, though no doubt for different reasons, have always preached to the faithful with regard to their *umma*. The latter must be upheld and succored, and due regard given to the rulers, who must be obeyed for fear of the greater evil of dissension and civil war. The doctrine of al-Husri appeals to these ingrained attitudes. Its very ambiguity increases its appeal, and it is perhaps in this profound ambiguity that we must seek the great success of totalitarian doctrines in the Arab East in modern times.

The second point on which al-Husri concentrated his efforts was to establish that Egypt was part of the Arab nation and to convince the Egyptians of this truth. Until fairly recently, Egypt was not considered, either by the Egyptians or by the Arab nationalists, as part of the Arab nation. Azoury, as has been seen, excluded it from the boundaries of his proposed Arab state, and the Sherif Husain did likewise in the claim he submitted to the British government which he said was based on the desires of the secret Arab societies. Amin al-Rihani, writing as late as 1937, adhered to the same boundaries.[91] So did Shakib Arslan in an address he gave at Damascus in the same year: he envisaged an Arab union among Iraq, Saudi Arabia, Syria, Palestine, and Transjordan, which the emirates of the Arabian Peninsula would join eventually. If Egypt, he said, found this Arab bloc existing on its eastern boundaries, "we do not think she would hesitate to link herself with this great Arab nation, with firm military and economic links." Again, he who did so much to encourage and organize resistance to the French in North Africa confined himself to saying that "our unity [with North Africa] is no more than religious, linguistic, cultural, and social." [92] And on the eve of the formation of the Arab League, Nuri al-Sa'id, in the scheme for Arab unity which he submitted to the British government in 1942, still excluded Egypt from his proposal.[93] It

---

[91] Anis Sayigh, *al-Fikra al-arabiyya fi Misr* (*The Arab Idea in Egypt*) (Beirut, 1959), p. 153.

[92] Shakib Arslan, *al-Wahda al-arabiyya* (*Arab Unity*) (Damascus, 1937). This address is quoted and summarized in Rossi, *op. cit.*, pp. 193–195. On Shakib Arslan see E. Lévi-Provençal, "L'Emir Shakib Arslan (1869–1946)," in *Cahiers de l'Orient Contemporain* (Paris, 1947), pp. 5–19.

[93] Nuri al-Sa'id, *Arab Independence and Unity* (Baghdad, 1943), pp. 11–12. Nuri al-Sa'id's conclusions are reprinted in J. C. Hurewitz, *Diplomacy in the Near and Middle East* (Princeton, 1956), II, 236–237.

is true that in an occasional rhetorical flourish, or in a burst of poetic license, Egypt was sometimes included in the domain of Arabism, as in the well-known poem by the Syrian Fakhri al-Barudi:

> *The country of the Arabs is my fatherland,*
> *From Damascus to Baghdad,*
> *From Nejd to Yemen,*
> *To Egypt and Tetuan.*

While the Arab nationalists never really envisaged Egypt as part of the Arab fatherland, the resistance of the Egyptians to such a prospect was always positive and forceful. Urabi rejected emphatically the rumors that, in his rebellion, he was intent on founding an Arab state, for in this, he said "there would be loss to all Islam and disobedience to the Prophet." [94] Muhammad Abduh called the Ottoman Empire a protective barrier "for the Muslims which, if it would disappear, they [*sic*] would become like the Jews, without protectors." On parting from al-Afghani in Paris, Abduh declared that the preservation of the Ottoman Empire was an article of religious belief, and that the duty to preserve it did not derive from such ideas as "the fatherland" or "the welfare of the country" or the like.[95] The nationalists, like Mustafa Kamil, deriving their notions from European sources, joined the traditionalists in defending the existence of the Ottoman Empire; for to them, Egypt's formal link with the empire was a guarantee and an obstacle against British desires fully to annex the country. Mustafa Kamil, in his book *The Eastern Question* (1898), attacked Blunt's *The Future of Islam* and its proposal of an Arabian caliphate as a nefarious British plot.[96] Again, in a speech at Alexandria in 1897, he attacked the Syrian immigrants in Egypt who filled the newspapers with attacks on the Ottoman Empire and foretold its end and the dethronement of the caliph, and nonetheless became surprised and angry when the loyal Egyptians despised and hated them.[97]

---

[94] Sati' al-Husri, *Ma hiya al-qaumiyya*, p. 203.

[95] Muhammad Rashid Rida, *Tarikh al-ustadh al-imam*, I, 912; C. C. Adams, *Islam and Modernism in Egypt* (Oxford, 1933), p. 62.

[96] *The Eastern Question* constitutes Vols. VII and VIII of Ali Fahmi Kamil, ed., *Mustafa Kamil Pasha fi arba'-a wa thalathin rabi'* (*Thirty-four Years of Mustafa Kamil's Life*) (9 vols.; Cairo, 1908–1911). The attack on Blunt appears in Vol. VII, pp. 27 ff.

[97] *Ibid.*, VI, 29.

Introduction

Mustafa Kamil was referring to the Christian Syrians who, of course, had no reason to love the Ottoman Empire and the principle of Muslim supremacy it embodied. In Egypt, under British occupation, they felt free to vent their dislike.

Mustafa Kamil's successor in the leadership of the Nationalist Party, Muhammad Farid, extended his attack to a Muslim like Rashid Rida who, a true instinct warned him—for he had little evidence to go on—was not perfectly loyal to the Ottoman Empire. He accused Rashid Rida, in 1911, of working under the guise of religion to propagate the idea of Arab independence and of being in league with the British to create a puppet Arabian caliphate, like the mock caliphate of the Abbasids under the Mamluks in Cairo, prior to the Ottoman conquest. He even confessed that his fear of the Arab Muslim and of the harm he might do to the caliphate exceeded his fear of Bulgarians, Greeks, and the like.[98] The Arabic edition of the Ottoman official report on Arab subversive activities, *La Vérité sur la Question Syrienne*, reproduces a Decentralization Party manifesto which denounces Abd al-Aziz Shawish for having written an article in which he said that the Arab Muslims were more harmful to the state than all the Christians.[99] In 1911, also, Ahmad Lutfi al-Sayyid, writing in his newspaper *al-Jarida*, said that he could not understand the meaning of an Arab question, and he contemptuously advised those who devoted their energies to the formation of a party to expound Arab grievances that they would do better to explain the Ottoman Constitution to the Bedouins.[100]

An eyewitness has recorded the strong feelings aroused in Egyptians during the war by the sight of Arab officers in Sherifian uniform; one evening, in a theater, he saw three such officers being abused and insulted by Egyptians of good family.[101] After the war and the disappearance of the Ottoman Empire, the Egyptian attitude was still skeptical. Abd al-Rahman Azzam recounted that once he was speaking to Zaghlul about Arab unity when Zaghlul interrupted him with a question: "If you add one zero to another and then to another, what sum will you get?" [102] In

---

[98] Anis Sayigh, *op. cit.*, p. 55, where the article is quoted.
[99] *Idahat 'an al-masa'il al-siyasiyya* (Istanbul, 1916), pp. 100–103.
[100] Anis Sayigh, *op. cit.*, p. 59.
[101] Abd al-Fattah abu'l-Nasr al-Yafi, *op. cit.*, p. 192.
[102] Quoted in Sati' al-Husri, *al-Uruba awwalan* (*Arabism First*) (Beirut, 1955).

1938, also, the periodical *al-Hilal* asked three prominent Egyptians what they thought of the idea of Arab unity. All of them, Ahmad Lutfi al-Sayyid, then Rector of Fuad University, Bahi al-Din Barakat, the Speaker of the Chamber of Deputies, and the poet Khalil Mutran, professed themselves skeptical of such an idea. Lutfi al-Sayyid went so far as to describe the idea as pure fantasy (*wahm min al-awham*).[103]

The traditionalists also continued to regard Islamic unity, rather than Arab, as the aim of all Muslims.

It was in Egypt, at the instance of Egyptian divines, that the Caliphate Congress of 1926 was convened. A representative view of the traditionalist attitude is found in an address given by Mustafa Ahmad Rifa'i al-Labban to the Young Men's Muslim Association entitled: "The duty of the Muslim toward his particular fatherland (*watan khass*) and toward his general fatherland (*watan 'amm*)." The speaker explained that the Egyptian had duties toward Egypt, which was the place where he lived, and to "our general fatherland, the Islamic world which extends from the farthest east to the farthest west." [104]

Again, in 1938, the Shaikh al-Azhar, Mustafa al-Maraghi, declared that he had no faith in the plan of Arab unity and that he did not favor it.[105] There were, of course, both political and doctrinal reasons for this attitude. Both King Fuad and his successor Farouk had the ambition to become caliph.[106] Soon after Farouk's accession to the throne a campaign seems to have been started to push his claim to the caliphate. A pamphlet which no doubt was part of this campaign, reproducing an essay by al-Afghani, *Islamic Union; Unity and Sovereignty*, had an epigraph and a foreword by the publisher in which it was asserted that the

---

[103] *Al-Hilal* (Dec., 1938), pp. 121–124. Lutfi al-Sayyid's views are on p. 123.

[104] The address is reproduced in Muhibb al-Din al-Khatib, ed., *al-Muntaqa min muhadarat jam'iyyat al-shubban al-muslimin* (*Select Addresses to the Young Men's Muslim Association*) (Cairo, 1930–1931), II, 250–259. The quotation is from p. 254.

[105] See E. Nune, "L'Idea dell'Unita Araba in Recenti Debattiti della Stampa del Vicino Oriente," *Oriente Moderno*, XVIII (1938), 411.

[106] See E. Kedourie, "Panarabism and British Policy," in Laqueur, *op. cit.*, pp. 100–111. Farouk admitted in 1942 that such ambitions had been nursed. See Fuad Abaza's account of an interview with him, "al-Ittihad al-arabi fi'l-qahira" ("The Arab Union in Cairo"), *al-Kitab al-thani* (*The Second Book*) (Cairo, 1950), p. 10.

best way to save Islam would be to unite under Farouk. "There will be no power for Islam," the epigraph said, "nor a union of those who utter the creed of the unity [of the Godhead] except by ranging themselves under the banner of the lord of the kings of Islam, our Lord His Majesty Farouk the First, the Caliph of the Muslims." The foreword also called Farouk the "Upright King and the Commander of the Faithful." [107] Again, at the Arab Muslim Parliamentary Congress dealing with Palestine, held in Cairo in 1938, there were shouts, obviously prearranged, acclaiming King Farouk as the Commander of the Faithful.[108]

PAN-ARABISM AFTER THE ANGLO-EGYPTIAN AGREEMENT

Sometime in the 1930's, after the conclusion of the Anglo-Egyptian Agreement of 1936, a few Arab nationalists began to consider seriously the possibility of including Egypt in the Arab national movement. Egypt was populous and rich, and if freed from British control she was likely to be a respectable power on the Middle Eastern scene. Some Syrians living in Cairo, together with some Egyptians such as Abd al-Sattar al-Basil, Abd al-Rahman Azzam, Mansur Fahmi, and Muhammad Ali Alluba gave their support to a Society for Arab Unity, which had first appeared among university students in Cairo, in 1936. As'ad Daghir, the Lebanese Christian who had been connected with the Arab nationalist movement since the First World War, and who became the secretary of the Society, tells us that the hopes which the nationalists had placed in Iraq for the realization of Arab unity had by then become dim, and that with Syria, Palestine, and the Lebanon occupied by foreign powers these countries could not do much for the movement. As'ad Daghir adds that the society drew material and moral support from Prince Faisal, the second son of Ibn Saud, who was no doubt glad to encourage any movement to diminish Hashemite influence in the Middle East.[109]

It was in those years that Sati' al-Husri himself engaged in a

[107] Jamal al-Din al-Afghani *al-Wahda al-islamiyya wa'l-wahda wa'l-siyada* (*Muslim Union; Unity and Sovereignty*) (Cairo, 1938). The publisher was Izzat al-Attar.

[108] *Oriente Moderno*, XVIII (1938), 589.

[109] As'ad Daghir, *Mudhakkirati ala hamish al-qadiyya al-arabiyya* (*My Memoirs Concerning the Arab Question*) (Cairo, 1959), pp. 242–243.

campaign to prove to Egyptians and others that Egypt was part of the Arab nation. He took violent issue with those like Taha Husain who then maintained that Egypt was really part of Europe[110] in its present culture but was pharaonic in its traditions. Taha Husain had said that the Egyptian was an Egyptian before anything else; Sati' al-Husri disclaimed any desire, as an Arab nationalist, to deprive Egyptians of their feeling for Egypt; Arabism did not rule out loyalty to Egypt. Why, then, did Taha Husain assume that these were irreconcilable opposites? Again, what did Taha Husain mean by pharaonism? Did he mean a restoration of the pharaonic language or the pharaonic religion? This was absurd, and Sati' could not bring himself to think that Taha Husain meant this. Could he, then, mean the protection of pharaonic archaeological remains? But in this case, why did he assume that Arabism entailed the destruction of the Sphinx and the Pyramids? Similarly, Sati' al-Husri ridiculed both Taha Husain's assertion that the Egyptians were unrelated to the Arabs by blood and that Egyptian history was an independent entity, unrelated to that of its neighbors. He then took the offensive and argued that language was a most powerful link between Egypt and the other Arab countries, and that Arab unity was not only a matter of sentiment, but was a vital interest to Egypt and those other countries.[111]

In an article which he published in a Baghdad newspaper in 1936, Sati' al-Husri explained that nature had endowed Egypt with all the qualities which made it incumbent upon the country to assume the leadership of the Arab national movement. It was in the heart of the Arab lands, it was the biggest of the existing Arab states, it had made greater progress than any in adopting modern civilization, it was the most important cultural center in the Arab world, its modern machinery of administration had been longest in operation, its literature was the best in quality

---

[110] Taha Husain has since completely changed his views and has become an advanced Arab nationalist; see his article, "al-Udaba' hum bunat al-qaumiyya al-arabiyya" ("Writers Are the Builders of Arab Nationhood"), *al-Adab* (Beirut, Jan., 1958), pp. 7–11.

[111] Sati' al-Husri, "Bain Misr wa'l-uruba" ("Between Egypt and Arabism"), in *Ara' wa ahadith fi'l-wataniyya wa'l-qaumiyya* (*Opinions and Addresses on Patriotism and Nationalism*) (Cairo, 1944), pp. 109–120. This article was first published in *al-Risala* (Cairo, 1938), and was followed by another, "Haul al-wahda al-arabiyya" ("On Arab Unity"), included in the same volume, pp. 121–130. The latter prolonged the controversy with Taha Husain.

and the purest in language. In short, Egypt, he claimed, was the natural leader of the Arabs.[112]

The outbreak of war, British encouragement of Pan-Arabism, and the unlikelihood of a restoration of the caliphate, all must have turned Farouk's thoughts to the leadership of the Arab national movement. In 1942, the Arab Union was formed, a society that would work for Arab unity. Obviously, this was with official encouragement, and prominent Egyptian personalities were associated with it. The society's secretary, Fuad Abaza, presented a memorandum to the chief of the Royal Cabinet in March, 1942, to explain the aims of the society. Arab unity, based on ties of language, the memorandum said, had been mooted previously; it came to the fore during the discussions on Palestine which took place in Cairo and in London in 1938 and 1939, and unity seemed to the society a worthy object, all the more so because their own views were reinforced by Mr. Eden's declaration, in February, 1942, in favor of Arab unity. According to the memorandum, Arab union would include Egypt, the Sudan, the Arabian Peninsula, Iraq, Syria, the Lebanon, Palestine, Transjordan, North Africa, and all other Arab-speaking countries. This, Abaza pointed out, definitely excluded non–Arabic-speaking Muslims, and therefore excluded the idea of a caliphate "of which no Arab country can, today, bear the heavy burdens, discharge the momentous responsibilities, or pay the exorbitant price." [113]

Obviously, the argument found favor with the King; in 1943, preliminary talks on Arab unity were held in Cairo, and Abd al-Rahman Azzam, later to be the first Secretary-General of the Arab League when it was set up in 1945, could write in a magazine article that Egypt was an Arab country even before the time of Christ, and that some Copts were even more Arab than the inhabitants of Mecca itself or of Madina.[114] The officers who carried out the *coup d'état* of 1952 took over this new element of Egyptian foreign policy, and even became its most zealous advocates. The Egyptian Constitution of 1956 states in its first article that "Egypt is a sovereign independent Arab state; it is a

---

[112] Sati' al-Husri, "Daur Misr fi'l-nahda al-qaumiyya al-arabiyya" ("The Role of Egypt in the Modern Arab Renaissance"), in *Ara' wa ahadith fi'l-wataniyya* . . . , pp. 131–134.

[113] Fuad Abaza, in *al-Ittihad al-Arabi* . . . *op. cit.*, pp. 6–8.

[114] Abd al-Rahman Azzam, "al-Wahda al-arabiyya" ("Arab Unity"), *al-Hilal* (Cairo, Sept.-Oct., 1943), pp. 462–463.

democratic republic; and the Egyptian people are an integral part of the Arab nation." Yet it would seem that for all this fervor, in spite of the fact that Gamal Abdel Nasser has been proclaimed the champion of Arabism and that the identity of Egypt is now submerged in a United Arab Republic, an ambiguity in Egypt's commitment to Arab nationalism still remains. It must not be forgotten that until 1943, or thereabouts, the idea was still extremely strange in Egypt. Among the Egyptians, the term Arab, as used in current speech, is derogatory, denoting a shiftless nomad, someone to be looked upon with contempt by a people who had been settled cultivators from time immemorial.

A curious illustration of the shift in the meaning of the word "Arab," deliberately attempted, then occurred in a guide to the Egyptian Parliament, the second edition of which appeared in 1943. In the first edition, the author explains, he described some members of Parliament as "Sheikhs of the Arabs," meaning the chieftains of Arab tribes. But Abd al-Sattar al-Basil, one of the prominent members of the Arab Union, had asked him to change the designation to "Sheikhs of the Bedouins," as he explains, "because he believes that the Egyptians of today are also 'Arabs.' " [115] When the movement to link Egypt to Arabism started, even its most fervent exponents such as Muhammad Ali Alluba disclaimed that it had any political significance; he looked on it, rather, as an attempt to realize cultural, spiritual, and scientific unity, a unity which would transcend geographical and political barriers.[116] Again, Makram Ubaid, the Coptic leader of the Wafd who, because of his religion, liked to curry favor with Muslims, whether Egyptians or not, and who at that time declared that the Egyptians were Arabs, was careful to say that the unity he envisaged was to be built round an ideal. It was not to mean, he asserted, that the different fatherlands of the Arabs would lose their personality or be merged in one great fatherland in which they would lose their identity.[117]

Even after the commitment to the Arab League, Egyptian

[115] Ahmad al-Sawadi, *al-Burluman fi'l-mizan* (*Parliament in the Balance*), (2d ed.; Cairo, 1943), p. 319.
[116] Muhammad Ali Alluba, "Ahamiyyat al-mu'tamarat al-arabiyya" ("The Importance of Arab Congresses"), *al-Hilal*, special issue on "Arabs and Islam in the Modern Age" (Cairo, 1939), p. 51.
[117] Makram Ubaid, "al-Misriyyun Arab" ("The Egyptians Are Arab"), in *ibid.*, p. 33.

doubts about Arabism were not to be stilled. The journalist Mustafa Amin, in an article in *Akhbar al-yaum* in January, 1951, was quite sarcastic about the idea of a united Arab state; he likened it to such chimeras as the transformation of deserts into gardens, or a single world state. In an inquiry held by the magazine *al-Musawwar*, in 1953, Abd al-Rahman Azzam stated, "We are Egyptians first, Arabs second, and Muslims third." He looked on the Arab countries as a "vital space" for Egypt, necessary for its security and its exports. Dr. Fikri Abaza declared: "We are old Egyptians, nothing else"; and Dr. Husain Kamil Salim said that they were Egyptians first and last, and that Egypt was a state before the world had ever heard of the Arabs.[118] Gamal Abdel Nasser, in his *Philosophy of the Revolution*, did not write of Egypt as being Arab, but of Egypt being at the center of three circles, of which one was Arab and the other two African and Islamic.[119]

The third point with which Sati' al-Husri is concerned in his writings on Arab nationalism is to prove that Arab nationalism and Islam are not incompatible. In his controversy with Taha Husain he was tackling modernist objections to Arab nationalism, but here he was endeavoring to banish the doubts which traditionalists had concerning the movement. When Husain rose in revolt against the Ottomans, in 1916, the Arab nationalists, to dissociate themselves from the Ottoman caliphate, had to emphasize that they were Arabs, that the solidarity they practiced embraced all Arabs, regardless of religion. This, of course, was dubious doctrine to traditionalists who stood by Islamic solidarity and condemned Arab nationalism (as had Mustafa al-Maraghi, the Sheikh of al-Azhar, in 1938[120]) or looked on Arab unity a trifle more indulgently, as a prelude to Islamic unity. The latter attitude was shared by Ahmad Hasan al-Zayyat, the editor of the Cairo periodical *al-Risala*.[121]

By the 1930's the Ottoman Empire was no more, and since Arab nationalism, if it was to get anywhere, had to capture the loyalties of peoples predominantly Muslim, there were serious

---

[118] Instances are quoted in Sati' al-Husri, *al-Uruba awwalan*, pp. 115, 127, 145.

[119] See no. 18 in the anthology.

[120] Nune, *loc. cit.*

[121] See Nabih Amin Faris, *Ghuyum arabiyya* (*Arab Clouds*) (Beirut, 1950), p. 91.

objections to divorcing Arabism from Islam and so allowing the impression to gain ground that Arabism and Islam were opposed to each other. Hence, Sati' al-Husri took up al-Maraghi's declarations and attempted to refute them. He pointed out that it was unrealistic to expect unity among Cairo, Baghdad, Teheran, Kabul, and the other Islamic centers, before realizing unity among those Islamic centers which were Arabic-speaking. The one, he argued, is the essential prerequisite of the other; therefore, to oppose Arab unity would be not only not to support, but actually to oppose, Islamic unity. But he went further: he actually denied that Islam, or any religion, could be the basis of a political structure. To cling to Islamic unity, then, or actually to prefer it to Arab unity, was either naïve or ill-disposed. Arab unity could in no way harm the cause of Islam, but would even promote it.[122]

In discussing the relation of Islam to Arab nationalism, Sati' al-Husri was dealing, albeit in a controversial and superficial manner, with the central problem confronting any serious theory of Arab nationalism. Such a theory would seek to replace Islamic loyalty—which, so far, has been the only one to move the Muslims—by loyalty to Arabism. But however "scientific" such theories claimed to be, however learned in anthropology, philology, and the other specialized subjects for which nationalists have such affection, the fact remained that Arab nationalism had to make place for Islam, to accommodate itself to it, or else risk to find itself exiled to the limbo of clever ideas which dazzle by their subtlety and astonish by their sterility. The "Arabs," in their majority, remained Muslim, and unless Arabism were made to seem consonant with their religion there was no prospect that it would make many converts. The practical men knew, without the support of any elaborate theory, that in actual fact the great strength of Arab nationalism was that it could draw on Muslim sentiment. Thus Nuri al-Sa'id, pleading the cause of Pan-Arabism with the British government in 1942, could write naturally: "All Arabs and particularly those of the Near and Middle East have deep down in their hearts the feeling that they are 'members of one another.' Their nationalism springs from the Muslim feeling of brotherhood enjoined on them by the Prophet Muhammad in his last public speech." [123]

---

[122] See no. 12 in the anthology.
[123] Nuri al-Sa'id, *op. cit.*, p. 8.

Introduction

Fadil al-Jamali, in a work devoted to pedagogy, could remark in passing, without feeling the need to justify and amplify, that "the Arab world comprises all the countries where Arab culture predominates, where the majority speak Arabic, and where the Islamic religion is prevalent." [124] Such an attitude is natural, more natural in fact than to define the Arab nation with reference to race, language, history, and so on; and it has, for its support, the sanction of history. At the beginning of Islam, and for some time thereafter, to be Muslim and to be Arab signified the same thing, and Arab converts had to attach themselves as clients to Arab tribes in order to find for themselves a place within the new Muslim polity. [125] To be Arab, then, and to be Muslim, naturally go together. Indeed, Rashid Rida, as will be recalled, based his preference for the Arabs over the Turks on zeal for Islam and a desire for its reform. But the official theory of Arab nationalism, such as it came to be after the First World War, abjured any exclusively religious criterion: the Arabs were a nation, it was argued, because they spoke the same language, lived in the same area, had a common ancestry, a common history, and so on. Yet, it was imperative for Islam to be incorporated within the theory. This was done by shifting the emphasis of Rashid Rida's argument slightly but significantly. It was now argued, as, for example, Abd al-Rahman Azzam did in a lecture of 1943, [126] that the ideals of Islam, as revealed by an Arab prophet, are the very ideals and values of modern Arab nationalism and that the Arab nation, now remembering its prodigious resurgence in the seventh century of the Christian era, desired once more to take its rightful place in the world and to resume the mission which Muhammad had inaugurated.

It was another ideologue, however, Abd al-Rahman al-Bazzaz, who explored the full implications of this argument and presented them in a logical, coherent, and almost perfect form. In a lecture given in Baghdad, in 1952, [127] al-Bazzaz asserted that Arab nationalism and Islam went together in every respect. "Is-

[124] Muhammad Fadil al-Jamali, *Wajhat al-tarbiya wa'l-ta'lim fi'l-alam al-arabi* . . . (*The Direction of Pedagogy and Education in the Arab World* . . .) (Baghdad, 1935), p. 5.

[125] See the excellent article by C. Snouck Hurgronje, "L'Islam et le Problème des Races," *Revue du Monde Musulman*, L (1922).

[126] See no. 13 in the anthology.

[127] Translated as no. 15 in the anthology.

lam," he said, "although it is a universal religion suitable for all peoples, . . . is undoubtedly a religion first revealed to the Arabs themselves; in this sense, it is their own special religion. The Prophet is from them, the Koran is in their language; Islam retained many of their previous customs, adopting and polishing the best of them." He said further that "the sending of the Prophet to the Arabs revived the Arab nation in its entirety and resurrected it." Al-Bazzaz protests against the attempt to divorce the Prophet from his Arab environment, and he asserts that the pre-Islamic Arabs must already have been a highly civilized people for a genius such as Muhammad to appear in their midst. A Muslim Arab need not disparage the history of the Arabs before Islam, so as to enhance and glorify it after Islam; between the two there is unbroken continuity, and "the Muslim Arab, when he exalts his heroes, partakes of two emotions, that of the pious Muslim and that of the proud nationalist." Al-Bazzaz sums up his attitude by means of a bold analogy: "We can say that the position of the Arabs in Islam is like that of the Russians in the communist order"! Clearly, though it is not impossible to disentangle the strands of Arab nationalism from those of Islam, it is impossible to disembody it from Islam.

As the theory now stands, Muhammad has become the founder of the Arab nation, and Islam itself the incarnation of the Arab national spirit. But if such is the case can a non-Muslim, who otherwise fulfills the necessary conditions, be considered fully an Arab? This would have been quite impossible if writers such as al-Bazzaz meant by Islam what the traditionalists understood by it, namely an unquestioning belief in a specific divine revelation superseding all previous revelations. But this is not what such modern writers mean by Islam; Islam they see as the product of the Arab national genius, and this view of things provides a solution for the non-Muslim's difficulty. He becomes fully Arab when he recognizes Muhammad as the hero of Arab nationalism and venerates Islam as the religion which enabled the Arab nation to assert its place in the world. In an address of 1947 which commemorated the anniversary of the Prophet's birth, al-Bazzaz said that "the Christian Arabs are as obliged as the Muslims to commemorate the anniversary in some way; because if Muhammad was a messenger and a leader to the Muslims, he was also a hero and a leader to the other [non-Muslim] members of the

Arab nation." [128] If Islam is to be regarded as the foundation of Arab nationalism, then, the demand that Christians should venerate it equally with the Muslims does not seem, at first sight, exorbitant. But such a demand is an ambiguous one, since Islam, even considered as the foundation of Arab nationalism, still remains a religion which is practiced by a group who are, and for centuries remained, the overlords of the Christians in Muslim countries.

Is not this demand, then, a secular version of the old arguments for Muslim supremacy? Such a conclusion may be suspected from the tone, for instance, in which al-Bazzaz speaks of the Christians in his lecture of 1952. "It also befits us," he said, "to make it clear that there is nothing in this national call of ours which need exercise the non-Muslims among the Arabs, or diminish their rights as good compatriots. Chauvinism, in all its aspects and forms, is incompatible with the nature of the Arabs. The non-Muslim Arabs used to enjoy all their rights under the shadow of the Arab state, from the earliest times, and the scope open to them was wide. The loyal nationalists among the Arab Christians realize this, and know that Islam and the civilization which accompanied it are an indivisible part of our national heritage, and they must, as nationalists, cherish it as their brother Muslims cherish it." That is not the tone of equal speaking to equal; rather, it is the voice of a tolerant superior, aware of his station, affably reassuring a timid subordinate.

To clinch the argument, al-Bazzaz quotes the words of Qustantin Zuraiq, a Christian Arab nationalist, who himself argues that the duty of every Arab, whatever his sect or community, is to sanctify the memory of Muhammad and to interest himself in Islam. This argument of Qustantin Zuraiq illustrates a curious and important feature of Arab nationalist thought. When Muslim writers argue that Islam and Arab nationalism are not incompatible, and even that each is implicit in the other, we can see that they are studying a vital problem which concerns them intimately. In the first place, they are trying to counter traditionalist objections; in the second place, they may also be trying to convince themselves that in being Arab nationalists they are also good Muslims, that what Islam enjoins nationalism also

---

[128] Abd al-Rahman al-Bazzaz, *Min ruh al-islam* (*From the Spirit of Islam*) (Baghdad, 1959), p. 103.

57

requires, and that therefore nationalism is a true substitute for a religious faith about which they have grown skeptical. Such preoccupations cannot trouble Christian writers, of course, yet we find them saying with even more vehemence and eloquence than the Muslims that the relation between Islam and Arab nationalism is intimate and that Islam should be the special object of veneration for all nationalists, no matter what their actual religion. Indeed, they have said this earlier and more frequently than Muslims. Qustantin Zuraiq was saying it as early as 1938,[129] and Michel Aflaq, the Damascus Christian founder of the Ba'th Party, reiterated the same point in a lecture of 1943.

The causes of this phenomenon are complex. The earliest Christian Arab nationalists, such as Negib Azouri, argued that in a future Arab state religion and politics would be separated. Though Edmond Rabbath, writing in the 1930's, considered Islam as one of the factors which had formed Arab nationality, he did not argue that Islam should be the basis of modern Arab nationalism. As Arab nationalism became an organized political movement, however, dictating the policies of states such as Iraq (the political leaders of which were Muslim), it was no longer open to Christian Arab nationalists who might wish to obtain a hearing to advocate an Arab nationalism divorced from Islam. Their attitude was perhaps decisively shaped by another factor. The loyalties of Christians, in a society organized on the millet system, had in the past been directed toward their own communities; but with the breakdown of this system the younger generation no longer found communal ties satisfying, and some of them transferred their affections to an Arab nation of which they claimed to be fellow members, along with the Muslims. This transference happened most frequently with Arabic-speaking Orthodox Christians, whose community was ruled by Greek-speaking clergy; and these men, from the middle of the nineteenth century onward, were encouraged by Russia, for her own ends, to look upon themselves as Arabs oppressed by Greeks.[130]

That the preoccupation of Arab Christian writers with Islam stems not only from their desire to prove themselves good Arab nationalists, but also from a spiritual crisis taking place inside

[129] See no. 14 in the anthology.
[130] See E. Kedourie, "Religion and Politics: The Diaries of Khalil Sakakini," in *St. Antony's Papers*, No. IV (1958).

their community, may be clearly illustrated by the views of one writer whose value, in this context, is all the greater in that he cannot be described as a nationalist. A small pamphlet bearing the title *Da'wat nasara al-arab ila 'l-dukhul fi'l-islam* (*A Call to the Christian Arabs to Embrace Islam*) appeared in Cairo, in 1931. It was published by the Muslim religious periodical *al-Fath*, in which the contents of the pamphlet had appeared previously as articles. The author was Khalil Iskandar Qubrusi, a Christian Orthodox who, from internal evidence, seems to have been of Palestinian origin. Qubrusi is not much concerned with politics. Believing that religion is necessary to man, he is yet profoundly dissatisfied with his own. He holds that primitive Christianity, which had originated in the East, was corrupted by the Europeans, who now seek to dominate the Eastern Christians. "Our religion," he says, "is now more like a childish toy with which we are distracted from the true worship of the Creator and led to the worship of various nationalities"; "the teachings of the Gospel do not tally with their teachings. They say: Hate, avoid, beware, detest, abhor, while the Gospel says: Love your enemies and bless those who curse you"; "the Christian religion in its Frankish dress has become the religion of slavery."

Qubrusi then proceeds to enumerate the various ways in which the European Christians have oppressed the Eastern:

> 1. Holiness is a preserve of the Westerners alone! Not a single Arab has been proclaimed a saint. Does this mean that we are all evil men, while some of them are saintly men?
> 2. Their monopoly of high religious office from that of cardinal to that of bishop. The sons of gods, no matter what their nationality, occupy these offices; but not the Arabs.
> 3. The sway exercised by foreign religious missions and missionary institutions over our own people and their trampling over the rights of the Arab clergy and the denial to these of the administrative independence which obtains in other countries.
> 4. The fact that no Arab sits in the religious courts and the communal council, while many foreigners are members.
> 5. Their begging for alms in the name of the Arab Christians, in order to lower their dignity and not out of benevolence. They rejoice in this falsehood in order to have an excuse for begging, and in order to expose the infirmities of the Arabs and their shame, and to swell up with pride.

And this is not all, for Qubrusi proceeds to remind the readers of the horrors of the Inquisition, which from 1481 to 1499 burnt at the stake 10,220 people, hanged 6,860, and condemned 97,023 more to other punishments.

In contrast to this corrupt and cruel religion, Qubrusi holds up for the reader's admiration a benevolent, egalitarian, democratic Islam, the Islam found in the pages of Lebon and other European enthusiasts. Since Christianity is corrupt and Islam pure, Qubrusi proceeds to argue, and since all religions have the same end, namely love of God and of man, then let the Arab Christians embrace Islam, and thus return to their pure original Christianity: "Since the religion of God has always been one among the ancients and the moderns, and has differed in nothing but its outward form, while its essence and truth are always one, namely what the whole world is commanded to do through the intermediary of the prophets and the messengers, and since the highest aim in religion is belief in God alone and his steadfast worship, as well as mutual aid and forbearance, and since the good is worthy to be loved wherever it is found, what harm would it do the Christian Arabs if they united in religion as they are united in race [with the Muslims] and we may then get away from this misleading faction, in fulfillment of His saying, glory be to Him: I have not taken as a support those who lead into error."

Qubrusi then exhorts his fellow Christians to embrace Islam as the true uncorrupted religion. This is not his only reason, however; he argues not only that Islam is pure religion, as Christianity is corrupt religion, but also that Islam is the religion of the Arabs. As the Eastern Christians are also Arab, equally oppressed, along with the Muslims, by Europeans, they should therefore embrace Islam and unite with the Muslims in withstanding European oppression. Thus he writes: "What harm would it do the Arab Christians if they should guide themselves by the light of Islam, which is a true Arab religion recognized even by European thinkers? If I call to it, it is because I bring tidings of a blessed union which is the foundation of strength, assuming, that is, that we intend to free ourselves completely from the yoke of British, Zionist, and foreign imperialism, so that there should be only Muslim Arabs and Christian foreigners." Again he writes: "I have therefore called you to Islam, your Arabian religion,

which God has sent down in your noble language. Be not therefore like a child whose sleep deepens as you try to wake him up,
or like those who have become careless through procrastination.
I am not calling you to give in to a passing whim or to a novel
opinion but to the exemplary path in which is to be found the
best both of eternity and of this world. Let souls be one, let all
hands coöperate, and let all dispositions be cordial, and all purposes be in harmony and concord, and peace be with you."

Qubrusi's motives, as can be seen, are mixed. He has a genuine
regard for Islam as a religion, but he also wishes his fellow Christians to adopt Islam because it is the religion of the Arabs. Can
it be that the Eastern Christians, Arabs as he asserts them to be,
would thereby become more perfect Arabs, or at least not give
rise to suspicions in Muslim breasts that they are in league with
Christian Europeans? To such questions, which this pamphlet
raises, there can be no categorical answers. All that may be said
is that the pamphlet gives evidence of unease among some Arabic-speaking Orthodox Christians, discontented with their own
lot, and of a desire to identify themselves with Muslims.

MICHEL AFLAQ AND THE BA'TH PARTY

In later writers, the need for such identification becomes much
sharper, but it also entirely loses the religious quality to be discerned in Qubrusi. Two attitudes of Arabic-speaking Christians
toward Muslim Arabs may now be discerned. The first, which
may be called moderate, is well exemplified by Charles Malik's
article, "The Near East: the Search for Truth," [131] and is one
that bends over backward in an attempt to "understand" the
Muslim Arabs, to be "fair" to them, to dissipate "misunderstand-
ings." Islam, it says in effect, is a great religion, and the Arabs
are a great people; and the Eastern Christians are best qualified
to interpret their needs and views to Europe and to effect a rec-
onciliation between the West and the Arabs, based on a restoration of their dignity and their national being. The second attitude, which may be called extremist, holds unequivocally that
Islam is inseparable from Arab nationalism, and that it is the
duty of all Arab nationalists to uphold and venerate it. Qustantin

---

[131] See no. 16 in the anthology.

Zuraiq's essay, mentioned above, is a classic statement of this attitude.

Nabih Amin Faris expresses the same thought when, in an address at the American University of Beirut, he says that "the birthday of the Prophet is the birthday of Arabism." [132] A later statement in the same vein is the address by the founder of the Ba'th Party, Michel Aflaq, given in Damascus in 1943 to commemorate Muhammad's birthday. In this address, Aflaq shows a conscious and total departure from orthodox religious attitudes and explicitly represents Islam not as a divine revelation but in part as a response to Arab needs at the time of Muhammad and in part as a foundation of Arabism. For Aflaq, "God" is an expression of man's need, a projection of his thirst for justice. Concluding his address, he said: "We, the new generation carry today a nonpolitical message, a belief and a creed, not mere theories and talk. Only those who suffer and those who believe will understand. We believe in God because we have great need for him. We did not start with this belief, but reached it only with great effort and suffering. How can any youth who has our aspirations not believe in God, that is, in justice and in the triumph of justice?" Such a conclusion Aflaq supports by a long, involved, precise, and quite novel analysis of Islam. In his opinion, there is a split in the Arab personality, a complete divorce between past and present; Islam, as reflected in the life of the Prophet, "is a faithful picture, a complete and true symbol of the nature of the Arab soul, its rich possibilities and its noble leanings. For this reason, it is right to consider it as able continuously to renew itself in its essence rather than in its form and expression."

It is Islam, he reasons, which enabled the Arabs to conquer themselves before conquering the world; yet Islam is not merely a historical event but "a permanent tendency within the Arab nation . . . which is aroused every time that matter controls spirit, and appearance essence, so that the nation comes to be at odds with itself, and [in this struggle] attains a higher unity and a healthy integration." Speaking of the life of the Prophet, Aflaq says: "The life of the Prophet, and it is that which represents the Arab soul in its absolute reality, cannot be known by the intellect but only by living experience." The way to under-

---

[132] See Nabih Amin Faris, *al-Arab al-ahya'* (*The Living Arabs*) (Beirut, 1947), pp. 61–68.

stand it is not to recite the verses of the Koran, but to live it. Unfortunately, however, heroism is nowadays unknown among the Arabs; nevertheless, it is the duty of every youth to try and emulate, however imperfectly, the life of the Prophet, because "Muhammad was the epitome of all the Arabs; so let all the Arabs today be Muhammad."

Aflaq goes on to argue that God could as well have chosen some people other than the Arabs; he could have chosen some other time in which to make his revelation. That he chose the Arabs at a specific and particular time proves that they alone had some essential virtues, and that at the particular time at which Muhammad announced his message they were ready to accept it and to carry it to the rest of mankind. To have delayed the victory of Islam for all those years was in order that the Arabs might attain the truth through their own efforts and experience. "Islam then," Aflaq affirms, "was an Arab movement and its meaning was the renewal of Arabism and its maturity." The language in which Islam was revealed was Arabic; it explained things according to the mentality of the Arabs; it praised specifically Arab virtues and fought specifically Arab vices: "The Muslim at that time was none other than the Arab, but a renovated and perfected Arab who has undergone evolution and attained perfection." Today, he explains, we call those people patriotic (*watani*) or nationalist (*qaumi*), par excellence, who have put their trust in their nation, know intimately that they belong to it, and accept the responsibility which this entails: "The Muslim was (similarly) that Arab who believed in the new religion because he had combined the necessary conditions and virtues so that he could understand that this religion represented the ascent of Arabism toward unity, power, and progress."

Aflaq quickly refutes the possible conclusion that Islam is to be confined to the Arabs, for although Islam is by its nature Arab, yet, he says, it is also humanist in its aims. The role of the Arabs in his scheme is a special one: it is to raise the other nations up to their own level. "The message of Islam," the author affirms, "is to create an Arab humanism." The distinctive feature of the Arabs is that their national awakening coincided with a religious message; their conquests were not made for the sake of material gains, but in order to fulfill a divine duty to bring about goodness and justice. This they can only achieve if they are strong, and the first condition laid down by Islamic humanism is that the Arabs should be strong and masters in their own country. "Islam is universal and eternal," writes Aflaq in another classic sentence, "but its universalism does not mean that it is open at any given time to all possible interpretations and tendencies; rather that at every critical period of history, and at every decisive stage of evolution, it is able to give expression to one of the infinite number of possibilities which it has contained from eternity. The immortality of Islam does not mean its stagnation."

In the present historical situation, Aflaq concludes, Islam shows the need to devote all efforts to the strengthening of the Arabs and the improvement of the conditions of the Arabs. For Aflaq, Islam *is* Arab nationalism, and any other kind of Islam is either degenerate or an imposition of Western imperialism; conversely, today the only defenders of Islam are the Arab nationalists. The Arabs, indeed, he goes on to say, have no need to distinguish between nationalism and religion because "the relationship of Islam to Arabism is not like the relation of any other religion to any other nationalism. When their national consciousness will awaken completely," he goes on, speaking of the Arab Christians, "and when they will regain their true uncorrupted characteristics, the Arab Christians will recognize that Islam constitutes for them a national culture in which they must immerse themselves so that they may understand and love it, and so that they may preserve Islam as they would preserve the most precious element in their Arabism." Aflaq, of course, does realize that today the actual fact is contrary to his wishes, but he exhorts the new generation of Arab Christians to strive for the realization of his ideal. Reverting to the relation between Islam and Arab nationalism, Aflaq explains that reforms are meaningless unless there is a psychological change, that is, unless the nation has faith in its own message and destiny. In early Islam there was indeed such a faith, namely belief in the one God, and it was from this belief that all progress stemmed. This is why he attaches such importance to Islam as a national faith. "We are celebrating," he says, "the memory of the hero of Islam and Arabism, and what is Islam but the child of sufferings, the sufferings of Arabism?"

So far, we have attempted to set out the development of Arab nationalist doctrine in the context of recent Middle Eastern history, of the critical situation of Islam when confronted by modern ideas, and of the heterogeneous nature of Middle Eastern population. But Arab nationalism is not only a doctrine that seeks to define the Arab nation and the boundaries of the Arab state; it is also a doctrine of political action. That is, associated with ideas about the nature of the Arab nation are to be found certain other ideas which recommend certain modes of action as most efficacious in realizing nationalist aims. This doctrine of political action, like the doctrine of Arab nationalism itself, appears fairly late, also in the 1930's, and since then it has been so redefined and perfected that today, in the publications of Michel Aflaq and the Ba'th Party, it constitutes a veritable corpus of maxims, recommendations, and attitudes.

Sati' al-Husri, as has been seen, attempted to define the characteristics of the Arab nation "objectively." The Arab nation, he believed, really existed, and this existence was grounded upon unity of language and history. But in a recent book he indicates that to prove the objective existence of the Arab nation is not enough, and so he comes to make a distinction between Arabism and the feeling of Arabism. Arabism, he points out, has existed from time immemorial; as for "the feeling of Arabism, [and the] thought concerning it, making it the axis of a definite policy," he concedes that this is a recent phenomenon.[133] If such a distinction is made, then it follows that Arab nationalists must fashion a policy for spreading and popularizing the feeling of Arabism, and it further follows that the attempts to define the objective characteristics of the Arab nation must be adjudged either useful or useless, according to whether they do or do not contribute to the success of such a policy. In fact, such attempts were never disinterested scientific exercises, but were undertaken precisely to promote the feeling of Arabism. As such, they fall into the second place, and the main preoccupation must be the feeling itself, which is clearly seen as the motive power whereby a powerful Arab state may be set up. Success will come if the feeling can be instilled into the Arab masses; should the masses remain indifferent, the Arab state would remain a dream.

Thus we see Arab nationalists, who were in control of the Iraqi State, making strenuous efforts to propagate the feeling of Arabism in the schools and in the army, by means of articles, books, and

---

[133] Sati' al-Husri, *al-Uruba awwalan*, p. 185.

broadcasts. One nationalist, Muhammad Mahdi Kubba, who was called by an observer of the Iraqi scene of the 1930's the Goebbels of the nationalists,[134] defined nationalist aims as follows: "The high aim which our national renaissance seeks to reach is the creation of a comprehensive Arab entity, unified in feelings and opinions, cultured in mind and thought, homogeneous in its parts, where individuals are equal in rights and duties, share the same sufferings and hopes, the good times and the bad. This will be done by strengthening the national spirit, and by planting its principles in the souls of the inhabitants of the Arab countries, which would thereafter be linked closely together in such a way as to have a common foreign policy, and as to be able to defend themselves against any dangers." [135]

The same idea is expressed more forcefully and concisely by Ali Nasir al-Din, who says that national consciousness means that the individual should feel that "he is the nation and the nation is himself," and when he expresses, without precaution or circumlocution, the idea that Arabism is a religion for the Arab nationalist. He goes on: "Paradise, which is promised to virtuous believers, is here on earth, just as hell, with which heretics and rebels are threatened, is also to be found here on earth." [136] This secular religion, centering on national feeling, is the logical conclusion of al-Afghani's utilitarian interpretation of Islam, and his emphasis on the unifying properties of *asabiyya*. With the nationalists, however, *asabiyya* is the product of national feeling, not of religion. The development of an Arab *asabiyya* is seen by the congress of Arab students in London, in 1946, as the essential prerequisite for the formation of an Arab state. They list the elements of this Arab *asabiyya* as follows:

1. Intellectual conviction respecting the Arab idea
2. Sentimental attachment to Arab legends, traditions, and history
3. The striving by the soul for an Arab aim which is impossible or quasi-impossible to realize
4. The direction of the will toward the realization of all this in a noble Arab way.[137]

[134] Umar abu'l-Nasr, *al-Iraq al-jadid* (*The New Iraq*) (Beirut, 1937), p. 79.
[135] *Ibid*
[136] Ali Nasir al-Din, *Qadiyyat al-arab* (*The Cause of the Arabs*) (Beirut, 1946), pp. 67, 105.
[137] *Conference of Arab Students in London* (Beirut, n.d.), pp. 20–21.

It is interesting to note that this emphasis on national feeling as the foundation of strong and prosperous states is precisely the point on which Mustafa Kamil seized in his attempt to rouse Egyptian nationalism against the British occupation. "Patriotism," he said in a speech of 1898, "is the most honorable link between individuals and the firm foundation on which are built strong states and powerful kingdoms. All the signs of civilization which you see in Europe are but the fruit of patriotism (*wataniyya*)." [138] Earlier, in 1893, in a magazine for schoolboys which he edited, Mustafa Kamil expressed the view that the feeling of patriotism should be stronger than the love of family.[139] It must follow that this encouragement of political emotions and their subordination to personal and family ties, must make the state the primary focus of loyalty, the ultimate source of happiness and well-being. Here too, Mustafa Kamil provides some early instances—which, in his case, it must be repeated, refer to Egypt and not to the Arab state. In an article in *al-Ahram*, in 1893, he explained that national unity is the source of all welfare, and in another article in his schoolboys' magazine, in 1894, he wrote that he who does not serve his fatherland (*watan*) will live a sad and morose life subject to the anger and the curse of God.[140] Another facet of such a view is that it is the state which is responsible for the happiness, progress, and welfare of society.[141]

It is worth observing that this exaggeration of the role of the state not only proceeds from the necessity to promote a strong national *asabiyya*; it is also a reflection of the traditional strength of state institutions in Muslim society, a strength which was enhanced beyond measure by the introduction of western reforms and techniques of government, in both the Ottoman Empire and Egypt, which greatly increased the scope of state intervention in private affairs and greatly weakened the autonomous institutions of society such as trade guilds and communal organizations. After the First World War, and particularly in the 1930's, the example of Fascist Italy and Nazi Germany increased the attraction of a strong, omnicompetent state to take charge of

---

[138] Ali Fahmi Kamil, *op. cit.*, VI, 138.
[139] *Ibid.*, I, 212.
[140] *Ibid.*, I, 286; II, 24–25.
[141] Mustafa Kamil's interview with Ali Mubarak in 1893, *ibid.*, II, 50.

national revival, as of the methodical organization of the wills and the powers of the citizens in its service. Thus, the Iraqi Director-General of Education, Sami Shawkat, devoted his efforts to propagandize the young in favor of Arab nationalism, and he continually exhorted them to subordinate life, and even sacrifice it, to bring about Arab unity.[142]

The Inspector-General of Education of Iraq in the 1930's, Fadil al-Jamali, shared the same views and attitudes. He deplored the fact that youth was unorganized and undisciplined, that Iraq had nothing to compare with the Nazi or the Fascist youth organization, or with the Russian *Komsomols*. "Such organizations," he said, "demand of the young faith, discipline, and united action, and these are the fundamental conditions of success."[143] It is on the young that al-Jamali pins his hopes for national regeneration; it is they who should spread nationalism among the masses and it is in schools that the task of defining the aims of Arab nationalism should be carried out.[144] Al-Jamali speaks of "the warm blood of youth" which the situation of the Arabs today requires; indeed, modern Arab nationalism is, par excellence, a movement of the young. Since what is required is a total renovation and reformation of Arab society, the task cannot be left to the old, hopelessly sunk in antiquated ways as they are, defending sectional and corrupt interests, and inclined to compromise and settle for the second best. Thus we see students and political organizations in the vanguard of political action, issuing statements of principles and declarations of policy, and setting the ideological pace which their elders must follow.[145]

---

[142] See his address to schoolboys, "The Profession of Death," no. 7 in the anthology.

[143] His views are quoted verbatim in Umar abu'l-Nasr, *op. cit.*, pp. 84–86. This quotation is from p. 84.

[144] *Ibid.*, p. 85

[145] See, for instance, the declaration of the First Arab Students' Congress in Europe in 1938, no. 8 in the anthology. The moving spirit behind this congress seems to have been Musa al-Husaini, later implicated in the murder of King Abdullah of Jordan. Among other members were Abd al-Rahman al-Bazzaz, whose work is included in this anthology and who became dean of the Law College in Baghdad; Abd al-Aziz al-Duri, later dean of the Higher Teachers' Training College in Baghdad; and Abd al-Ghani al-Dalli, later to become Iraqi ambassador to Morocco and Tunisia and a member

All these aspects of Arab nationalism, its activism, its accent on youth, its emphasis on the state as the regulator of private and public life, its depreciation of private loyalties at the expense of public, are admirably illustrated by Michel Aflaq and the Ba'th Party which he founded in Damascus in 1940. The word *ba'th* means resurrection, and in a religious context it denotes the resurrection of the dead at the Last Judgment. But its meaning also connotes: to rouse, to excite, to put in motion, to vivify, and it is thus a very suitable title for an activist, dynamic, and radical party. The motto of the Ba'th Party is: "One Arab nation with an eternal mission." [146] The constitution affirms that "the Arabs form one nation" and that this nation "is characterized by virtues which are the result of its successive rebirths," that its mission is eternal and "reveals itself in ever new and related forms through the different stages of history." The Party believes that nationalism "is a living and eternal reality" which intimately unites the individual to his nation and sets up in him a will to freedom and unity.

The Party is revolutionary, moreover; only by struggle and revolution can the aims of Arab nationalism be realized: "To rely on slow evolution and to be satisfied with a partial and superficial reform is to threaten these aims and to conduce to their failure and to their loss." An essential condition of being an Arab is to have faith in belonging to the Arab nation, and any traitor to Arabism is not an Arab. Property, the constitution says, will be regulated and limited by the state, which shall also control internal and external trade. The state is responsible for protecting, developing and helping it. "Procreation is a trust given, in the first place, to the family, and then to the state." "Marriage is a national duty." Teaching is the exclusive function of the state, and a "national Arab stamp will mark all the aspects of intellectual, economic, political, architectural, and artistic life."

These directives of the Party are amplified and given body by the writings of Aflaq, the Party's ideologue. He is firm in

---

of the Development Board. There were other well-known leaders from Syria, Lebanon, and Palestine, also two Egyptians, one of them a Christian, probably Syrian by origin.

[146] See the Constitution of the Ba'th Party, no. 19 in the anthology.

rejecting all piecemeal reforms, all tinkering with Arab society as it exists at present. In his article on "Aspects of Revolution" [147] he says that revolution is "a powerful psychic current," a "mandatory struggle, without which the reawakening of the nation is not to be understood." It is not only because conditions in the Arab world are bad that a revolution is necessary; rather, it is that revolution is the only way by which the Arabs can renew themselves and find spiritual fulfillment. This insistence on violence, on the virtues of struggle, as such, Aflaq justifies at a metaphysical level. Progress, development, he argues, can take place only if opposites clash. In his address commemorating the birth of the Prophet he says that the idolators of Quraish had their part to play in the revelation of Islam equally with Muhammad's supporters: they were necessary to the realization of Islam.[148] Hence, for Aflaq, political action is an uncompromising assertion of true principles; there can be no middle way: "Either we will bring something new and important which will transform the life of the Arabs from humility to glory and from degeneration to progress, or our attempts shall have failed: we do not recognize a middle solution." [149]

The Arab nation, he again says, must be totally remodeled.[150] And this remodeling must proceed without mercy; the nationalists, he says, "are merciless to themselves, merciless to others. If they discover in their own views a mistake, they correct it without fear or shame, for they aim at the truth and not to benefit themselves. If they find the truth anywhere, then [for its sake] the son will deny his father and the friend abandon his friend." [151] Again, he says that successful national action is one that leads "to a powerful hate, a hate unto death of those persons who embody an idea contrary to the idea of [the nationalist]. . . . An inimical theory is not found on its own; it is embodied in individuals who must be annihilated so that it too may be annihilated. The existence of an enemy of our

---

[147] No. 21 in the anthology.

[148] The idea of struggle as a necessary feature of progress is one of the components of the doctrine of nationalism. See E. Kedourie, *Nationalism* (London, 1960), chap. IV.

[149] Michel Aflaq, *Fi sabil al-ba'th* (*Toward the Ba'th*) (Beirut, 1959), p. 95.

[150] *Ibid.*, p. 92.

[151] *Ibid.*, p. 18.

idea vivifies it and sends the blood coursing in us. Any action that does not call forth in us living emotions and does not make us feel the spasm of love, the revulsion of hate, that does not make our blood race in our veins and our pulse beat faster is a sterile action." [152]

Two notable consequences at least flow from this: namely, that it is the young who must carry out the revolution and that its end is the establishment of love among all members of the Arab nation. It is the young who are the source of salvation, for the old are hopelessly immured in their selfishness and cowardice and can know neither the spasm of love nor the revulsion of hate: "What the old generation and those whose spirit is weak see as imperfection in youth is nothing but perfection itself, and what they consider perfection in old age is nothing but imperfection itself. Youth is qualified by life itself to remain free from all cowardly, self-seeking, defeatist influences, because life does not allow him these things. When youth is past and the environment begins its work to influence and anesthetize the young man, in order to bring him down to the level of impotence, acquiescence, and pessimism, binding him by all kinds of conventional and artificial bonds so as to make him into a domestic animal, when people begin to tell him that he is beginning to mature and attain perfection, that he has become more accomplished and acquired new qualities, then, in reality, the young man will start to be a loser and his vitality to weaken." [153]

It is clear from this that Aflaq considers politics as a means of effecting a change of heart among the Arabs, in fact, of instituting the reign of love among them. His mercilessness, he says, is accompanied by love, love for those errant Arabs whose real will accords with nationalist aims, even though their actions denote the contrary: "our mercilessness has for its object to bring them back to their true selves which they ignore, to their hidden will which they have not yet clearly discerned and which is with us, even though our swords are raised against them." [154] It is for this reason that he proclaims in an eloquent

---

[152] *Ibid.*, pp. 40–41.

[153] *Ibid.*, p. 155. This quotation is from an essay of 1955. There is remarkable consistency and continuity in Aflaq's views, as may be seen from the quotations above, which span the period from 1935 to the present day.

[154] *Ibid.*, p. 103.

essay that "Nationalism is love before everything else." [155] It is only when the Arabs love one another, their nation, and their soil with an absolute and unquestioning love that they will find salvation, and that their weaknesses and difficulties will fall away from them. This uncompromising vision of a super-human and transformed life as the end of political action gives Aflaq a stature which other Arab nationalist writers do not possess. He, at the end of half a century of searchings and gropings, shows himself as the writer who, however small his output, provides a doctrine which contains all the necessary and classic features of nationalism.[156]

[155] No. 20 in the anthology.
[156] On these classic features see Kedourie, *Nationalism*.

Writers on Arab Nationalism

Rashid Rida

Islam and the National Idea [1]

THE FOLLOWING questions were set by an Indonesian correspondent:

1—Is it true that there are hadiths which forbid the national idea (al-fikra al-wataniyya wa'l-qaumiyya)?

2—Do the sayings [of Muhammad], "There is to be no tribal feeling (asabiyya) in Islam," and "There is none among us who calls for the ideals of the jahiliyya," clearly prohibit nationalism (wataniyya)?

3—Is there a dividing line between tribal feeling and nationalism, and is nationalism included within tribal feeling? What is the meaning of tribal feeling for the Arabs?

4—What is the attitude of Islam toward nationalism, and does the latter contradict Islamic union, and what is to be understood by Islamic union?

5—It is well known that the Sheikh Muhammad Abduh, the great philosopher, is the father of nationalism and the nationalists, since it was in his house in Helwan that Sa'd [Zaghlul] grew up and the great men of Egypt met. What do you, his disciple and biographer, think of this?

6—What kind of nationalism should adorn a Muslim youth?

Rashid Rida replies:

Asabiyya [tribal feeling] is derived in Arabic from 'isba, a man's qaum [kin group], around whom they rally; that is, they protect and defend him whether he be the oppressor or the oppressed. 'Isba originally meant the relatives of a man who would mourn him; its meaning gradually widened.

[1] Al Manar, XXXIII (1933), 191–192. (S. G. H.)

It is derived from *'isb*, which is the convolvulus that winds itself up round a tree or some such thing. It is well known that Islam necessarily forbids taking the part [*ta'assub*] of relatives, of a kin group or a homeland, when they are oppressors. It also forbids enmities and dissensions among Muslims who might take the part each of their own kin group or their town or their region against their brother in religion and against others, exception being made of those against whom a war is justly waged. The Prophet made this clear in his saying "*Asabiyya* consists in a man helping his kin group (*qaum*) in oppression," quoted by the Imam Ahmad. It is also well known that Islam necessarily imposes on its people hostility toward foreign aggressors and the duty to fight them. Indeed all the doctors have declared that the Holy War would become an obligation incumbent on every individual if the enemy should attack the Muslims or should occupy some of their regions. This is in order to repulse oppression. It is therefore a sign of great ignorance that this should be forbidden and the prohibition be justified by the fact that the *asabiyya* of the *jahiliyya* was forbidden in certain hadiths, such as the *asabiyya* which manifested itself when the Aus and the Khazraj who were among the Helpers fell out among themselves. This, in brief, is the answer to the first three questions.

As for the modern idea of nationalism, it is nothing but union of the inhabitants of a homeland who may be different in religion, who coöperate in the defense of their common homeland and in preserving its independence or in winning it back when it is lost, and in increasing its prosperity. Such an idea does not manifest itself in Indonesia as it does in Egypt. Regarding it Islam considers that it is the duty of Muslims to defend those of other religions who come under their rule and to treat them on a basis of equality, according to the just rulings of the Shari'a. How then can Islam prohibit the coöperation of Muslims and non-Muslims in the defense of the country, in the preservation of its independence, and in the care for its prosperity? During the caliphate of Umar, the Companions went so far as to exempt the *dhimmis* [the protected people] who took part in war with them from the payment of the poll tax. As for the kind of nationalism that should adorn the Muslim youth, it is that he should set a good example to the inhabitants of his homeland irrespective of their religion and sects, and that he should coöperate with them in every legitimate action to further the independence of the homeland and to raise it up in learning, virtue, strength, and wealth, according to the rules of Islamic law which lays down that rights and duties devolve on the nearest relatives and then on those nearest to them. The Muslim youth must not forget, while serving his homeland and his people, that Islam has honored him and exalted his position by making him a brother to hundreds of millions of Muslims in the world; he is a member of a body bigger than his people, his own personal homeland is only a part of his religious homeland, and he must therefore seek to make the progress of the part a means toward the progress of the whole.

Abd al-Rahman al-Kawakibi

2 The Excellences of the Arabs[1]

BECAUSE THE SOCIETY [of Umm al-qura] is concerned only with the religious renaissance it has found it necessary to pin its hopes on the Arabian Peninsula and its dependencies, and on its people and their neighbors, and to lay before the eyes of the Muslim nation the characteristics of the peninsula, of its people and of the Arabs in general, in order to eliminate political and racial fanaticism as well as to explain why the society has shown preference for the Arabs. We therefore say:

1. The peninsula is the place from which the light of Islam originated.

2. It contains the exalted Kaaba.

3. In it is found the Prophet's Mosque and the holy ground of his house, pulpit, and grave.

4. The peninsula is the most suitable center for religious policy since it lies halfway between the Far East of Asia and the Far West of Africa.

5. Of all countries it is the most free of racial, religious, or sectarian intermixture.

6. It is the most removed of all the Muslim countries from the vicinage of foreigners.

7. The peninsula is most worthy to be a land of free men, owing to its remoteness and natural poverty which preserve it from the greedy and the ambitious.

8. The Arabs of the peninsula have Islamic unity because religion appeared among them.[2]

---

[1] *Umm al-qura* (Cairo, 1931), pp. 193–197. *Umm al-qura* (another name for Mecca) was first published in Cairo in the periodical *al-Manar* in 1901–02. (S. G. H.)

[2] Including the tribes who dwell in Mesopotamia and those who have emigrated to Africa.

9. The habit of religion has become ingrained in them because religion is more compatible with their social customs than with those of others.

10. Of all Muslims they are the most knowledgeable in the principles of Islam as they are the oldest to practice it; many hadiths give witness to the strength of their faith.

11. The Arabs of the peninsula are the most zealous of all Muslims in preserving religion, in supporting it, and in glorying in it, especially as that zeal for the Prophet's cause is still alive among them in the Hijaz, in the Yemen, in Aman, in Hadramaut, in Iraq, and in Africa.

12. The religion of the peninsula Arabs is still governed by the right example of the ancients, free of excess and confusion.

13. Of all other Muslims, the peninsula Arabs possess the strongest *esprit de corps* and are the most proud because of the Bedouin characteristics which they possess.[3]

14. The princes of the peninsula Arabs descend from noble fathers and mothers and are married to noble consorts of good birth; their honor remains untainted.

15. The peninsula Arabs are the most ancient of nations in having a polished civilization, as is shown by the proliferation and the excellence of their wisdom and their literature.

16. Of all Muslims, the peninsula Arabs are the best able to bear hardships in order to attain their aims, and to undertake travel and residence abroad because they have not succumbed to the servile habits of luxury.

17. The peninsula Arabs preserve better than all other peoples their race and customs; for though they mingle with others they do not mix with them.

18. The peninsula Arabs are, of all the Muslim nations, the most jealous of their freedom and independence and those who most reject oppression.[4]

19. Of the Arabs in general. Their language, of all the languages of the Muslims, takes greatest care of knowledge; it is preserved from extinction by the noble Koran.

---

[3] On the strength of this they still levy the *kharaj* in the guise of a present from those who have to contribute it.

[4] This is the reason for the resistance offered to the Ottomans by the Yemenites and their followers.

20. The language of the Arabs is the language common to all the Muslims, who number 300 million souls.

21. The language of the Arabs is the native language of 100 million people, Muslim and non-Muslim.

22. The Arabs are the oldest of nations in following the principles of equality in rights and in eschewing great disparities in society.

23. The Arabs are the oldest of peoples to practice the principle of consultation in public matters.[5]

24. The Arabs know best, of all people, the principles of socialist living.

25. The Arabs are amongst the most noble of people in respecting treaties, and the most humane in keeping faith, and the most chivalrous in respecting the rights of vicinage, and the most generous in the doing of good deeds.[6]

26. The Arabs are of all nations the most suitable to be an authority in religion and an example to the Muslims; the other nations have followed their guidance at the start and will not refuse to follow them now.

---

[5] The Koran bears testimony for them in this regard in the story of Balkis and Solomon—Peace be on Him—when she said, addressing her advisers: "O Chiefs! Give me advice respecting my affair: I never decide an affair until you are in my presence." They said: "We are possessors of strength and possessors of mighty prowess, and the command is yours, therefore see what you will command." She said: "Surely the kings, when they enter a town, ruin it and make the noblest of its people to be low, and they (always) do."

[6] To prove this it is enough to mention the cordiality shown by the inhabitants of the peninsula to the European travelers, except for the deed Ibn Sabah committed as a result of which, two years later, he was awarded the title of Pasha, and the preference of the Jews for the immigration into Arab lands; also the fact that the Arab lands of the Ottoman Empire such as Mosul, Mardin, Nasibin, and the Arab towns in the vilayet of Aleppo did not participate in the recent Armenian incidents. The events that took place in the Lebanon, in Damascus, and in Aleppo in the last century were not the result of religious or racial fanaticism but of the infatuation of some Druses with the English and of some Christians with Napoleon III.

Negib Azoury

3 Program of the League of the Arab Fatherland

THERE IS NOTHING more liberal than the league's program.

The league wants, before anything else, to separate the civil and the religious power, in the interest of Islam and the Arab nation, and to form an Arab empire stretching from the Tigris and the Euphrates to the Suez Isthmus, and from the Mediterranean to the Arabian Sea.

The mode of government will be a constitutional sultanate based on the freedom of all the religions and the equality of all the citizens before the law. It will respect the interests of Europe, all the concessions and all the privileges which had been granted to her up to now by the Turks. It will also respect the autonomy of the Lebanon, and the independence of the principalities of Yemen, Nejd, and Iraq.

The league offers the throne of the Arab Empire to that prince of the Khedivial family of Egypt who will openly declare himself in its favor and who will devote his energy and his resources to this end.

It rejects the idea of unifying Egypt and the Arab Empire under the same monarchy, because the Egyptians do not belong to the Arab race; they are of the African Berber family and the language which they spoke before Islam bears no similarity to Arabic. There exists, moreover, between Egypt and the Arab Empire a natural frontier which must be respected in order to avoid the introduction, in the new state, of the germs of discord and destruction. Never, as a matter of fact, have the ancient

---

[1] *Le Réveil de la Nation Arabe dans l'Asie Turque en Présence des Intérêts et des Rivalités des Puissances Étrangères, de la Curie Romaine et du Patriarcat Oecuménique* (Paris, 1905), pp. 245–247, 248. (S. G. H.)

Arab caliphs succeeded for any length of time in controlling the two countries at the same time.

The Arab fatherland also offers the universal religious caliphate over the whole of Islam to that sherif (descendant of the Prophet) who will sincerely embrace its cause and devote himself to this work. The religious caliph will have as a completely independent political state the whole of the actual vilayet of Hijaz, with the town and the territory of Medina, as far as Aqaba. He will enjoy the honors of a sovereign and will hold a real moral authority over all the Muslims of the world.

One of the principal causes of the fall of the vast empire of the Arabs was the centralization in a single hand of the civil and the religious powers. It is also for this reason that the caliphate of Islam has become today so ridiculous and so contemptible in the hands of the Turks. The successor of the Prophet of Allah must enjoy an incontestable moral prestige; his whole life must be of unblemished honor, his authority suffering no diminution, his majesty independent [of anything other than itself]. His power also will be universal; from his residence he will rule morally over all the Muslims of the universe who will hurry in pilgrimage to the sanctuaries of Mohammed.

[*About the position of the caliph, Azoury offers a word of explanation.*]

The caliph of Islam must be either the sovereign of all the Muslims of the earth united in a single state, which has always proved impossible, even under the first caliphs, or, quite simply, the sovereign of a country entirely Islamic. There is indeed no country more Islamic than the Hijaz, and there are no towns more suitable than Medina and Mecca to receive the Supreme Head of the believers.

Anonymous

4 Announcement to the Arabs, Sons of Qahtan[1]

See how on the day of battle we fill
the universe with flame and fire

O SONS OF QAHTAN! O Descendants of Adnan! Are you
asleep? And how long will you remain asleep? How can you remain deep in your slumber when the voices of the nations around
you have deafened everyone? Do you not hear the commotion
all around you? Do you not know that you live in a period when
he who sleeps dies, and he who dies is gone forever? When will
you open your eyes and see the glitter of the bayonets which are
directed at you, and the lightning of the swords which are drawn
over your heads? When will you realize the truth? When will
you know that your country has been sold to the foreigner? See
how your natural resources have been alienated from you and
have come into the possession of England, France, and Germany.
Have you no right to these resources? You have become humiliated slaves in the hands of the usurping tyrant; the foreigner
unjustly dispossesses you of the fruit of your work and labor and
leaves you to suffer the pangs of hunger. How long will it be
before you understand that you have become a plaything in the
hand of him who has no religion but to kill the Arabs and
forcibly to seize their possessions? The Country is yours, and they
say that rule belongs to the people, but those who exercise rule
over you in the name of the Constitution do not consider you
part of the people, for they inflict on you all kinds of suffering,
tyranny, and persecution. How, then, can they concede to you any

[1] Manifesto of Arab nationalists disseminated from Cairo at the beginning
of the First World War, printed by Ahmad Izzat al-A'zami, *al-qadiyya al-
arabiyya* (*The Arab Question*) (Baghdad, 1932), IV, 108–117. (S. G. H.)

political rights? In their eyes you are but a flock of sheep whose wool is to be clipped, whose milk is to be drunk, and whose meat is to be eaten. Your country they consider a plantation which they inherited from their fathers, a country the inhabitants of which are their humble slaves. Where is your Qahtanic honor? Where your Adnanian pride?

The Armenians, small as their numbers are when compared to yours, have won their administrative autonomy in spite of the opposition of the Turkish state, and they will presently become independent. Their people will then become self-governing, free and advanced, free and active in the social organization of humanity, in contrast to you, who will remain ever enslaved to the descendants of Genghis and Hulagu who brought to an end your advanced Arab government in Baghdad, the Abode of Peace; and to the descendants of Tamerlane who built a tower composed of the heads of eighty thousand Arabs in Aleppo. Till when will you go on acquiescing in this utter humiliation, when your honor is made free of, your wives raped, your children orphaned, your habitations destroyed, so that the Byzantine capital should be defended, your money taken to be spent in the palaces of Constantinople, full as they are with intoxicating drink, musical instruments, and all kinds of wealth and luxury, and your young men driven to fight your Arab brethren, sometimes in the Yemen, sometimes in Kerek, sometimes in the Hauran, thus reinforcing the persecutions of the Turks while you remain silent and accept this tyrannous imposition? Why do you shed your blood at the behest of the Turk in fighting your brethren, while you refuse it for the safeguard of your rights and the honor of your race, as the Armenians have done and are still doing? Have you forgotten that:

> *High honor is not safe from injury*
> *until blood is shed in its defense?*

Have you not seen the confirmation of this in the Armenians whom the Turks respect as they do not respect you, and to whom they give rights which they would not give you? Has your Arab blood become congealed in your veins, and has it changed into dirty water? You have become, by God, a byword among the nations, a laughingstock of the world, a subject of mockery and derision among the peoples. You have almost become proverbial in your humility, weakness, and acquiescence in great loss.

Compare how well the Turks treat the Armenians and how they seek to humor them, with the harsh treatment which they reserve for you Arabs. See how the Turkish government adopts the stance of obedience before them, how it humbly begs them to accept more than their due share of parliamentary representation. As for you, O how we grieve for you! The government directs against you those armies which had been defeated on the Russian front and in the Balkans, in order to kill you, destroy your liberty, destroy your noble Arab race, and finally to finish you off, as though it can have no power but over you. Consider the expedition sent to Iraq: its purpose is to kill your innocent Arab brethren, destroy their prosperous homes, stain the purity of their honor, and despoil them of their dear possessions, in short to reënact what they did in the Hauran, Kerek, and the Yemen. What is the reason of all this? Is it not because you have sunk into passivity and accepted the yoke of the Turks? Till when will you remain acquiescent in these oppressions, witnessing all the while the annihilation of your people? See how these corrupt tyrants set the Imam Yahya upon the Idrissi in order to ruin the Yemen, how they set ibn al-Rashid upon ibn-Saud in order to destroy the Arabs of Nejd, how they sow enmity between the Sherif of Mecca and his neighbors in Asir and Nejd, how they use the State's resources, its arms and its soldiers—who have been defeated in every war and seem to have no power but over Arabs—in order to give support to some Arabs in their quarrels with other Arabs. . . .

O sons of Qahtan! Do you not know that man is meant to live here on earth a goodly life, in honor and prosperity, a life full of spiritual values, and that he founds states which safeguard these things, the most precious gift of God to the sons of Adam, to which they hold very fast? What, then, is the value of life, when honor is stained, possessions robbed, and souls destroyed? What is the meaning of a life spent in humiliation and subjection, without honor, without possessions, without enjoyment of liberty and independence? Is there any use or honor in undergoing all this under the banner of the Crescent?

Arise, O ye Arabs! Unsheathe the sword from the scabbard,   85 ye sons of Qahtan! Do not allow an oppressive tyrant who has only disdain for you to remain in your country; cleanse your country from those who show their enmity to you, to your race and to your language.

Constantinople has afflicted you with the curse of its most malevolent coadjutors in tyranny such as Arif Bey al-Mardini, who falsely claims to be one of you, since no one among you is willing to become an instrument in your enemies' hands to inflict suffering upon you . . . , and Bakr Sami Bey, who used to stand guard over Jawid Pasha's room when he was governor of Trebizond, and Jawid Pasha, the leader of the Iraq expedition, and such other descendants of Genghis and Hulagu, who slaughtered your upright and pure ancestors, destroyed their flourishing civilization, trampled with the hooves of their horses on the books of their libraries, or else stopped up the course of the Tigris with the great number of these books which they flung into it. The descendants have destroyed what the ancestors left standing, and have thus prevented Arab civilization from recovering its scattered elements and returning to its former glory.

O ye Arabs! Warn the people of the Yemen, of Asir, of Nejd, and of Iraq against the intrigues of your enemies. Be united, in the Syrian and Iraqi provinces, with the members of your race and fatherland. Let the Muslims, the Christians, and the Jews be as one in working for the interest of the nation and of the country. You all dwell in one land, you speak one language, so be also one nation and one hand. Do not become divided against yourselves according to the designs and purposes of the troublemakers who feign Islam, while Islam is really innocent of their misdeeds. . . .

Unite then and help one another, and do not say, O ye Muslims: This is a Christian, and this is a Jew, for you are all God's dependents, and religion is for God alone. God has commanded us, in his precious Arabic Book and at the hand of his Arab Adnanian Prophet, to follow justice and equality, to deal faithfully with him who does not fight us, even though his religion is different, and to fight him who uses us tyrannously. Who, then, have tyrannized over the Arabs? Have the Christian Arabs or any others sent armed expeditions to the Yemen, to Nejd, or to Iraq? Is it not the band of Constantinople who fight you and seek to exterminate some of the Arabs by means of sword and fire, and others by means of quarrels and dissensions, following the maxim "divide and rule"?

O ye Muslim Arabs, you make a great mistake if you think that this tyrannical, lawless government is Islamic. God says in His precious Book: the unbelievers are the tyrants.

Every tyrannical government is an enemy and a foe to Islam; how more so, then, if the government destroys Islam, considers it lawful to shed the blood of the people of the Prophet of Islam, and seeks to kill the language of Islam in the name of Islamic government and the Islamic caliphate? He who seeks proof has only to read the book *A New Nation* by Ubaidullah, the creature of the unionists, a book which they have used as one of the preliminaries for the destruction of Islam. Therefore, he who supports these unionists because he considers them Muslims is in clear error, for none of them have done a good deed for Islam. Indeed, most of them have no root in that Turkism for the sake of which they are fighting the Koran. They are merely Turks by virtue of this counterfeit language they speak, which derives what is best in it from the sacred Arabic tongue and the sweet Persian tongue. Fanatic in its cause, they fight the Koran and the tradition of the Arabic Prophet. Is this the Islam which it is incumbent on them to respect? It is not notorious that they seek to kill the Arabic language? Did they not write books to show that it must be abandoned, and that prayers and the call to prayers should be made in Turkish? And if Arabic dies, how can the Koran and the traditions live? And if the Book and the traditions cease to be known, what remains of Islam?

And O ye Christian and Jewish Arabs, combine with your brethren the Muslim Arabs, and do not follow in the footsteps of him who says to you, whether he be one of you or not: The Arab Muslims are sunk in religious fanaticism, therefore we prefer the irreligious Turks. This is nonsensical speech which proceeds from an ignorant man who knows neither his own nor his people's interest. The Muslim Arabs are your brethren in patriotism, and if you find among them some who are seized with an ugly fanaticism, so likewise are such to be found among you. Both sides, indeed, have learnt it from the non-Arabs. Our ancestors were not fanatical in this sense, for Jews and Christians used to study in the mosques of Baghdad and the Andalus like brethren. Let them, both sides, aim at tolerance and at the removal of these ugly fanaticisms. For you must know that those who do not speak your tongue are more harmful to you than the ignorant fanatics among the Arabs, since you can reach understanding with the Arabs who are your brethren in patriotism and race, while it is difficult for you to reach agreement with these contemptible creatures[2] who are at the same time your enemies and the enemies of the Muslim Arabs. See how, when you are friendly to them, they maltreat you, look down on you, and withhold your rights. Combine with your fellow countrymen and your kin, and know that ugly fanaticism will inevitably disappear. A day will come when fanaticism will disappear from our country, leaving no trace, and that day shall be when our affairs will be in our own hands, and when our affairs, our learning, and the verdicts of our courts will be conducted in our own language. If we are united, such a day is not far off.

Know, all ye Arabs, that a *fada'i* society has been formed which will kill all those who fight the Arabs and oppose the reform of Arab lands. The reform of which we speak is not on the principle of decentralization coupled with allegiance to the minions of Constantinople, but on the principle of complete independence and the formation of a decentralized Arab state which will revive our ancient glories and rule the country on autonomous lines, according to the needs of each province. This state will begin by liquidating some flattering foxes among the Arabs who are, and have always been, the means whereby these murderous minions have trampled on our rights, as the world will see when they proceed to bring about the disasters they have in store for us.

---

[2] The word *uluj*, which I translate here "contemptible creatures," means a thing that is eaten or chewed. (S. G. H.)

Sherif Husain of Mecca

5 Territorial Demands Made on the British Government[1]

[*Translation of a letter (no. 1) from the Sherif of Mecca to Sir Henry McMahon, His Majesty's High Commissioner at Cairo.*]

To his Honour,   July 14, 1915

WHEREAS THE WHOLE of the Arab nation without any exception have decided in these last years to live, and to accomplish their freedom, and grasp the reins of their administration both in theory and practice; and whereas they have found and felt that it is to the interest of the Government of Great Britain to support them and aid them to the attainment of their firm and lawful intentions (which are based upon the maintenance of the honour and dignity of their life) without any ulterior motives whatsoever unconnected with this object;

And whereas it is to their (the Arabs') interest also to prefer the assistance of the Government of Great Britain in consideration of their geographical position and economic interests, and also of the attitude of the above-mentioned Government, which is known to both nations and therefore need not be emphasised;

For these reasons the Arab nation see fit to limit themselves, as time is short, to asking the Government of Great Britain, if it should think fit, for the approval, through her deputy or representative, of the following fundamental propositions, leaving out all things considered secondary in comparison with these, so that it may prepare all means necessary for attaining this noble pur-

[1] Official English translation: Document No. 1 from "Correspondence between Sir Henry McMahon, G.C.M.G., G.C.V.O., K.C.I.E., C.S.I., His Majesty's High Commissioner at Cairo, and the Sherif Husain of Mecca, July 1915–March 1916, Miscellaneous No. 3 (1939) (Cmd 5957)." Reproduced here by special permission of the Controller of Her Britannic Majesty's Stationery Office. (S. G. H.)

pose, until such time as it finds occasion for making the actual negotiations:—

Firstly.—England to acknowledge the independence of the Arab countries, bounded on the north by Mersina and Adana up to the 37° of latitude, on which degree fall Birijik, Urfa, Mardin, Midiat, *Jezirat (Ibn 'Umar), Amadia,* [2] up to the border of Persia; on the east by the borders of Persia up to the Gulf of Basra; on the south by the Indian Ocean, with the exception of the position of Aden to remain as it is; on the west by the Red Sea, the Mediterranean Sea up to Mersina. England to approve of the proclamation of an Arab Khalifate of Islam.

Secondly.—The Arab Government of the Sherif to acknowledge that England shall have the preference in all economic enterprises in the Arab countries whenever conditions of enterprises are otherwise equal.

Thirdly.—For the security of this Arab independence and the certainty of such preference of economic enterprises, both high contracting parties to offer mutual assistance, to the best ability of their military and naval forces, to face any foreign Power which may attack either party. Peace not to be decided without agreement of both parties.

Fourthly.—If one of the parties enters upon an aggressive conflict, the other party to assume a neutral attitude, and in case of such party wishing the other to join forces, both to meet and discuss the conditions.

Fifthly.—England to acknowledge the abolition of foreign privileges in the Arab countries, and to assist the Government of the Sherif in an International Convention for confirming such abolition.

Sixthly.—Articles 3 and 4 of this treaty to remain in vigour for fifteen years, and, if either wishes it to be renewed, one year's notice before lapse of treaty to be given.

Consequently, and as the whole of the Arab nation have (praise be to God) agreed and united for the attainment, at all costs and finally, of this noble object, they beg the Government of Great Britain to answer them positively or negatively in a period of thirty days after receiving this intimation; and if this period should lapse before they receive an answer, they reserve

---

[2] * Former reading: "Amadia Island (Jezireh)." *

to themselves complete freedom of action. Moreover, we (the
Sherif's family) will consider ourselves free in word and deed
from the bonds of our previous declaration which we made
through Ali Effendi.

[*Translation of a letter (no. 5) from the Sherif of Mecca to Sir
H. McMahon, His Majesty's High Commissioner at Cairo.*]

November 5, 1915

(In the name of God, the Merciful, the Compassionate!)

TO HIS EXCELLENCY the most exalted and eminent Minister who is endowed with the highest authority and sound-
ness of opinion. May God guide him to do His Will!

I received with great pleasure your honoured letter, dated the
15th Zil Hijja[3] (the 24th October, 1915), to which I beg to
answer as follows:

1. In order to facilitate an agreement and to render a service
to Islam, and at the same time to avoid all that may cause
Islam troubles and hardships—seeing moreover that we have
great consideration for the distinguished qualities and dispositions of the Government of Great Britain—we renounce our
insistence on the inclusion of the *vilayets* of Mersina and Adana
in the Arab Kingdom. But the two *vilayets* of Aleppo and Beirut
and their sea coasts are purely Arab *vilayets*, and there is no
difference between a Moslem and a Christian Arab: they are
both descendants of one forefather.

We Moslems will follow the footsteps of the Commander of
the Faithful Omar ibn Khattab, and other Khalifs succeeding
him, who ordained in the laws of the Moslem Faith that Moslems should treat the Christians as they treat themselves. He,
Omar, declared with reference to Christians: "They will have the
same privileges and submit to the same duties as ourselves."
They will thus enjoy their civic rights in as much as it accords
with the general interests of the whole nation.

2. As the Iraqi *vilayets* are parts of the pure Arab Kingdom,
and were in fact the seat of its Government in the time of Ali
ibn Abu Talib, and in the time of all the Khalifs who succeeded
him; and as in them began the civilisation of the Arabs, and as
their towns were the first towns built in Islam where the Arab

---

[3] No. 4.

power became so great; therefore they are greatly valued by all Arabs far and near, and their traditions cannot be forgotten by them. Consequently, we cannot satisfy the Arab nations or make them submit to give us such a title to nobility. But in order to render an accord easy, and taking into consideration the assurances mentioned in the fifth article of your letter to keep and guard our mutual interests in that country as they are one and the same, for all these reasons we might agree to leave under the British administration for a short time those districts now occupied by the British troops without the rights of either party being prejudiced thereby (especially those of the Arab nation, which interests are to it economic and vital), and against a suitable sum paid as compensation to the Arab Kingdom for the period of occupation, in order to meet the expenses which every new kingdom is bound to support; at the same time respecting your agreements with the Sheikhs of those districts, and especially those which are essential.

3. In your desire to hasten the movement we see not only advantages, but grounds of apprehension. The first of these grounds is the fear of the blame of the Moslems of the opposite party (as has already happened in the past), who would declare that we have revolted against Islam and ruined its forces. The second is that, standing in the face of Turkey which is supported by all the forces of Germany, we do not know what Great Britain and her Allies would do if one of the *Entente* Powers were weakened and obliged to make peace. We fear that the Arab nation will then be left alone in the face of Turkey together with her allies, but we would not at all mind if we were to face the Turks alone. Therefore it is necessary to take these points into consideration in order to avoid a peace being concluded in which the parties concerned may decide the fate of our people as if we had taken part in the war without making good our claims to official consideration.

4. The Arab nation has a strong belief that after this war is over the Turks under German influence will direct their efforts to provoke the Arabs and violate their rights, both material and moral, to wipe out their nobility and honour and reduce them to utter submission as they are determined to ruin them entirely. The reasons for the slowness shown in our action have already been stated.

5. When the Arabs know the Government of Great Britain is their ally who will not leave them to themselves at the conclusion of peace in the face of Turkey and Germany, and that she will support and will effectively defend them, then to enter the war at once will, no doubt, be in conformity with the general interest of the Arabs.

6. Our letter dated the 29th Shaual, 1333[4] (the 9th September, 1915), saves us the trouble of repeating our opinions as to articles 3 and 4 of your honoured last letter regarding administration, Government advisers and officials, especially as you have declared, exalted Minister, that you will not interfere with internal affairs.

7. The arrival of a clear and definite answer as soon as possible to the above proposals is expected. We have done our utmost in making concessions in order to come to an agreement satisfying both parties. We know that our lot in this war will be either a success, which will guarantee to the Arabs a life becoming their past history, or destruction in the attempt to attain their objects. Had it not been for the determination which I see in the Arabs for the attainment of their objects, I would have preferred to seclude myself on one of the heights of a mountain, but they, the Arabs, have insisted that I should guide the movement to this end.

May God keep you safe and victorious, as we devoutly hope and desire.

27th Zil Hijja, 1333.

---

[4] No. 3.

6 Vindication of Arab National Rights[1]

Your Excellency,

FOR GENERATIONS NOW, the Arab nation has been suffering under the Turkish yoke. History has not recorded an instance of a people who have suffered the kind of enslavement and torture which this nation has endured, though it is guilty only of constituting the majority in the Ottoman Empire. The Turks have, in consequence, looked upon it as a danger to the dominance of their race, and have treated it like a dangerous enemy. After the loss of some European provinces, they even began to intensify this treatment, since the fact that Arabs were in the majority became a matter beyond discussion. Thus, the Arab element, deprived of its rights and subjected to tyranny and atrocity, came to decrease in significance and to be enfeebled in its own country, compelled to seek in other Arab countries the life which the Turks were denying it. When the European war was declared, foreign control disappeared from the Turkish Empire, and the Turks gave full rein to their hatred and anger; they began to implement an orderly plan to annihilate the Arabs. No sentiment stood in their way, no law prevented them. To this end, they made lawful every divinely prohibited means; they used hanging, exile, prison, torture, dispersal of families, confiscations, verdicts *in absentia*, and similar persecutions.

His Majesty the King, my master, tried his utmost to persuade the Turkish government to revert to the path of truth and justice,

---

[1] Memorandum by the Foreign Office of the Arab government of the Hijaz to the Secretary of State, United States of America, 1917, from Amin Sa'id, *al-Thaura al-arabiyya al-kubra* (Cairo, 1934), I, 317–318. (S. G. H.)

but his efforts proved vain. He therefore overthrew the yoke of tyranny and proclaimed the independence of the Arabs, in his capacity as the head of the House of Quraish, that house from which have issued all the houses which sat on the throne in the Arab countries, from the Umayyads to the Abbasids and the Fatimids. His Arab people followed him, and only a few months elapsed before he founded an army, set up an administration, and expelled and annihilated all that was Turkish in the Hijaz. Medina, however, the religious standing of which absolutely prevents its bombardment and forcible conquest, he was content to blockade. His armies today are stationed in Syrian territories where they engage in operations which are all victorious and successful.

The new kingdom has struggled for two years past to rescue a race worthy of respect, owing to its glorious history and its beneficent influence on European civilization. It cannot but expect sympathy and friendship from the great American nation. It hopes that the government of the great Republic will grant it the same recognition granted by the Allied Powers, especially now that the United States has joined the war on the Allied side. His Majesty, my master, attaches great importance to this recognition, which will be the first practical example of the principle of national liberation which President Wilson has endorsed, and which your country has joined the war to realize.

There is no need here to recapitulate.

It is not necessary to mention the occasions when the nations have in the past admitted to their number, that is, to international society, a people struggling for its freedom and independence before the end of its struggle. I need only recall here the Treaty of London of 1827 which recognized the independence of Greece while the Turks were still considering the Greeks as their subjects.

A free constitution will be promulgated for the Arab Kingdom at the end of the war, which will guarantee equality of rights to all inhabitants without distinction of creed or religion. Any Arab country which will, after its deliverance from the Turkish yoke, announce freely and out of its own choice its desire to join this kingdom will be granted internal autonomy and will form a union with the Hijaz based on broad democratic principles.

For all these reasons the New Kingdom considers itself entitled in every way to the sympathy and help of the great Republic, and I would ask Your Excellency to inform your government of the hopes of the Arab nation.

Sami Shawkat

7 The Profession of Death[1]

TOMORROW, your headmaster Mr. Darwish al-Miqdadi will visit the Ministry of Defense to discuss with its senior officials the curriculum of your military studies. Do you know what these studies are and why they are introduced this year into the curricula of our schools? I have called you together today to explain this point.

We often hear and read that there is no political independence without economic independence, or that there can be no independence without knowledge. But Egypt, whose income has for many years now exceeded her expenditure by millions of pounds, and who has the best universities and schools and the greatest scholars in the Near East, has had her independence delayed up to now. The treasuries of the Indian rajas contain hundreds of millions of gold pieces and vast numbers of precious stones; India herself has more than twenty-five large universities from which graduate annually thousands of young men with diplomas in higher studies. Yet India is a colony. The proportion of the educated in Syria amounts to 76 per cent, and the majority of her population is not different in progress, civilization or culture from the peoples of southern Europe, but in spite of this, unfortunately, we still find her deprived of independence. On the other hand, the Afghans, who lead the life of the fourteenth century and whose treasuries have never been filled with gold, are independent. And here is our neighbor, the Kingdom of Saudi Arabia, whose inhabitants live on dates and camels' milk,

[1] This is an address given to the students of the Central Secondary School, Baghdad, in the autumn of 1933; printed in Sami Shawkat, *Hadhihi ahdafuna* (*These Are Our Aims*) (Baghdad, 1939), pp. 1–3. (S. G. H.)

in whose schools no modern arts are taught, and whose culture has not crossed the boundaries of religion; she too is independent. And Arab Yemen is also independent, in spite of her lack of money.

Money and learning, therefore, are not all that is needed for the independence of nations, nor are they the only axe with which to strike down the walls of imperialism and sever the chains of humiliation.

But . . .

There is something else more important than money and learning for preserving the honor of a nation and for keeping humiliation and enslavement at bay.

That is strength.

Strength is the soil on which the seed of justice burgeons; the nation which has no strength is destined to humiliation and enslavement. Riches without strength are a cause of humiliation and enslavement; as for knowledge without strength, it only produces crying and weeping on the part of the weak, and mockery on the part of the strong. This weeping and mocking will sometimes go on for tens, even hundreds, of years, as has happened in India and other countries.

Strength, as I use the word here, means to excel in the Profession of Death.

The nation which does not excel in the Profession of Death with iron and fire will be forced to die under the hooves of the horses and under the boots of a foreign soldiery. If to live is just, then killing in self-defense is also just. Had Mustafa Kemal not had, for his revolution in Anatolia, forty thousand officers trained in the Profession of Death, we would not have seen Turkey restoring in the twentieth century the glories of Yavouz Sultan Selim. Had not Pahlavi had thousands of officers well versed in the sacred profession we would not have seen him restoring the glory of Darius. And had Mussolini not had tens of thousands of Black Shirts well versed in the Profession of Death he would not have been able to put on the temples of Victor Emmanuel the crown of the first Caesars of Rome.

In the Balkans, the Albanian nation is independent, and in the Near East Arab Iraq is independent; in Albania the reed has prospered and in Iraq the cedar. The reed bush casts its shade over no more than a few centimeters of ground, no matter how tall it grows; but the cedar tree, after only a few years of growth, casts its shade over tens and hundreds of meters. Iraq's horizon of hope extends to all the Arab countries, whereas it is not in the power of Albania to look beyond its boundaries. Sixty years ago, Prussia used to dream of uniting the German people. What is there to prevent Iraq, which fulfilled her desire for independence ten years ago, from dreaming to unite all the Arab countries?

On the banks of this great river which we see morning and evening Harun al-Rashid established his throne, and from this sandy shore he ruled more than 200 million souls. We will not deserve to take pride in him and to claim that we are his descendants if we do not restore what he built and what the enemies of the Arabs destroyed. The spirit of Harun al-Rashid and the spirit of al-Ma'mun want Iraq to have in a short while half a million soldiers and hundreds of airplanes. Is there in Iraq a coward who will not answer their call? Your military studies this year, oh youths, are those lessons of strength which the country needs and which our glorious history demands. If we do not want death under the hooves of the horses and the boots of the foreign armies, it is our duty to perfect the Profession of Death, the profession of the army, the sacred military profession. This year, the lessons will be confined to the Central Secondary School in the capital, but in the future they will extend to all the secondary schools in the country, as well as to all the teachers' training colleges.

On then, oh young men, to Strength. On to the perfection of the sacred Profession of Death. Lift up high the banner of Faisal, the successor of Harun al-Rashid.

8 Arab Pledge, Definitions, Manifesto[1]

I. OUR NATIONAL PACT

I AM AN ARAB, and I believe that the Arabs constitute one nation. The sacred right of this nation is to be sovereign in her own affairs. Her ardent nationalism drives her to liberate the Arab homeland, to unite all its parts, and to found political, economic, and social institutions more sound and more compatible than the existing ones. The aim of this nationalism is to raise up the standard of living and to increase the material and the spiritual good of the people; it also aspires to share in working for the good of the human collectivity; it strives to realize this by continuous work based on national organization.

I pledge myself to God, that I will strive in this path to my utmost, putting the national interest above any other consideration.

II. FIRST PRINCIPLES

The Arabs: All who are Arab in their language, culture, and loyalty [defined in a footnote as "national feeling." S. G. H.], those are the Arabs. The Arab is the individual who belongs to the nation made up of those people.

---

[1] "Mu'tamar al-tullab al-arab fi uruppa" ("Conference of the Arab Students in Europe"), *Al-qaumiyya al-arabiyya—haqiqatuha—ahdafuha—wasa'iluha* (*Arab Nationalism—the Truth about It—Its Aims—Its Means*) (Beirut, n.d.). This conference was held in Brussels in December, 1938. (S. G. H.)

The Arab Homeland: It is the land which has been, or is, inhabited by an Arab majority, in the above sense, in Asia and Africa. As such it is a whole which cannot be divided or partitioned. It is a sacred heritage no inch of which may be trifled with. Any compromise in this respect is invalid and is national treason.

Arab Nationalism: It is the feeling for the necessity of independence and unity which the inhabitants of the Arab lands share [a footnote adds: "The Arab emigrants abroad are included in this definition." S. G. H.]. It is based on the unity of the homeland, of language, culture, history, and a sense of the common good.

The Arab Movement: It is the new Arab renaissance which pervades the Arab nation. Its motive force is her glorious past, her remarkable vitality and the awareness of her present and future interests. This movement strives continuously and in an organized manner toward well-defined aims. These aims are to liberate and unite the Arab homeland, to found political, economic, and social organizations more sound than the existing ones, and to attempt afterward to work for the good of the human collectivity and its progress. These aims are to be realized by definite means drawn from the preparedness of the Arabs and their particular situation, as well as from the experience of the West. They will be realized without subscribing to any particular creed of the modern Western ones such as Fascism, Communism, or Democracy.

The Arab National Idea: It is a national idea which proscribes the existence of racial, regional, and communal fanaticisms. It respects the freedom of religious observance, and individual freedoms such as the freedom of opinion, work, and assembly, unless they conflict with the public good. The Arab national idea cannot be contradictory to the good of real racial and religious minorities;[2] it aims rather at treating all sincere patriots on the principle of equality of rights and duties.

[2] A footnote to the text deals with a particular minority and runs as follows: "The interests of the Jews settled in the Arab lands are not in opposition to the interests of Arab nationalism. But Zionism is directly opposed to Arab nationalism; we must resist it. Should the Jews who are settled among the Arabs not resist it openly and in earnest, then they will be an enemy to the Arabs." (S. G. H.)

III. FOREIGN ELEMENTS IN THE ARAB COUNTRIES

We have said that the Arab countries belong to the Arabs and that benefits therefrom must accrue to them. By Arabs we mean those whom the political report has included under this appellation. As for those elements who are not Arabized and who do not intend to be Arabized but are, rather, intent on putting obstacles in the way of the Arab nation, they are foreign to the Arab nation. The most prominent problem of this kind is that of the Jews in Palestine.

If we looked at the Jews in Palestine from an economic angle we would find that their economy is totally incompatible with the Arab economy. The Jews are attempting to build up a Jewish state in Palestine and to bring into this state great numbers of their kind from all over the world. Palestine is a small country, and they will therefore have to industrialize it so that this large number of inhabitants can find subsistence. And in order to make their industry a success they will have to find markets for their products. For this they depend on the Arab market; their products will therefore flood the Arab countries and compete with Arab industries. This is very harmful to the Arabs.

Moreover, Palestine, placed as it is between the Arab countries in Asia and Africa, occupies an important position in land, sea, and air communications. A foreign state in Palestine will impede these communications and have a harmful effect on commerce. And even if the Jews in Palestine presented no danger other than the economic, this would be enough for us to oppose them and to put an end to their intrigues, so that we may ensure for our country a happy and glorious future.

Among the dangerous alien elements in the Arab countries are the foreign colonies such as the Italians in Tripolitania, the French, and the Frenchified Jews in Tunisia, Algeria, and Morocco. The danger of these elements is akin to that of the Jews in Palestine, even though less prominent and less critical.

Edmond Rabbath

9 The Common Origin of the Arabs [1]

A COMMON ORIGIN, whatever may be said of it, inspires the unity [of the Arabs].

This is not to say that one could speak of an Arab race. Here, but to a smaller extent than elsewhere, the inevitable mixture of blood has produced what, in the case of France, has been called the "ethnic synthesis" which seems to have been the fate of most European countries. Marcellin Boule, in a now-classic definition, means by "a race," "The continuity of a physical type which manifests affinities of blood, and which represents an essentially natural grouping, neither having nor being able to have anything in common with a people, a nationality, a language, or habits, these being concepts which correspond to purely artificial groupings which are in no way anthropological and which depend only on history, of which they are the product." [2] Racial unity, as may be seen, is not essential to national existence. In a famous lecture, "What is a Nation," Renan defined it in these brilliant words: "A nation is a soul, a spiritual principle. Two things which, truth to say, are really one, constitute this soul, this spiritual principle. One lies in the past, the other in the present. One is the common possession of a rich legacy of memories, the other is the actual willingness, the desire to live together, the will to improve the inheritance which has been received intact. Man . . . does not improvise. The nation, as much as the individual, is the outcome of a lengthy past made up of efforts, of sacrifices, and of devotion. . . . To share the common glories of the past,

[1] Edmond Rabbath, *Unité Syrienne et Devenir Arabe* (Paris, 1937), pp. 43–69. (S. G. H.)
[2] *Les Hommes Fossiles*, p. 320.

to have a common will in the present, to have done great things together, to want to go on doing them, such are the essential conditions of being a people. . . . The Spartan song: We are what you were, we will be what you are, is in its very simplicity the short and compendious anthem of every fatherland. . . ."

However, when a community of blood exists, it undoubtedly strengthens national unity. The peoples who have it do not have to wait for the work of time, for historical circumstances, for the tenacious will of a dynasty such as that which "in a thousand years made France," to realize their national unity. They carry this unity in themselves, in their ethnic consciousness, in the voice of the blood. It will be invincibly realized when those factors which have been favorable to other peoples in the past will, in turn, make it possible.

But can one dare today, considering the new horizons which are constantly revealing themselves to ethnology, to assert the existence of pure races, of organic species constituting those "essentially natural groupings" of which Marcellin Boule speaks? The violent or peaceful contact among peoples has powerfully modified human anthropology. And which people did not, during the course of its past, undergo the mixing processes of history?

Among the Arabs, however, these inevitable changes are much less pronounced than elsewhere.

It is commonly agreed to classify the Arabs with the Semitic group.[3] In it are generally included those peoples who were called Syrians or Aramaeans in the north; Babylonians and Assyrians in the east; Arabs in the south; Phoenicians, Edomites, Hebrews, Moabites, and so forth, in the west.[4] "The areas which they inhabited or which they still inhabit are bounded by the Taurus, the Persian Gulf, the Indian Ocean, the Red Sea, Egypt, and the Mediterranean. The whole of this is called the Fertile Crescent because it constitues a semicircle open to the south, with the desert in front and the mountains behind."[5]

---

[3] According to Bertholon and Chantre the true Arabs are brachycephalous (Aryan branch) and not dolychocephalous (*Recherches anthropologiques dans la Berbérie Orientale* [Lyon, 1913]). Ethnologists have not concurred in this view: "The anthropological picture which one has of the Arabs is that of tall men, with dolychocephalous heads, with a long face and black hair and eyes." (Eugène Pittard, *Les Races et l'Histoire*, p. 433).

[4] The Egyptians considered Sennacherib's Assyrians as Arabs (Herodotus II, Ch. CXLI).

[5] Dr. Rappoport, *Histoire de la Palestine* (Paris, 1933).

Whence come the Semites? Not from Central Asia, as it used to be asserted, but actually from the Arabian Peninsula. Winkler, an authority on the subject, is categorical. "The home of the Semites," he affirms, "is Arabia." [6] Sprenger before him also maintained that "all the Semites are Arabs." [7] In successive eras, starting with the earliest antiquity, under the pressure of over population (Winkler), or more simply, of climatic variations which caused persistent famine, their migration waves overflowed periodically in the neighboring countries, overwhelming the native populations, or evicting them from their country of origin. Four times in history the Semitic wave broke its dam and spread outside. The first migration, called Babylonian, is lost in the night of time. It went in the direction of the Tigris and Euphrates valley and reached northern Babylonia, where the Sumerians and Akkadians had to surrender.[8]

The second time, it invaded the countries of the west, especially Canaan. This is the migration of the Amurru, or western Semites. The known history of Palestine goes back to that period.

Toward the fourteenth century B.C. the Aramaean invasion took place in Syria. In northern and central Syria small, semi-independent kingdoms were founded. The history of Damascus began then.

Finally, in the seventh century of our era, the conquests of Arab Islam were started from Medina. This is the last Semitic

---

[6] *Geschichte Babyloniens und Assyriens.* See, by the same author, *Die Volker Vorderasiens* (in *Alte Orient*, I, 2, I, 10).

[7] *Leben und Lehre des Mohammad* (Berlin, 1869), pp. 241–242. See, by the same author, *Die Alte Geographie Arabiens* (Bern, 1875), pp. 293–294. This is the most widespread view: E. Meyer, *Geschichte des Altertums*, Vol. I, 2, pp. 386–387; Weber, *Arabien vor dem Islam*, pp. 3–4. Other writers as well have expressly stated that Arabia was the cradle of the Semitic race. English writers also share the same view: Burton (*A Sketch of Semitic Origins*), Clay (*The Empire of the Amorites*). See, however, against this view: M. Hartmann (*Die Arabische Frage*). But Guidi (*Della sede primitiva dei popoli semitici* in *Acti della R. Ac. dei Lincei* [Rome, 1879]) inclines to favor the region of the southern Euphrates. He agrees with Noeldeke, however, in attributing a common ancestry to the Semitic races.

[8] "Since the dawn of historical time, that is, since the Sumerians came from the south, 3,500 years at least before our era, and occupied the ground on which Ur and Eridu stood, the Semites of Arabia have never ceased to overflow into Mesopotamia and Arabia, in the same way as the Bedouins are trying to do today." (R. Blanchard, *Asie Occidentale*, Vol. VIII of P. Vidal de la Blache and L. Gallois, *Géographie Universelle*, p. 232.)

invasion, the most violent, the most widespread, and the most durable.[9]

In the intervals between these brutal population movements, a slow and peaceful penetration went on, through the groupings which inhabited the Arab periphery. Whenever their Semitic origins became diluted or began to fade, the peninsula, both a laboratory and a reserve, would again inject young blood to remind them of their Arab origins. Semite and Arab are therefore synonymous appellations. They express the same biological reality, the unity of a race which has not stayed put in its original home. "Contemporary Arabia does not contain within its natural limits . . . the whole of the Arab race." [10] The latter has, long since, gone beyond its prehistoric boundaries and occupied new territories where, thanks to it, majestic civilizations were founded. They have been called Babylonian, Assyrian, or Phoenician. In truth, they were Arab, Arab in the spirit which conceived them, Arab in the hands which set them up.[11]

It is certainly true that these peoples, in the course of their peregrinations, came up against other races and fell under their moral and physical influence. Mixing with these races, they lost the purity of their early characteristics. But if their history is closely considered, it cannot be denied that these adulterations are small and without great influence over the whole, at least in those countries which are strung out round the peninsula. From the first Babylonian migrations, the Semites who come from Arabia have always met on their path other Semites who had come before them. By means of struggle or mutual help which takes place between the newcomers and the old occupiers, they have necessarily come into contact with one another. Their inevitable fusion, invariably consummated in history, does not blot out their ethnic characteristics. It rejuvenates them and enables them to adapt themselves to their new situation, a process all the more

[9] Rappoport, *op. cit.*, pp. 35–36.

[10] Pittard, *op. cit.*, p. 432.

[11] It will be observed, not without astonishment, that no lasting civilization could be founded in Arabia proper. At least history has not yet been able to find convincing traces of such, apart from the Yemen, the Arabia Felix of the ancients, where it seems that advanced kingdoms saw the light of day. In contrast, the Semites set up, all around the periphery of their original home, brilliant millenary civilizations which prove, contrary to Ibn Khaldun's view (in his *Prolegomena*), the ability of the Arab race to build and perpetuate.

easy and rapid in that it is effected between groups having the same origin.

But the invasions which originated from outside the Arab countries, from the west or the south, from the north or the east—and in this part of the world they succeeded one another ceaselessly through the centuries—obviously did bring new blood. They encroached on the homogeneity of the Semitic race, which was subjugated for a time. In Iraq, they "encapsulated" it with Persian or Indian elements, in Syria and Palestine with a sediment of extremely varied lineages separated from the peoples who had trampled over their soil. But the Arab-Semitic race, because it is prolific, rooted in the soil, and constantly renewed by infiltration from the desert, has remained the dominant one. The foreign elements have changed it only at the surface. Indeed, their cultural and social manifestations endured only for a short time. Slowly, the Arab wave would cover them once more. Without opposing any resistance, they let themselves be absorbed by it, to be lost and forgotten.

All the same, the landslides constituted by the foreign armies, however small their weight, have impressed on the Arab countries ethnic modifications which diminish a little the purity of their race. Today they are no longer the direct descendants of a common ancestor, but "the congregation of similar individuals descended from parents of the same blood." [12]

Popular tradition indicates this when it divides the Arabs into two categories, the *ba'ida* (extinct) Arabs, a pure race of whom the traces subsist only in the Yemen and Hadramaut, and the *musta'riba* (Arabized) Arabs who constitute the majority of the Arabs in history.

It would therefore seem rash to bring forward the unity of the Arab race, at a moment when scholars agree in accepting the disappearance of pure races. In spite of the fact that the argument from the unity of the race favors the Arab nation, we would prefer instead of the term "race" the more generic term "origin," that is, *Arab origin*, or, if it is preferred, *Semitic origin*, which is the same thing.

Racial unity, or unity of origin, cannot, by itself, constitute the nation. Race is a corporeal element "which constantly falls

---

[12] Pittard, *op. cit.*, p. 4.

apart . . . which is exposed to attack by that which produced it, namely environment and heredity." [13] Further, it is the characteristic of human progress to liberate gradually the individual from the influence of the soil and of blood, in raising him up toward an ideal which men of different races could share. Spiritual effort lessens the intensity of physical reactions. It liberates man from the instincts of his race. "Within the skull which does not change, the brain is modified." [14] Under the *facies* of the ancestor a new soul will live.

Hybrid races may form a united nation. And it is the glory of France to supply so magnificent an example of a people eminently homogeneous in spite of the diversity of the old races which compose it.

COMMON CIVILIZATION

When ethnic similarity is allied to a *common civilization,* it then gives birth to an ideal type of nation. This other distinctive trait of a nation is found in the Arab case. It constitutes its preponderant characteristic. It is the spiritual and social foundation of the Arabs as a nation.

"What seems to me to be the essential characteristic of a civilization," writes Maurice Croiset, "is the way in which it realizes social organization." [15] Civilizations may be distinguished from one another by the manner, by the procedures, which they employ to attain this end. Each one has its own instruments, fashioned by the coördinated efforts of past generations. Such are language and its literary expression, art, customs, religions, which are the substance of every civilization, investing it with its own individuality and its specific originality.

The astonishing history of the Arabs, wrongly called Islamic, is known. Their empire, which they founded in less than twenty years, is greater than that of Rome and is the work of their race and their faith. During an irresistible advance, they expelled the Byzantines from Syria and the Persians from Iraq. Thereafter the Empire, under a multiplicity of forms, whether unitary or

---

[13] Henri Berr, foreword to Pittard, *op. cit.,* p. viii.
[14] *Ibid.,* p. vii.
[15] *La Civilisation de la Grèce Antique* (Paris, 1932), p. 2.

feudal, broken apart or reunited, included a collection of areas with no center of its own, constantly crossed and recrossed by the armies and orders of the caliph, from whose capital the ideas, the winds of passion, the taste and fashions of the court, the religious heresies, the *fetwas* of the ulema, spread in all directions. Civil or foreign war was endemic and kept Syrians and Hijazis, Iraqis and Yemenites, Bedouins and settled people at odds between themselves. Victories and defeats, invasions and conquests, inspired common joy and sadness, marriages and interbreeding, commerce and caravans, fairs and pilgrimages, helped the work of time in bringing together the scattered elements of this vast whole. From generation to generation, the Arab whole became conscious of its being and increased in coherence and vigor.

In spite of the centuries of decadence, in spite of the Turkish regime, and later on in spite of foreign dominance, the legacy of a complete and sumptuous civilization would maintain unity among the Arabs, and would act as a buttress and a *raison d'être* for their national feeling. A religion national in its essence, an intensely living tongue, identical habits and institutions, a commonly shared aesthetic—such are its typical and dominant constituents.

Religion, it is true, is far from constituting an indispensable condition of the national link. But in the initial formation of nations, it does play a considerable historical role, which helps them to evolve and reinforces the collective feeling. Islam, which the majority of the Syrians profess, draws them to the other peoples of the peninsula, morally as well as socially. It creates a religious solidarity among them which prepares the way for their political association and makes them confront the foreign invader instinctively.

But Islam, quite apart from its social consequences, which are similar to those of any other religion, enjoys a special political characteristic which seems to have been desired by its founder. Islam shows itself to be Arab in the first degree; take some of its fundamental ordinances, such as the prohibition against reading the Koran in any but its Arabic text (now, however, becoming weaker), or the numerous political institutions (the caliphate, for example, which according to a hadith must fall to a descendant of Quraish), or the religious institutions (such as the pilgrimage to Mecca, the heart of Islam). The profound changes which are now taking place in some non-Arab Islamic countries illustrate the characteristic of Islam. Must we not, in fact, see in the policy of the governments of Ankara and Tehran an attempt, sometimes conscious, at national reaction against Arab Islam? Under cover of a so-called religious modernization, this policy pursues no other end but the emancipation of Turkish or Iranian thought from the Arab influences which have enveloped it for centuries, stifling its national originality which is derived from its ancient history. The authors of this policy, taken with the non-religious spirit, seem to find at the bottom of Islam a collection of rules and precepts which serve to strengthen the spiritual imperialism of the Arabs. Does not such a fear—however chimerical it seems—express, however, a fundamental trait which essentially belongs to the religion of Mohammad the Arab?

Another constituent of Arab civilization is language. This is the national factor, par excellence.[16] Is not language, in a way, a fatherland? The contemporary evolution of the great Western societies shows it in a striking manner. A centripetal force with irresistible effects, language attracts its followers and brings forth in them a psychological state which is soon frozen into a society and institutions which are covered with its individual coloring.[17] A linguistic renaissance is at the basis of almost all the national liberation or restoration movements, at the origin of pan-Germanism as of fascism. Perhaps this has also been the cause of the "Alsatian malaise," and is occasioning today the slow but inevitable falling apart of historic Belgium. Before as after the war, most of the great states were trying to assimilate, through language, their ethnic minorities. Russification, Germanization, Turkization, Arabization, . . . all these neologisms of contemporary politics represent a series of actions and events which are an

---

[16] "Language invites unity, but does not compel it." (Renan, *Qu'est-ce qu'une nation?*)

[17] This is the view of the Italian professor, Giorgio del Vecchio: "We must consider the concept of the nation to be essentially founded on two elements. The first is of a psychological nature: that unity of thought and of feeling which constitutes national consciousness, and implies the belief in a common destiny, cemented by the memory of the great actions and the incidents of a common past. There is also another element which is as though the tangible exteriorization of the first: language. . . . If these two elements, namely, national consciousness and language, its exteriorization, are realized, then we have the concept of the nation." (*Lezioni di Filosofia del Diritto* [Roma, 1936], p. 290.)

index of the intimate correlation which makes national unity depend on language. When one considers the historic role which language has played in the formation of states, one is astonished that it has not been regarded as the one factor in the formation of nations, since the other factors on which there is agreement, such as race or the general will, are, as even their protagonists concede, uncertain and of passing importance.

From this point of view, the Arabic language brings together, over considerable areas, populations which would otherwise have followed divergent paths. Established at its source, so to speak, within a Sacred Book which is the religious and social foundation of Arab and Muslim life, it has remained throughout the millennia immutable in its general lines, stable but open to extension, expressive, but also rich in its vocabulary and flexible in its subtle and acute distinctions.

For some two thousand years it has not changed in the least. If it has become fragmented, as in fact it has, into two different varieties, the literary and the spoken language, the latter always draws sustenance from the former, finding in it strength and new expressions. In spite of the passage of the centuries, literary Arabic remains free from any radical change. If contemporary style is different from that of the Koran, the language used remains the same.

At the time when the ancient writers were glittering with their greatest brilliance, pre-Hijra Arabic was producing its own masterpieces. This is the very same Arabic which is still being used as a medium by the literate of the Arab world, from the Maghrib to Iraq. The genius of the language, its syntax, and its forms are everywhere the same. The same grammatical rules govern it, as they governed the old Koranic prosody. What a unique privilege in the world, this eternal maturity!

But, as elsewhere, the ignorant mass, influenced by its locality and by geographical isolation, has impressed on its own speech secondary and often picturesque modifications. To the Western Arabist, the alliterations and ellipses which abound in the different dialects seem to constitute the elements of a language on its own. He hastens to classify them under various rubrics: Syrian Arabic, Egyptian Arabic, and the like . . . , while in fact these variants of the same language are, with a little care, understood by all Arabs, without any distinction.

111

In spite of the rapidity with which the language is spoken and the inaccuracy of the expressions, the same permanent substance is found in it. One cannot therefore speak of distinct Arabic idioms or dialects, because none of them has sufficient individuality to make it qualify as such. Popular speech is always being nourished at the source of the written language. There is even a tendency today among the educated classes to try to use in conversation as classical an Arabic as possible.

It is true that the action of time and distance might, in the long run, subject regional dialects to a divergent development, which would increase their distance from the original trunk. This is the case with existing European languages which are derived from two or three fundamental languages: some of them, such as Greek and Latin, are dead, and the others, such as the various dialects of the barbarian tribes of the fifth century, are forgotten.

But thanks to the Koran, the *summa* of the principles of right speech, Arabic has been spared this degeneration. The protective works with which the Prophet surrounded it—the prohibition to translate it, its daily reading by the believers, the scrupulous respect in which its intangible form is held—have preserved it eternally against the treachery of time and the ignorance of men. It is to its venerable language that the Arabs come back in any reviving region. In their literary or periodical works they make it a matter of honor to adopt the "Book," this breviary of impeccable style, as their model. The writers are adopting more and more classical turns of phrase, and systematically reject the use of vitiated or foreign terms. When such a tendency, now still timid, will have become generalized, the danger of linguistic disintegration, which the Koran has so far powerfully worked to prevent, will become no more than a memory. Already, it contributes greatly to the cohesion of the Arab countries.

Before such a language could have become common and exclusive to those who use it, and dear and sacred to them, there were required centuries of history and tradition, of enthusiasms and misfortunes felt in unison, which have created and remolded the Arab personality, nourished its spirit and its dreams, and fashioned its ideal.

Customs and mentality are fashioned in the image of religion and of the past. A link of reciprocal solidarity binds together these social facts. Wherever Islam came, it established in the

The Common Origin of the Arabs

Arabic-speaking countries equivalent modes of thinking, of feeling, of living, without affecting those differences of a secondary order which are produced by climate and geographical environment, and which are of no importance in relation to the whole. This is because Islam, more than any other religion, is not content with regulating the spiritual and moral life of men, but their relations, and their intellectual and social activity as well.

This identity of customs and mentality is expressed in everyday life, as in the numerous manifestations of a social, political, and intellectual character, the harvest of which, peculiarly rich and as yet virgin, will tempt those sociologists who will take the trouble to observe things Oriental from a point of view other than that of philology and erudition.[18] To take one side only of these phenomena, namely literature and art, the mirrors in which is generally reflected social life, it is striking to observe the homogeneous character of Arab societies, in spite of the distances which separate and divide the regions which give them shelter.

It is a significant symptom that there is not and has never been a Syrian, an Iraqi, or a Hijazi literature. Everywhere there is only one Arabic literature, inspired by the same genius, having its roots in the same thinking. In form as in substance, it has the same physiognomy, almost totally free from autochthonous modifications.

The literary schools in each country are, in addition, composed without distinction of writers originating from the most distant Arab areas.

This literature, by means of the ideas which nourish it, of the painters who give it color, of the satires which agitate it, reflects Arab life in various epochs; it rarely reflects life under the tent, but rather prefers that of the societies of Damascus, Baghdad, Cairo, in turn joyful or sad; and in modern times it reflects the life of these countries in their latest development.

The literary composition which, if it had existed, might reproduce as faithfully as possible this general similarity, is undoubtedly the novel, whether in prose or verse. After having gone through brilliant epochs in the past—*The Thousand and One Nights*, *Antar*, and similar works—today it suffers an almost total eclipse.

---

[18] This is the aim that the *Revue des Études Islamiques*, which has appeared in Paris since 1925, has set for itself, under the editorship of Professor L. Massignon.

At the most, there are some modernist writers in Egypt who try their hand at short stories characterized by a somewhat unskilled realism. In order to form an idea of the social life we must still remain content with poems, satires, newspaper articles, and notably with those popular songs which have so great an influence over the mentality of the masses. Folklore, vast in quantity and not well known, contains some fragments of these, scattered but so evocative of the mentality and the feelings of the people.

This contemporary literature, which has just been reborn and which is read and discussed with equal intensity on all sides, indicates habits of thought, concepts, and modes of feeling and living equally dear to all those readers to whom it gives sustenance, without any distinction. Egyptian or Yemenite, Muslim or Christian, poet or singer, any Arab who writes in the language of the Koran will reach millions of Arabs who will share his hatreds and his aspirations.

Similarly, in art the Arabs show everywhere a similar conception of the beautiful. The homogeneous character of Arab architecture and music—those two areas where their art has been exercised with great ease—has already been remarked upon. From Granada to Damascus the same style, obedient to the uniform taste of each epoch, erects minarets harmonious in proportion, and calmly meditative mosques surmounted by subtly, strangely shimmering domes. The contemporary music of an Um-Kulthum or an Abd al-Wahhab, whose pastoral modulations depress the Europeans and give them a sense of anguish, occasion alike in the Arab of Egypt or the shepherd of Syria the same aesthetic emotion as in the time of al-Isfahani (*Kitab al-Aghani*).

This is an Arab, but in no way an Islamic, art. It is felt and appreciated only in the Arab countries, to the exclusion of the other Islamic peoples whose aesthetic departs more and more from the traditional imitation of Semitic art, in order to go back to the more ethnic sources of inspiration which predate their conversion to Islam.

Customs dictate the meaning of institutions, which are not always imposed by an interested legislator but are often of the natural framework of social life which extends and stabilizes them.

It is in this area that similarity, resulting from religion, is most striking. In all the latitudes, the Arab family, to cite only a topical example, is similar in its general lines. The laws which preside over its formation, its development, and its continuance or dissolution (death or divorce), are drawn from the same moral principles which inspire its profound design. The Koran, supported by the Sunna and the teachings of the jurists, constitutes its exclusive charter.[19] This common origin and common legislation explain why many of the problems resulting from the conflict between conservatism and modernism, which has become more and more pressing, occur in a different manner in the Arab countries from the way they arise in Turkey or Persia.

Such is the case with the emancipation of woman, which in the Arab countries encounters arguments in its favor drawn from the history of Arab societies, both before and after Islam, in which woman enjoyed a relative liberty and an active role, while her Turkish or Persian sisters remained plunged in the darkness of the *gynaeceum*. In order to free woman from the harem and lift the heavy veil which covers her face, the Turks of Ankara have been compelled to adopt the habits of the West wholesale, while for the Arabs to attain the same end it is sufficient to go back to the sources of their history and to seek inspiration in examples given by their tradition.

Examples of this kind can be multiplied indefinitely. They would show the homogeneous and specific character of the family, and, after that, of the institutions and customs of the Arab countries.

So intimate a social and affective life as this, directed by a definite will which increasingly asserts itself every day—does it not contain the unmistakable signs of a profound national vitality? But our time is avid for realism. Modern sociologists assert that the bases of modern nations are composed of elements more stable and, so to speak, more tangible than moral characteristics. A nation that will live is one that rests on a complex substratum of interests and material needs which national feeling, in fact, does nothing but reproduce. Unless it is supported, disciplined, and continuously *recharged* by the harmony of concordant and contented economic interests, the collective will to live would

---

[19] If, however, religion, from the time of the Prophet, orders its structure, it is far from having given birth to the institutions which it now regulates. Most of these (clan, tribe, paternal authority, etc.) may be found in their pure state in pre-Islamic Arab societies.

weaken, in the long run, and cause the disintegration of the social whole which holds it up.

MATERIAL UNITY

The Arab fact conforms also to this rule of sociological research, which is finding increasing favor. The economic laws which regulate the Arab world correspond to an imperious geographical determinism. They are the result of a complex of political conditions which have remained unchanged ever since the remote past.

Arab Asia, which shelters the nucleus of the nation, has a particular physiognomy marked by a complete physical indivisibility. Continuous and well-emphasized boundaries define it from all sides. It is like an immense deep saucer surrounded by a belt of mountains, broken by faults in the rock which facilitate access, and by difficult beaches; and in the center green protuberances are scattered which here and there break the monotony of its limitless steppes.

A longitudinal chain crosses it to the west, through Syria. It flattens out in Galilee and becomes a plain, at the level of the sand in the Sinai peninsula.

It gathers up its links again starting from the Gulf of Aqaba, the observatory of the Hijaz, and traces out in a straight line exactly parallel to the Red Sea, an abrupt shield behind which the holy cities of Islam shelter. Beyond Aden stunted hills continue their miragelike profiles until the Hadramaut. Then the limitless desert, the waste seashore, until Oman and Bahrain are reached, where begin, to the north, the fertile valleys of the Tigris and the Euphrates, cradle of the world, which ensure the historic linking of the Persian Gulf with the Syrian plains. Few countries possess a system of natural boundaries so well arranged and so continuous through many latitudes.

In the middle of this circle, which was closed by nature, are means of communication which make it easy for the natives to keep the complementary regions in contact.

In spite of what is commonly believed, the Arabs have never found the desert impassable. Even more than the Sahara, of which the same has been said, the Arabian sands are ceaselessly

crossed, like the sea, along well-established routes, by long caravans of travelers and by the tireless Bedouins, those incomparable
carriers of goods, ideas, and new blood. Thanks to the camel, the
"ship of the desert"—a hackneyed but expressive metaphor—and
increasingly today thanks to mechanical science, these vast areas
of the different Arab regions are put into contact with one
another, in much the same way as oceans or railways serve to
connect various regions. This is why none of them can be separated from the whole, whether historically or politically. Each
one of them is incapable of being understood unless its neighbors
are also understood. They are the product not only of their own
peculiar contingencies, but also of laws, in the elaboration of
which they had all, without distinction, participated. Such a phenomenon explains both their community of civilization and culture, and their social and political institutions, lasting for centuries. It also explains a profound state of affairs which is at the
origin of the peculiarly severe economic conditions from which
some countries placed on the circumference of the peninsula,
notably Syria, have suffered.

This is because, from the economic point of view, the Arab
areas do not constitute individual entities independent one from
another. The work of the centuries has established among them
a veritable division of labor. A common system links their economies, which complement and sustain one another. Without
going back into the past, it is enough to think of the active commerce which, before the war, provisioned the towns of Arabia
from central Syria and the ports of the Hijaz, or Mesopotamia
from northern Syria and Mosul, and of the opposite movement
which spread through the markets of Damascus and Beirut local
produce such as cereals and oleaginous grains, skins, guts, live-
stock, all destined for the Egyptian market. Produce circulated
freely, without any obstacle, giving sustenance to the regions and
contributing to the mutual prosperity of the whole. Today, customs barriers erected between the Arab countries have broken
its economy. In order to live, each country must turn in upon
itself, with all the resulting anemia, stagnation, and misery which
afflict most Arab countries.

In truth, as this brief survey has tried to show, the Arab bloc
of the Near East presents a remarkable unity. There, as else-

where, but even more so, geography rules human life, in all its various forms, whether social, political, economic, or ethnographic. Each part shares in the life of the whole. Commerce and invasions, race and religions, customs and ideas, these manifestations of social activity, once begun, are diffused within the area by a thousand invisible channels with a high rate of circulation, maintaining and renewing national life.

Countries which meet and find one another in such important areas of moral, social, and economic life, are inevitably led to unite. The community of civilization and of origin, maintained and reinforced by a continuing common history and by naturally identical interests, has remained alive throughout the different regimes that have weighed down upon the Arab countries. It predestines these countries to a common life, to be lived in a broad national association and to correspond to their political aspirations and their material and moral needs.

The Arab nation is a social fact not to be denied. It is the fateful end result of history and ethnography, and inevitably it tends toward a political existence. Having already passed the initial stage, its general lines begin to emerge from the depth of the centuries that have traced it out unalterably. Neither political objections nor the schemes of adverse forces can deflect its irresistible advance toward the realization of its necessary destinies. The wisest policy consists in admitting its existence and in reckoning with the unsuspected and striking effect which the powerful idea of Arab unity makes.

No longer occupying the original area of its religious and cultural expansion, the Arab nation has become conscious of its being and its necessities and has retreated beyond Sinai, between the Mediterranean and the Indian Ocean. This was its original home, the place where its racial power is still concentrated. Its will to live is in conflict with the ambitions of the Western powers dominating large sections of its territory and exercising on it their tentacular pressure.

People have spoken of the Greek miracle. With greater awe, they might remember the Arab miracle, the survival of which today produces its political effects. This is the tenacious vitality of a race supremely assimilatory, a vitality which has been transmitted to a mass of peoples spread through two continents and has given them its language and its faith, its own civilization, fashioned with their help. This full history itself had to end up by forming a new nation, which soon will constitute one of the most important factors of Mediterranean civilization in the Near East. And this will be the historic event of the twentieth century.

Abdullah al-Alayili

10 What Is Arab Nationalism?[1]

ARAB NATIONALISM is the consciousness of the Arabs of their complete social existence, a consciousness which is internal and not merely external objective knowledge, so that the image of the Arab community as a spiritual and living complex is ever-present to their conscience. Every Arab must feel with an instinctive compulsion the strong existing connections and ties, in such a way that the community is transferred for him from the externality of life to the internality of the soul.

I do not intend this definition to be restrictive, for nationality, as I have already pointed out, may be defined linguistically or legally or according to its visible results only, without reference to the existence of any pure feeling. But this approximate definition makes two things clear. (1) In nationalism it is necessary for every individual to feel that he is not separate from his community, either in fact or emotionally, and that it is constantly present to his imagination even when he is far from his fatherland and alone. This is also the way of holding it dear and of loyally striving in all that concerns its welfare, though this will not be accomplished until we know how to make of the soul of every Arab something like the camera obscura, a photographic apparatus which will register the shadows of the objects set before it in a clear and stable likeness. (2) It is necessary for nationalism to predominate in the individual in such a manner that it becomes his sole guide, as if it were a compulsive instinct. This compulsive state is the national guarantee which will paralyze the other tendencies, should they attempt to find an outlet, and

---

[1] Abdullah al-Alayili, *Dustur al-arab al-qaumi* (*The National Constitution of the Arabs*) (1st ed.; Beirut, 1941), pp. 88–95. (S. G. H.)

the desires of the intellect should they stir into expression. In this way nationalism is transformed into something which possesses the imaginative power of religion; nay, it becomes a religion with all that the word connotes and entails. Then the people will feel that it is homogeneous and one and that it has a fundamental natural right to freedom and independence.

The factors that contribute to the creation of national feeling are as follows:

Language, which greatly enhances a people's (*sha'b*) consciousness of its unity. Language works toward creating the national link in two ways. (1) It is a means of communication which enables the people to exchange ideas, so that the tendencies and feelings of its members become akin one to another, serving thus as a powerful link which makes the nation (*umma*) share in sorrows and hopes, enables it to preserve its past and its glories and to record its social, political, and literary history so that the coming generations may be acquainted with it, and also guides the nation toward a future hidden in the womb of time. (2) Language is a national custom which cements amicable relations among all members of the people, so that they feel as though they were one family. For it often happens that if someone hears another language being spoken he feels the speaker to be alien to him, and he might even go so far as to hate him because he is foreign, both to his ears and to his heart.

This influence of language in creating a unified homogeneous nation may be scientifically explained by the fact that language is an instrument for the dissemination of thoughts and feelings. A man hears an idea being expressed, and finding it agreeable embraces it; or else a man hears a sad mourner and has a certain melancholy feeling. This dissemination of thought and feeling only language can effect. The society in which only one language is prevalent must, of necessity, be stamped with its peculiar imprint, and its members must be refined anew in its furnace. For language, as I believe, consists of thoughts and feelings expressed in vocables which you may read or hear, thereby becoming attracted to them, because it is also the history of the thoughts and the emotions which have touched our ancestors with their currents, and have then come down to us, and because it is an instrument for the dissemination of thoughts and feelings. The 121 duty of nationalists who are imbued with a burning and true belief is to persuade society by all possible means to free itself from all languages except the one which it is desirable to impose, attachment to which must be fanatical. The fanaticism we mean is the deepest and most violent it is possible to conceive. In such a fanaticism we must mingle hate and contempt for anyone who does not speak that national language, which we hold sacred and venerate as a high ideal. The mystical must enter into everything with which we seek to inspire all hearts. To succeed in a nationalist sense, therefore, we must seek aid from mystical inspiration.

It would be apposite here to quote in illustration a story recounted by Rention [?] in his book, *The Unrest of the Near East*, when discussing Zionism. He said: "Toward 1860 there was a young Jewish student in the small town of Lushki, in Russia. His name was Eliezer; he finished his studies in Paris in 1877 and heard Gambetta speak, at a time when republican principles in France were undergoing a variety of changes. When this student heard Renan speak at the Sorbonne on the greatness of the Hebrew language, he fell wholeheartedly in love with that language, and it came to occupy a sacred place in his heart. He then started to call for the return to Hebrew among the Jews, and to preach the necessity of imposing it in the household and of fanatical attachment to it in society. He became an author and called himself Ben Yehuda; he looked with contempt on those Jews who, to start with, met his call with mockery. At last, he came to an agreement with a young Polish nobleman who, like himself, was burning for the same ideal, and they published two newspapers called *Glory* and *Hope*. Baron Edmond Rothschild also helped him afterward until he made a reality of his preaching and imposed the language as he wished. It was as a result of this that the Jews began to think of resurrecting their golden dream and even, like Theodore Herzl, the author of the Zionist national gospel, to carry out propaganda for the fatherland seriously, persistently, and eagerly."

Since language is the essential pillar on which a stable national edifice is erected, we must attend to its welfare by different educational, scientific, artistic, and literary means. The vitality of the common ideal derives from the vitality of the language, and the love of the people for the language derives from the ability

122

of that language to express the most hidden intimations, the most inarticulate instincts, and the most tumultuous feelings as they rage within their hearts. Our intoxication with our language results from the fact that it reflects the exact picture of our various feelings and emotions.

This is what, of old, endeared the Arabic language to the ancestors, for in it they found everything they could desire. In order to make it a language full of life, expressing all the feelings that it should express, we must labor to make it so that it can become matter fit for thought, art, literature, and emotion. In order to attain this aim the Arabs must bestow their care on linguistic collections and encyclopedias. I have indicated many ways of perfecting the language in the book *Introduction to the Study of the Language of the Arabs.*

Interest. Interest, when it is fused with ideals and hopes, is a powerful factor making for the unity of groups. It is always one of the causes of a union or a social grouping, because it is based on natural selfishness, without which man would not have roused himself to strive for anything.

Those who hold the materialist theory of history have attempted to explain all the actions of man by means of material interests. They have been able to prove that if religions are analyzed minutely they are found to safeguard particular interests which adopt this or that form of religion. If a group finds the safeguard of its interests in Christianity, it will become fanatical because it seeks to preserve its material interests, insistently and selfishly. In this sense, a group, and its interests, are found in Islam and in every religion.

Since interests are common within the great Arab fatherland, the religions which in the past were adopted to safeguard interests have now no function except as regards morals and behavior. Union, in spite of diversity of religious belief, is imposed by common interests within the common fatherland. In any event, what objection is there to our having one national creed and various religions, that is, various moral philosophies?

The Geographical Environment. This factor is effective in two ways. (1) Climate has a great influence over mentality and temperament; uniformity of climate usually creates in people 123 mutual and temperamental similarity and conduces to peaceableness and mutual understanding. (2) The nation is totally or partly encompassed by natural barriers. In modern times, rapid communications have abolished the importance of some of the barriers. Nationalists have considered, however, that the nation has to exist in a defined environment which enables its members to live in full intercourse, because lack of relations between fellow countrymen creates estrangement and unfriendliness. In spite of the ease with which people can cover vast distances in modern times, we still find moral estrangement among the different groups who live in far-flung countries like Russia, Brazil, the United States; this is because of the great distances which separate one part of the nation from another, and this frequently results in differences in customs which greatly militate against a nation's consciousness of its unity.

If we try to isolate the effects of natural barriers on the unity of the nation and its feeling of independence we will find that barriers have no essential value except when they are accompanied by a difference of climate. It is therefore possible to replace natural proximity by artificial proximity by means of fast transport. If natural barriers had by themselves any essential importance they would have continued to exist, no matter how powerful other factors might have been. What is important is the geographical environment as a whole, the relationship between nation, climate, and soil. Because the geographical environment of the Arabs is extensive and the barriers between the Arab nations are such as will be abolished by rapid communications in the modern age, we must (1) Link all Arab areas by means of a communications network which guarantees rapid movement and replaces natural proximity by artificial; (2) Encourage travel and tourism for individuals and groups, because travel diminishes differences, especially if they are group differences. I will go so far as to say that travel ought to be made an educational, pedagogical, and national duty.

Ancestry. There is no doubt that the tie of blood is the oldest tie within the human group, and the most far-reaching in the history of man. Men became differentiated according to it, in ancient times, and on it were founded their international relations. But the course of evolution occasioned a change in the essence of state authority which reduced the importance of this tie; for whereas the state used to be characterized by its authority over persons, afterward its most important characteristic came to be its authority over territory. This transition was of great importance in endowing nationality with social significance.

But in spite of this evolution in the authority of the state, in spite of the fact that there is no pure race in the world, owing to the intermingling of races by means of migrations, intermarriage, and international movements, and in spite of the fact that the modern state is somewhat easygoing in naturalization matters, we nevertheless see that the tie of blood is still important, up to a point, as a factor enabling a people to feel its unity. The idea of blood kinship is a factor in uniting the hearts of a people and harmonizing its inclinations, and the similarity of bodily shapes and formations induced by blood kinship facilitates the idea of a common ancestry.

If we examine the circumstances of some modern states such as America or Belgium, which are mixtures of different kin-groups so complex that it is very difficult to judge which constitutes the majority, we will see that they have agreed to impose the most powerful kin-group of those composing the state, and to glory in it as do the English kin-group in Great Britain, a state which consists of Celts, Normans, English, and Welsh. Common ancestry has been, and still is, a factor that makes the nation feel its unity. We in the Arab fatherland have a number of groups descended from one ancestry, and since the Arab group is the most important, we must then make it a foundation of the state and glory in it.

However, the lesser kin-groups in the Arab whole to which we allude are not so important as those found in other national wholes; further, they are to be found in certain areas only, such as geographical Syria, all other areas being considered purely Arab. Add to this that the majority in Syria itself is Arab, and the Arab race has succeeded in imposing its habits, customs, mentality, and language over other races whose relation to their ancestors is now as remote as that of humanity to Adam.

It is biologically established without doubt that racial characteristics do not subsist in the same form over a long period of time, but undergo essential variations. How much greater these variations would be, then, if these characteristics fell under the 125 influence of a powerful current engulfing them in its violent tide. However this may be, it remains true that the characteristics of those other races have fallen into obscurity, and only the characteristics of the Arab race still subsist and are vital. It is therefore mere mental confusion to disregard reality in favor of sophistries and misleading errors. No doubt, to discuss the details of the minor races [in the Arab fatherland] may lead to the creation of racial personalities in different regions.

This would confront us with one of two conclusions: either the importance of ancestry is abolished within the mixed nationality, or the Arab ancestry, in all its manifestations, which still lives in its descendants is imposed over all. Otherwise, the dead are resurrected at the expense of the living, the minority at the expense of the majority, and the other races are given dominance, although the Arab race is, in fact, the dominant one by virtue of its warm vitality and its movement, not by virtue of ancient statues and remains. This would be to act illogically.

History. This factor is of great importance in creating a unified and concentrated feeling, because it is the register of the events, good or bad, which have happened to the nation in succession. When a group go back to their history, their feelings and ideas go back to certain fixed points. The common rejoicings and common sorrows of the past constitute the memories of a common life to which everybody returns unified in thought and feeling; they also preserve the customs of the nation, its aims, and its ideals.

Since the different groups in the Arab fatherland have been involved with one another from ancient times, they have one common history. Every group is involved with every other, so much so that it is impossible to write a regional history of the Arab countries. The history of Syria is involved with that of Iraq, the history of Hijaz with Egypt's, and these with all the totality of the Arab regions. It must be understood that historical unity is not sundered or weakened by the quarrels or rivalries which may have taken place, for there is no nation which has not experienced such quarrels and rivalries among its different groups. Witness Prussia, which was involved in quarrels with other German principalities; in spite of this, German unity has not disintegrated. What is important in history are the general forces; as for private quarrels, these may even occur between two members of the same family. This compels us to correct the writing of history which still expresses many animosities productive of unconscious hatreds, especially among the young.

Customs. Similarity of customs results, of course, from racial, historical, and geographical unity; and there is no doubt that the very fact of your seeing somebody behaving in the same way as you do will bring you nearer to him. Agreement in customs is the result of agreement in thought, inclination, feeling, and emotion. Language is considered a national custom, [in this instance] a custom purely Arab. The national edifice cannot be erected without these units, for they coöperate in order to bring about a strong national link which does not flag or weaken. Nationalist thinkers have been accustomed to give them equal importance, although customs are unequal in their effects and their results. To me, the most important is the [unity of] geographical environment, followed by mutual interests, then by common language. The others merely fortify the effects of these. A nationality may be brought forth which has neither a history nor qualities, but it cannot be brought forth without an environment (geographical); this may be seen in the Jewish nation (*umma*) in which the different factors and causes have coöperated to make it into a nation with a particular nationality (*umma dhat qaumiyya*), but it was not destined to be one.

It has been agreed to define nationalism as an emotion and a feeling far removed from intellectual causation. The member of the nation loves the fatherland because he loves it; if he loves it for some other reason, then the love will also disappear if the reason disappears. The Arab, then, loves his fatherland and its different regions with a pure love because it is a fatherland; he loves it without any ulterior considerations.

Muhammad Jamil Baihum

11 Arabism and Jewry in Syria[1]

ANSWERING A QUESTION addressed to him during a conference on the Concepts of Freedom, Mr. Jumblat replied as
follows: "It is impossible to accept solutions which require the
expulsion of the Jews from Palestine, since any solution on nationalist principles must ignore the rights of those others who are
not members of the nation. Nationalism proclaims my right alone,
ignoring the rights of everybody else." This is a declaration which
recognizes frankly the Jewish right to Palestine and advocates in
a comprehensive manner an attempt to strike a bargain with the
Jews in order to solve the problem on the basis of this right of
theirs, and without further consideration. We do not know if
Mr. Jumblat bestows this right on the Jews by reason of their
conquest of the Holy Land with Western support, or whether he
seeks this right for them in ancient history. In the first instance,
we beg him to allow us to put this question to him: "If somebody attacked you and occupied a part of your palace in al-
Mukhtara, would you resign yourself to the *fait accompli*, and
would you think it fair and just to bargain with him in order
to reach a solution on the basis of his staying in your house and
his sharing of your property, knowing well that nothing would
satisfy him except to occupy the whole palace at the first opportunity? Or would you revolt against this usurper, and gather all
your strength to eject him, humiliated and defeated, out of your
palace, and so regain your self-respect?" In the latter case
(that is, if Mr. Jumblat recognizes the right of the Jews to
Palestine on the basis of ancient history), it will be necessary to

[1] *Al-uruba wa'l-shu'ubiyya al-haditha* (*Arabism and Modern Shu'ubiyyas*)
(Beirut, 1957), pp. 145–171. (S. G. H.)

review this history before him in order to prove that the Arabs have more right to the country than the Jews because they preceded them in it, and that they had in Syria and beyond it kings and states, even before Islam called upon them to conquer the world.

This is an important matter which is seldom known by the graduate of foreign schools. The reason is that the Old Testament, which the Jews composed on the principle that they were the chosen people, gives a picture of Jewry which deludes the reader into the belief that this constitutes the history of the whole world. Some followers of divine scriptures have fully recognized the Old Testament in spite of the blemishes which it contains, blemishes which do Israel no credit and their prophets no honor. Others, however, have been more cautious and have denied that the Torah in which they believe is among the myths at the disposal of the Jews. In any event, all followers of divine scriptures have succumbed to Jewish influence in their view of history; they have indeed believed in their prophets and looked on ancient history through their windows and have become the mouthpiece of Jewish views. The consequences of this have been that the Jews, though dispersed and humiliated for thousands of years, have been able up to now to preserve their domination over those who hold sacred the books of the Old Testament and who devote themselves to studies in their schools and institutes. This explains how the Americans became greatly interested in the books of the Old Testament, ever since they became concerned with Eastern affairs and started to study the history of Eastern peoples and countries. As soon as they became interested in Orientalism their universities placed the history and language of the Hebrews in the forefront of their studies. Foreign religious missions spread throughout the East, carrying with them this message, and among other things they confused the thoughts of the young and weakened in them the immunity against the Zionist danger which threatened the country.

A Beirut paper has lately published an article entitled, "Are These Hebrew Schools?" which we would like to reproduce word for word in the course of this inquiry. The newspaper said: "There is among the books which are taught in the schools of the foreign missions a French booklet entitled *The Creation*, which deals with what is known as sacred history. It begins with the life of Abraham and ends with the life of Moses, describing also the lives of David, Solomon, Nahum, Jehoshaphat, Jesse, Jacob, and others. In order to make sure that the student understands the requirements of knowledge, a page in this booklet is filled with examination questions and answers. Further, such schools have made this booklet a required text for terminal examinations, so that the student cannot be promoted unless he shows his knowledge of the booklet and its contents. Does the Ministry of Education know about this booklet? And does it know what purpose it serves?"

It is therefore incumbent on us, in this war between us and Zionism which still goes on, that we end our discussion with Mr. Jumblat with a historical account to prove that the Holy Land, which was the birthplace of Christ and Christianity and a first *qibla* for Muhammad and the Muslims, never was Jewish, as the Jews represent it in the Old Testament and as those who drink knowledge from Jewish sources still represent it. On the contrary, the Holy Land was a fatherland for the Arabs before the coming of the Hebrews; it was a fatherland for them even when the Jews were in Palestine, and it so remained until Arabism overspread Palestine during the Islamic period.

THE JEWS IN PALESTINE AND SYRIA: THE PERIOD OF TEMPORARY HOSPITALITY

The Torah recounts that Abraham migrated from the land of the Chaldees to Palestine, the fatherland of the Canaanites, in the second millennium before the birth of Jesus Christ. A famine then spread in Palestine and compelled the Hebrews, Abraham's tribe, to emigrate to the valley of the Nile. They went to Egypt and severed all connection with the land of the Canaanites. While they were in Palestine, the Hebrews had been considered as foreign refugees to such an extent that a piece of land bestowed upon them by the inhabitants as a place to bury their dead was considered purely as a gift. This is, in fact, what happened when the *sheikh* of the village allowed Abraham to be buried in the cave of al-Kafila [the Biblical Machpelah which Genesis 25:9 records Abraham as having bought from a Hittite]. The Jews, however, tried, in spite of this, to deceive the world into believing that their relation with Palestine dated from that period, that is, from the second millennium before the birth of Jesus Christ. They support this argument by the contention that Genesis makes Palestine a holy land because of Abraham's residence in it. The whole world went along with them in this belief, on the basis of the Holy Scriptures, whereas in fact the Hebrews were at that period mere aliens in the land of the Canaanites.

THE RETURN FROM EGYPT TO PALESTINE

When the Hebrews came into Egypt they were nomads, and they found in Egypt blessings which they had never known before. No sooner, however, had they satisfied their hunger and thirst than they became tyrannical rebels. The Egyptians therefore found their yoke very heavy and were scandalized by Hebrew selfishness and cruelty. They therefore chased them out, about the year 1215 B.C. When the Hebrews were expelled from Egypt, they made for the land of the Canaanites, where they had dwelt before, but they could not reach it because the Moabites and the Midianites barred their way. They had therefore to remain forty years in the wilderness, suffering hardship and deprivation, until an opportunity offered and they swooped down on the Canaanites who had been their hosts and benefactors, and carved out for themselves a piece of Palestine. The Hebrews at that time were divided into tribes headed by elders who were called the judges. These tribes then spent some time in constant quarrels among themselves careless of the civilization of the Canaanites around them. If perchance they united it was only to burn prosperous cities and to kill men, women, and children in the name of Jehovah, the god of the Jews. They did not even spare the cattle, in compliance with the so-called sacred revelation which they fraudulently put into the mouth of Moses, saying, "Exterminate the inhabitants of the land and do not spare them. Do not enter into a covenant with them. Kill the men, the women, and the nurslings, the cattle, the sheep, the camels, and the asses" (Exodus 134:15).[2] The inhabitants of Palestine could no longer

---

[2] No such reference is to be found in Exodus. Exodus 34:12–13, a passage which bears some resemblance to the above quotation, runs as follows:

"Take heed to thyself, lest thou make a covenant with the inhabitants of the land whither thou goest, lest it be a snare in the midst of thee:

tolerate them and began to persecute them exactly as the Egyptians had done before, after having been a toy in the hands of the Hebrews, who excited enmities among them and played them off one against the other.

THE GOLDEN AGE OF THE HEBREWS

The Canaanites in Palestine wished to be rid of the tyranny and the cruelty of their neighbors, the Hebrews, and they decided to expel them. Circumstances, however, were not favorable, because the pressure made the Hebrews forget their divisions and their tribes and unite against their enemies under the standard of King David of the tribe of Judah, in the years 1010-930 B.C. They then, from 970–930 B.C., came under the standard of Solomon, the son of David, and conquered another part of Palestine. During that period Solomon built the temple in Jerusalem and the golden age of the Jews came into prominence. They still sing the praises of this age, deceiving the world into believing that it is the apogee of human history. In fact, even in their golden age the Hebrews were still considered by their neighbors the Canaanites as intruders; as Bloch [?] says, "The Jews did not then control an area of Palestine more extensive than 120 miles." As for the title of king by which they addressed Solomon, it was bestowed on whoever headed a tribe; thus, the Old Testament mentions the existence of fifty kings in Palestine, each one of whom was the leader of a handful of people. Further, their golden age was very short-lived and did not last longer than the reign of Solomon, the son of David. This is not merely the result of Palestine's military situation, vis-à-vis the neighboring powers, but also of the constant rivalries and quarrels of the Jewish tribes and of their selfishness and cruelty which led both compatriots and strangers to hate them. Indeed as soon as Solomon, the son of David, died, his kingdom split into two states, the state of Judah in Jerusalem and the state of Israel in Samaria, which engaged in constant war. This enabled the inhabitants of the plain to

---

"But ye shall destroy their altars, break their images, and cut down their groves."

It may be remarked that Deuteronomy 20:14, 19–20, specifically prohibit the killing of women, children, and cattle, also the cutting of trees.

132   (S. G. H.)

regain their independence and aroused the ambitions of the states then existing in Iraq. Among the consequences of this were that Assyria conquered Israel, between 721 and 715 B.C. The Kingdom of Judah then fell to Nebuchadnezzar, the king of Babylon, in 585 B.C. Thus nothing but memories remained of the golden age of the Hebrews. Such an outcome occurred because Babylon was watching their oppressions and their corruption and tried to extirpate them. Babylon not only destroyed Jerusalem and razed Solomon's temple and transported its sacred treasures to Babylon, but also transported a great many of the Jews to its capital. Thus, certain annihilation befell the Hebrews as a punishment for their corruption in the land and their hatred for its inhabitants, as is explained in their Torah, in the books of Jeremiah and Ezekiel.

THE JEWS OF PALESTINE IN THE SHADOW OF THE CONQUERORS

When the Babylonians occupied Palestine and put an end to all Jewish independence, they annexed it to their kingdom and it remained part of Babylon until the latter passed into the possession of Cyrus, the king of Persia, when Palestine became one of his provinces. But Cyrus, the son of Esther, the Jewess, did not himself have occasion, as the king of Babylon did, to witness the oppressions of the Hebrews in Palestine; he took pity on them and allowed those who were in compulsory residence in Babylon to go back to Palestine; he also allowed those who returned to set up a government enjoying a measure of autonomy and attached it to the fifth of the Persian provinces. In addition, he allowed them to practice their religion freely; they rebuilt Solomon's temple in Jerusalem, and with Persian power they regained for this city some of the spiritual importance it had for their ancestors, in spite of the resistance offered by the inhabitants of the land with the Amonites at their head.

It deserves to be mentioned here that though Cyrus liberated them from the Babylonians, their upper class and the majority of their middle class preferred to stay in Babylon because of the financial and the commercial connections they had made there. Those who chose to return were mainly the poor, and their num- 133

ber did not exceed forty thousand. All the same, this small number who returned from exile and homelessness to Palestine had
hardly begun to taste self-government and freedom when they
became a source of irritation for their neighbors. Their situation
in those ancient times was like that of the present day, like a
sparrow escaped from his cage and knowing no bounds to the
liberties he takes. Their neighbors then remembered the early oppressions of the Hebrews. In spite of this they were not grateful to
the Persians. No sooner had Alexander the Great advanced to
occupy Palestine, in 333 B.C., than they received him as a deliverer
and opened the gates of Jerusalem to him. And so it was afterward with every new conqueror. Such will also be their attitude
soon enough toward England and America, the two countries that
have protected them in modern times and have built for them
their new homeland, over the bodies of the Arab martyrs. Such
will also be their attitude toward France, which has lately begun
to protect them in order to spite the Arabs for their support of
Algeria.

After Alexander's death, the fate of Palestine was the same
as that of the rest of Syria which fell to the Seleucids. In that
period the Jews were enabled to reëstablish by force a measure
of independence under the leadership of the Hasmonean family,
but this independence did not last long: Pompey soon attacked
Palestine, in the year 63 B.C., and made it into a Roman province.
It was then that Jesus Christ appeared, addressing his people: "I
am the Messiah whom you expect, the King of Israel." His message was a vital necessity required by the age, because the Israelites
had filled Palestine with corruption to the extent of making
Solomon's temple, as well as other places, a center for usury and
worse. It was natural that they should oppose and become the
enemies of him who was preaching lofty morals and calling for
the renunciation of this mortal world. Before Herod, they accused
Jesus Christ of preaching rebellion and sedition against Rome,
and his imprisonment and the order for his crucifixion followed.
The fact is that Jesus, the Son of Mary, was the bearer of a message calling for love and good works; as for any plot against the
rulers, this was characteristic of the Jews themselves. It was they
who lit the fires of revolt, a little after the death of Christ, and
engaged in disorders from 64 to 70 A.D.; they brought upon themselves the punishment of Titus, who swooped down on them

and ordered the destruction of Jerusalem and the burning of Solomon's temple, which was turned to dust, no stone remaining upon another.

Still, the existence of a small number of Jews in Palestine remained a source of irritation for the Roman Empire and the cause of successive disorders. When they revolted a second time, in 115 A.D., the Emperor Hadrian attacked them again and transformed their new temple into a temple dedicated to Jupiter and Venus and called Jerusalem Aelia Capitolina. In spite of this, the Jews did not learn from what had befallen them and did not appreciate the extent of their weakness; they imprudently rose up once again in a sweeping revolt against Rome, under the leadership of Bar Kochba, in 132 A.D. The Romans fell on them in strength and again destroyed Jerusalem, burning its buildings and demolishing their temple. They also drove many of the Jews to exile like cattle and, under penalty of death, prohibited them, by order of the Emperor Hadrian, from reëntering Palestine.

THE JEWS IN SYRIA AND THEIR CONSPIRACY AGAINST CHRISTIANITY

When the Romans exiled the Jews from Palestine, they took refuge in Syria, and some of them emigrated to the Arabian peninsula. They brought with them all kinds of vice and disorder. Then came the Byzantines, who succeeded the Romans in Syria, inheriting from them their desire for revenge on the Jews for their proceedings and conspiracies. The Byzantines became even greater enemies of the Jews, since they set themselves up as protectors of Christianity, for the destruction of which the Jews had been energetically watching and scheming. The Jews rose in Antioch, during the reign of the Emperor Heracles mutilating the Patriarch and his followers in the most dreadful manner; they then turned on the Christian inhabitants of Tyre and killed them and destroyed their churches; they did the same in Caesarea and elsewhere. Their hatred of the Christians was such that when the Persians advanced against Byzantium, they not only volunteered in the Persian army, in order to deliver Jerusalem, but when the Persians were victorious over the Byzantines in Dara and Bosra, in 611 A.D., they became exceeding glad and actually bought from 135 the Persians, as Jurji Zaidan recounts, eighty thousand Christian captives and put them to the sword!

But their iniquity was visited on themselves; shortly afterward, the Byzantines attacked the Persians, vanquished them, and expelled them from Syria, just as the Glorious Koran had prophesied to the Muslims when they became exceedingly sad at the defeat of their brethren the Byzantines, the people of the Book. When the Byzantines triumphed, they cruelly revenged themselves on the Jews and expelled them from the whole of Syria. The majority of the Jews followed the earlier emigrants who had gone to the Arabian Peninsula, and others spread over the countries of the world. Thus the Jews had spent forty years in the wilderness before they could enter Palestine. They had hardly conquered part of it and spread corruption there when they made Palestine a tasty morsel for the conquerors. Their fate was expulsion from Palestine and from all Syria, and dispersion over the whole world. As for the Arabs, who had been in the land for thousands of years, they were able to live peacefully with all the conquerors except the Jews, and they coöperated with all of them until Syria became theirs exclusively and Damascus the capital of one of their great empires.

ARABISM IN SYRIA BEFORE ISLAM

The Jews wrote their scriptures, their psalms, and their Talmud by the hand of their rabbis; they wrote their history with the ink of their spirit, which is impregnated with selfishness and arrogance. These productions, full of the stories of their prophets, their tribes, and their kings, came to deceive people, especially those people who believe in their Torah, into thinking that they were God's chosen people, that ancient history is no more extensive than their own history, and that Palestine is part and parcel of this history. They have made them believe that Palestine, which was theirs two thousand years ago, must therefore remain theirs eternally. In addition, the Jews have been able to conjure up from nowhere, in people's imaginations, a picture of their golden age in Palestine, drawn from the Torah; and this picture appears as a myth comparable to nothing else in history, the picture of an age when God put at the disposal of their rulers men, genii, and beasts, and spread over the world wisdom and light incomparable. And some of the modern believers in their scriptures who have fallen under their spiritual influence share their sentiments and their beliefs and support them in their demands.

In fact, the argument of the Jews with respect to their rights in Palestine, which is based on their immigration into it two thousand years ago, is "an argument not worthy of consideration or attention," as is textually recorded in the report of the King-Crane Commission which came to Palestine in 1919 to ascertain the wishes of the population in Syria and the Lebanon. And this argument, supposing that it were valid, is rather in favor of the Arabs than of the Jews, because the Arabs preceded the Jews in Palestine. Robinson, in his book *The History of Israel*, has written about the Arabs of Palestine: "They migrated into Palestine three thousand years before the birth of Christ, coming from the Arabian Peninsula; in spite of this their features and their looks are still apparent in the physiognomy of their descendants." Add to this the fact that the Arab element in Palestine was able in some regions to preserve its independence continuously, even during the golden age of the Jews, so that when the Jewish conquerors were gradually evacuated from Palestine the region came within the zone of influence of the Arab states, until finally it became purely Arab after the great Arab upsurge through Islam.

Moreover, the golden age of the Jews in Palestine, which they painted as though it were surrounded by majesty and glory, was really a poor age. If people would only liberate themselves from the influence of this picture which the Jews have framed with a frame of religion, they would be convinced that the golden age of the Jews, which did not exceed forty years, that is, Solomon's reign, was of no account in comparison with the periods of other conquerors, whether in ancient or in modern times. Further, if they would consult history they would find that this golden age is in debt to the Canaanite Arabs for its civilization, as it is in debt to them for its religion.

In his book, *History of the Arabs*, Philip Hitti writes what may be summarized as follows: "In Midian near Sinai, Moses married an Arab woman who was the daughter of a Midianite priest. This marriage was one of the most important events in history; she used to worship a god called Yahweh, and she taught 137 her husband this religious rite. Moreover, Job, who has composed the highest poetry in the ancient Semitic world, was not a Hebrew but an Arab. Shulit also, who has immortalized her beauty with the *Song of Songs* attributed to Solomon, was most probably an Arab from the tribe of Qaidar." This is a proof of the existence of the Arab people in Syria since the Jews returned to it and of its enjoying a measure of civilization.

The archaeological excavations in Palestine have confirmed Robinson's view that this part of Syria, like the rest, was inhabited for thousands of years before the birth of Christ by people who had come in successive waves from the Arabian Peninsula. In inner Syria they were known as the Amorites, in coastal Syria as the Canaanites; from these came the Phoenicians, who were still known as Canaanites until the days of Christ, as is proved in the glorious Koran when it mentions the healing of a Canaanite woman by Christ, in the neighborhood of Tyre and Sidon. Indeed, when Abraham came to Palestine—and he is the ancestor of the Arabs as well as of the Hebrews—this part of Syria was included in the country of the Canaanites; and when Moses left Egypt to return to Palestine, the Edomites, who also come from the Arabian Peninsula, stood in his path; they used to rule over the southeastern part of Palestine, and they compelled him to take another route. They remained enemies of the Jews, against whom they struggled in the days of David and Solomon, and in the days of Jehoshaphat and Isaiah; when Nebuchadnezzar, king of Babylon, defeated the Jews, the Edomites not only took another part of Palestine but spread southward until they reached the neighborhood of Egypt. In that period, the name of the Arabs occurred as such in a decree issued by Shalmanezzar the Assyrian on the occasion of his attack on Damascus, in 854 B.C. In this decree, among the names of his allies is mentioned Jundub, an Arab prince. The Torah also mentions the Arabs quite often. Dean Stanley was perhaps thinking of these Edomites when he said the following in his book *Sinai and Palestine:* "The custom was reversed in Palestine. Usually it is the conquerors who expel the inhabitants of the conquered land into the mountains, while the Palestinians were actually able to retain the plains, when they were attacked by the Jews whom they pushed into the mountainous regions." The Edomites, during the Roman period, had taken Petra as a capital. When their state declined, just before the fourth century A.D., they were succeeded by the Nabateans who spoke Arabic but wrote Aramaic, which was then the language of politics and civilization.

Contemporary with the Nabateans was another Arab state in Tadmur, ruled by the Al Sumaidhagh. When Petra passed into the control of the Seleucids, the successors of the Romans in Syria [*sic*] in 106 A.D., Tadmur began to take the place of the Nabateans in commercial traffic between the Near East and the Middle East, and attained the same degree of prosperity and fame; history still repeats the name of Zenobia, the queen of Tadmur, and of her husband who vanquished Shapur, the king of Persia, both of them Arabs.

Side by side with the Nabateans was another Arab state, that of the Abajira in al-Ruha. Abajira is the plural of Abjar which, etymologically, is a "distended belly." This state was founded in 132 B.C. and remained in existence for four centuries, playing as great a role as Tadmur in the relations between the Romans and the Persians. Its most famous king, Abjar V, was the contemporary of Jesus Christ. Tradition has it that this Abjar was suffering from an illness which the doctors were unable to cure; he sent to Jesus Christ, inviting him to al-Ruha to cure him, and Christ replied with a letter blessing him and his city and promising to send one of his disciples to cure him. The tradition further says that Thomas the Apostle fulfilled this promise and sent his brother Adda to al-Ruha, and Adda cured the king and taught him the way of salvation. In an article which Mr. Asad Rustum published in *Saut al-Mar'a* in 1956, he claimed that the Abajira were Arab; but the Metropolitan Suwairius Ya'qub Toma mentioned in his history of the Syriac Church of Antioch that these Abajira were Syriac. Desirous of pursuing the point, I approached His Eminence the Metropolitan and asked him if the names of the kings of the Abajira, such as Abd b. Qaz'ur, Wa'il, and Bakru, were not sufficient indication that these people were Arab, considering the further fact that they were named Abjar; the Metropolitan, however, denied this and insisted that they were Syriac, and that in Syriac Abjar means "lame."

It seems, then, that the Arabs had other states in Syria, dating from before the birth of Jesus. The most famous were the Jeturites whose capital was 'Anja, in the Bekaa; they are mentioned in Genesis 25:15 as the descendants of a son of Ishmael, 139 the son of Abraham. Their arrival in Syria coincided with the attack of the Jews on the Phoenicians, who expelled them from northern Palestine; in those conflicts the Jeturites sided with the Phoenicians and clashed with the Jews. Perhaps the French author Dussaud had them in mind when he wrote in his book *The History of the Arabs:* "The presence of the Arabs in Syria goes back further than its domination by the Greeks." His proof for this was that when Alexander advanced into Syria the Arabs were in occupation of the Lebanon. It seems that the Arabs did not then occupy Palestine and the Lebanon, but that for periods of time circumstances helped them to control the whole of Syria. Jurji Zaidan pointed this out in his book *The Arabs before Islam,* where he said: "One gathers from the study of the history of Byzantium that the towns of Syria were frequently under the control of the Arabs, especially those towns near the desert, such as Homs, Hama, Damascus, and al-Ruha, as well as the towns of Hauran and al-Balqa'. When Pompey reached Egypt in the first century B.C., Homs was in possession of an Arab state."

Although the Seleucids and the Byzantines were able to destroy the Nabateans, Tadmur and the Abajira, and other Arab states, they opened the way, however, for a new Arab migration which spread over Syria and, in the Byzantine period, gave it an Arab physiognomy. This is because the existence of the above-mentioned Arab states barred the way to many Arab tribes and prevented them from entering Syria, so that when the Nabateans and Tadmur were no more, these tribes began to move toward Syria in the hope of finding in the land of civilization the honor and prosperity which their ancestors had found. Two events chanced to take place then, in the Arabian Peninsula, each of which played an important part in the migration of the tribes toward the north: in Arabia Felix the irrigation dams, Ma'rab being the most famous, were destroyed at about the time of the birth of Christ. Livelihood became difficult as a result, and some Yemenites felt the urge to leave the country. Khuza'a came to Mecca, the Aus and the Khazraj settled in Yathrib, and the Lakhmids and the Ghassanids in Syria. Some of the Lakhmids also went to Iraq, and the Banu Amila, as Abu al-Fida relates, went to the Syrian coast and occupied the mountain in southern Lebanon, which is known by their name. In the Hijaz and its neighborhood the Banu Adnan increased in numbers, and they pushed each other in waves toward the north. The Sulaih, the Rayyan, the Daj'am, the Tanukh, the Safa, the Kalb, the Jarm, the 'Ilaf, and other tribes settled on the outskirts of Syria. The Banu Tanukh founded an Arab emirate on the ruins of the Nabatean state, in which they were succeeded by their fellows, the Banu Sulaih who are from Quda'a; they possessed the hinterland of Syria under the name of B. Daj'am while the B. Safa took control over Hauran. Other tribes advanced toward Diar Bakr and Diar Rabi'a. These places used to have foreign names, but the Arab tribes gave the territories they conquered their own names.

Toward the end of the second century A.D., the Yemenite Ghassanids were victorious over the emirates of the B. Daj'am who are from Adnan; they took Bosra in Syria as their capital. At the same time the Lakhmids, who are from the B. Tanukh, went to Iraq and were able to spread their domination over the area of the Najaf, taking al-Hira as their capital.

Thus the Arabic language spread over the whole of the Fertile Crescent as never before. Renan dates the spread of the Arabic language in Syria to this period, in an article published in 1882, in Volume XIX of the *Journal Asiatique*, where he said: "The conquest of Syria by the Arabic language goes back to a great historical event. I refer to the migration of a large number of Arab princes to Syrian towns at one and the same time, while the Byzantine authorities were trying to lay the bases of their power." At the time of Jesus Christ the Arabic language was one of the languages current in Jerusalem, as appears from the Acts of the Apostles 2:9. It then spread outside Syria into some parts of Iraq, into Diar Bakr, and into al-Ruha. But its spread in Syria was perhaps greater than elsewhere because Arabism had placed its own stamp on Syria, and it was almost an Arab province. This is what made Count Sforza write as follows, in a book published in 1938: "If you had asked Byzantium, you would have learned that Syria over which she ruled was an Arab country ruled by Arab princes who with their people formed the majority of the people."

It is worthy of mention that political circumstances in that period were similar to present circumstances, and gave the Arabs weight in Middle Eastern politics. For in that time two great camps were engaged in a struggle in the East, the first being the 141

Ceasars of Byzantium, the rulers of Syria, and the second the Sassanid Chosroes of Persia, who were rulers over Iraq; this struggle between the two blocs was very similar to the struggle between the Eastern and the Western bloc today. Each of these camps had to seek the support of the Arab state which was within his zone of influence: the Ghassanid in Syria, which was a Byzantine province, and the Lakhmid in Iraq, which was a Persian possession. They had to bestow on these two states many benefits, and arm and develop them. This was a great opportunity for these two Arab states to progress, to prosper, and to enjoy a civilization equal to that of the Ceasars and the Chosroes. The temples of Tadmur and its historical remains are still to be seen, and they indicate the state of civilization of that city. As for al-Hira, Gustave Lebon has greatly extolled its life of ease and luxury and has described its palaces in his book *Arab Civilization* as the most beautiful of Oriental buildings; he said that they compare in magnificence with the palaces of the Chosroes.

It happened then, at the beginning of the sixth century A.D., that there sat on the thrones of Persia and Byzantium at the same time two great rulers, Anu Shirwan and Justinian. The great struggle between these two shed glory and greatness on their two allies, Mundhir b. Imru' al-Qais, the king of the Ghassanids in Syria, and al-Harith b. Jubla, the king of the Lakhmids in Iraq. All this greatly increased the importance of the Arabs in general and enlarged the area of their domination, which stretched from the frontiers of Egypt to those of Persia, sometimes within the framework of the two empires and sometimes outside it. Palestine was within the Ghassanid zone of influence. Some years ago archaeological remains were discovered there, and one historian thought it probable that they were Ghassanid relics. The importance of the Arabs to the two camps was due not only to the reliance of each of them on his ally in Syria or Iraq but also to the care that each of them took to win the whole of the Arabian Peninsula, with the help of his Arab ally. In this instance, too, the Jews have played a great part, and no wonder; as the [Arab] proverb has it: ["The tribe of] Tha'laba leaves its traces everywhere."

They [the Jews] had taken refuge in Syria, in the second century A.D., when the Byzantine Emperor Hadrian issued an edict forbidding them to enter Palestine. But they were destined to be in Syria what they were in Palestine, to wage a war on the state and on Christianity, and to aid the enemies of the Christians. The consequence of this was that when the Byzantines reconquered Syria from the Persians, at the beginning of the seventh century A.D., the Byzantines persecuted the Jews and put restrictions on them, so that some of them emigrated to the Arabian Peninsula and settled either in Hijaz or in Yemen. Both here and there, while in alliance with the Persians, they waged a merciless cold war over Byzantium and over Christianity. They also began to proselytize for their religion. When the Yemen was Judaized—and to the Arabs it was what the caliphs were to the Muslims—and other tribes were also Judaized, the whole of the Arabian Peninsula, with the exception of some Christian tribes, became the ally of Persia against the Byzantines. At that period Islam appeared, confirming the previously revealed divine scriptures. Muhammad, therefore, because of this spiritual link, was won over to Christianity, and the Byzantines became its protectors against Persian Zoroastrians. He carried with him, subsequently, the whole Arab Peninsula, away from the political support of the Persians to Byzantium. This was not effected, however, without a violent struggle between Islam and Judaism, which made the two camps, the Persian and the Byzantine, pay great attention to the Arabs and compete with different means for their alliance. It was not long, however, before the Arabs rose up with Muhammad in their mighty revolt, and they turned into masters after having been followers. And as they successively pushed out the Byzantines from Syria, Egypt, and the Maghreb, they also destroyed the throne of Persia; and then there followed the well-known spread of Arabism everywhere.

SUMMARY OF HISTORY'S VERDICT
CONCERNING PALESTINE

From the first part of this article it has become clear to us that the Jews in Palestine passed through the following stages:

1. The history of the Hebrews up to the year 1000 B.C. was characterized by cruelty and destruction; their raids on their neighbors were a black spot in the history of nomad attacks on civilization.

143

2. When they imbibed culture and religion from the Canaanites and set up the state which their scriptures and their Torah have surrounded with an aura of glory, it was in fact weak and devoid of greatness, except what is found in their scriptures. It was so small in area that even in their golden period, the period of David and Solomon, it did not reach to the Mediterranean except in a small area near Jaffa, as Wade recounts in his *History of the Old Testament*. Its weakness was such that one wave coming from the east was enough to destroy the foundation of this alleged glory and to make the Jews successively slaves to Assyria, Babylon, and Persia.

3. When Cyrus, founder of the Persian Empire, allowed them to return to Palestine and to practice their religion freely, "they had become so little known that if the most intelligent of travelers had visited Palestine and Syria in the fifth century B.C., he would have never heard of the Jews," as Dr. F. Jackson wrote.

4. Ever since Alexander the Great assured his domination over Syria, in 333 B.C., the Jews were no longer of any importance, and they remained until the birth of Islam, that is, for a period of about 1,175 years, bent under the yoke of the Romans, the Seleucids and the Byzantines. Their conspiracies and seditions sometimes bore fruit in exceptional circumstances, only to collapse after a short while.

5. In the second century A.D., the Jews were forbidden to enter Palestine by a decree issued by the Byzantine Emperor Hadrian. This decree remained in force throughout the Byzantine period; indeed, the Byzantines were so careful to prevent the Jews from entering Jerusalem that when the Byzantine Patriarch Sofronius had to surrender to the Arabs, he stipulated that the keys of the city be given to the Caliph Umar b. al-Khattab personally; by so doing he wanted chiefly to obtain a promise from the Muslims to abide by Hadrian's decree. The Caliph answered his desire, came to Jerusalem, and signed a document presented by the Patriarch in which he engaged not to allow any Jews to enter Jerusalem.

6. The Jews welcomed every conqueror with hymns of praise and glory. They kept no promise and had no gratitude. When Cyrus triumphed over Babylon, and when Alexander the Great triumphed over the Persians, as well as when Chosroes defeated Heracles, the Jews welcomed the victor; afterward they welcomed

the Muslim conquest with great joy and became the spies of the Muslims in all their conquests though they had previously been the bitter enemies of Muhammad, rousing the tribes against him in order to kill his message in its cradle.

Moreover, Arabism in Palestine and in the rest of Syria was not only a thousand years older than Hebraism but, through the Canaanites, the Edomites, and others, remained in existence all the time the Jews were present in Palestine and after their evacuation from it. It went on to increase and flourish until the great Muslim wave overspread it.

When Abraham came to Palestine, in the second millennium B.C., Syria was inhabited by Canaanites who had come from the Arabian Peninsula a thousand years earlier.

At the foundation of the enlarged state of Israel in Jerusalem, and during its golden period, the Palestinian Canaanites were able to confine it to the interior, so that it had no outlet to the Mediterranean except in a small area near Jaffa.

Since the time when Syria came under the control of Alexander the Great (333 B.C.) until it became purely Arab, during the Muslim conquest in 637 A.D. (that is, through a period of about a thousand years), Arabism was prominent there and was powerful through the numerous Arab states which succeeded one another. It spread from Upper Egypt and the eastern desert to Diar Bakr and Iraq. Consequently, as soon as Muhammad preached his message, he turned his people's face toward Syria and especially to Jerusalem, which he made his first *qibla* and which he took as the first stage of his ascent. He had also openly preached its reconquest, as the Koran records: "O people, enter the holy land which God has promised you and do not turn back and become the losers."

As for the Zionists, who have come falsely pretending that they had more right to Palestine than the Arabs, and who have filled the earth with cries and lamentations, "most of them are Khazars who became Jews in the middle of the eighth century A.D.," as Griffith Taylor said in a lecture given to the British Association for the Advancement of Science. What right had they to Palestine? he wondered.

However, although we base ourselves on history to prove that the Arabs had more right to Palestine than the Jews, we do not believe that proofs are sufficient to ensure its return from those 145 who took it by force, so long as the law of the jungle still prevails in the world and so long as right is dominated by might. The aim of this exposition has been to show those who dwell among the Arabs, and those outside Arab countries who have been taken in by Zionist propaganda and have been bewitched by the magic of Jewry, that the historical arguments of the Jews are not based on the truth and that in any event they do not constitute a right to expel a people from their country, barefoot and naked, in order to replace them with the scum of the earth. The purification of Palestine depends on strength alone. Such a thing is not difficult for the Arabs, even though the Jews and the West support each other. Only yesterday we thought it difficult to evacuate the French from Syria and the Lebanon; we then thought it difficult to expel France by force from Morocco, Tunisia, and Algeria; we did not believe it possible to extricate Transjordan from the embrace of Great Britain and to expel Glubb Pasha or to liberate Iraq from the British army of occupation, or to expel Great Britain from Egypt. We used to think all this almost unattainable, whenever we compared our forces with the gigantic forces of the West.

But what was difficult became easy when the will was there and the circumstances were propitious. Had the Arab lands settled down quietly under the imperialists and given in to apathy and despair, accepting solutions which were less than full independence, they would still have been suffering under the burden of imperialism. Therefore, we beg those who advise negotiation with the Jews and who incline to make peace with them, whether on conditions made at the Bandung Conference or elsewhere, to believe with us that any negotiation with the Zionists who, whenever peace is mentioned, turn all smoothness, is defective as a solution and will end by breaking up the unity of the Arabs and dividing their united world. And as the poet said: "Snakes, smooth though they may be to the touch, yet, when they turn on you, there is hurt in their fangs."

Sati 'al-Husri

12 Muslim Unity and Arab Unity

I HAVE READ and heard many opinions and observations concerning Muslim unity and Arab unity, and which is to be preferred. I have been receiving for some time now various questions concerning this matter: Why, it is asked, are you interested in Arab unity, and why do you neglect Muslim unity? Do you not see that the goal of Muslim unity is higher than the goal of Arab unity, and that the power generated by Muslim union would be greater than that generated by Arab union? Do you not agree that religious feeling in the East is much stronger than national feeling? Why, then, do you want us to neglect the exploitation of this powerful feeling and to spend our energies in order to strengthen a weak feeling? Do you believe that the variety of languages will prevent the union of the Muslims? Do you not notice that the principles of communism, socialism, Freemasonry, and other systems unite people of different languages, races, countries, and climates; that none of these differences have prevented them from coming to understanding, from drawing nearer to one another, and from agreeing on one plan and one creed? Do you not know that every Muslim in Syria, Egypt, or Iraq believes that the Indian Muslim, the Japanese Muslim, or the European Muslim is as much his brother as the Muslim with whom he lives side by side? Whence, then, the impossibility of realizing Muslim union? Some say that Muslim unity is more powerful than any other and that its realization is easier than the realization of any other. What do you say to this? Some pretend, mistakenly, that the idea of Arab union is a plot the aim of which is to prevent the

[1] From *Ara' wa ahadith fi'l-wataniyya wa'l-qaumiyya* (*Views and Addresses on Patriotism and Nationalism*) (Cairo, 1944), pp. 88–98. (S. G. H.)

spread of the idea of Muslim union, in order to isolate some of the countries of the Muslim world and facilitate their continued subjugation. What is your opinion of this allegation?

I have heard and read, and I still hear and read, many similar questions which occur in conversations, in private letters, or in open letters. I have therefore thought to devote this essay to the full discussion of these problems and to the frank explanation of my view concerning them.

I think that the essential point which has to be studied and solved when deciding which to prefer, Muslim unity or Arab unity, may be summarized as follows: Is Muslim unity a reasonable hope capable of realization? Or is it a utopian dream incapable of realization? And assuming the first alternative, is its realization easier or more difficult than the realization of Arab unity? Does one of these two schemes exclude the other? And is there a way of realizing Muslim unity without realizing Arab unity? When we think about such questions and analyze them, we have, in the first place, to define clearly what we mean by Muslim unity and by Arab unity and to delimit without any ambiguity the use of the two expressions.

It goes without saying that Arab unity requires the creation of a political union of the different Arab countries the inhabitants of which speak Arabic. As for Muslim unity, that naturally requires the creation of a political union of the different Muslim countries, the inhabitants of which profess the Muslim religion, regardless of the variety of their languages and races. It is also well known that the Muslim world includes the Arab countries, Turkey, Iran, Afghanistan, Turkestan, parts of India, the East Indies, the Caucasus, North Africa, as well as parts of Central Africa, without considering a few scattered units in Europe and Asia, as in Albania, Yugoslavia, Poland, China, and Japan. Further, there is no need to show that the Arab countries occupy the central portion of this far-flung world.

Whoever will examine these evident facts and picture the map of the Muslim world, noticing the position of the Arab world within it, will have to concede that Arab unity is much easier to bring about than Muslim unity, and that this latter is not capable of realization, assuming that it can be realized, except through Arab unity. It is not possible for any sane person to imagine union among Cairo, Baghdad, Tehran, Kabul, Haiderabad, and Bukhara, or Kashgar, Persia, and Timbuctoo, without there being a union among Cairo, Baghdad, Damascus, Mecca, and Tunis. It is not possible for any sane person to conceive the possibility of union among Turks, Arabs, Persians, Malayans, and Negroes, while denying unity to the Arabs themselves. If, contrary to fact, the Arab world were more extensive and wider than the Muslim world, it would have been possible to imagine a Muslim union without Arab union, and it would have been permissible to say that Muslim union is easier to realize than Arab union. But as the position is the exact opposite, there is no logical scope whatever for such statements and speculations. We must not forget this truth when we think and speak concerning Muslim unity and Arab unity. The idea of Muslim unity is, it is true, wider and more inclusive than the concept of Arab unity, but it is not possible to advocate Muslim unity without advocating Arab unity. We have, therefore, the right to assert that whoever opposes Arab unity also opposes Muslim unity. As for him who opposes Arab unity, in the name of Muslim unity or for the sake of Muslim unity, he contradicts the simplest necessities of reason and logic.

Having established this truth, to disagree with which is not logically possible, we ought to notice another truth which is no less important. We must not forget that the expression "unity," in this context, means political unity; and we must constantly remember that the concept of Islamic unity greatly differs from that of Muslim brotherhood. Unity is one thing and affection another, political unity is one thing and agreement on a certain principle another. To advocate Muslim unity, therefore, is different from advocating the improvement of conditions in Islam and different also from advocating an increase in understanding, in affection, and in coöperation among Muslims. We can therefore say that he who talks about the principle of Muslim brotherhood, and discusses the benefits of understanding among the Muslims, does not prove that Muslim unity is possible. Contrariwise, he who denies the possibility of realizing Muslim unity does not deny the principle of Muslim brotherhood or oppose the efforts toward the awakening of the Muslims and understanding among them. What may be said concerning the ideal of brotherhood is not sufficient proof of the possibility of realizing Muslim unity. Further, it is not intelligent or logical to prove the possibility of realizing Muslim unity by quoting the example of Freemasonry 149

or socialism or communism, because the Freemasons do not constitute a political unity and the socialist parties in the different
European countries have not combined to form a new state. Even
communism itself has not formed a new state, but has taken the
place of the Czarist Russian state. We have, therefore, to distinguish quite clearly between the question of Muslim brotherhood and that of Muslim unity, and we must consider directly
whether or not it is possible to realize Muslim unity in the political sense.

If we cast a general glance at history and review the influence of
religions over the formation of political units, we find that the
world religions have not been able to unify peoples speaking
different languages, except in the Middle Ages, and that only in
limited areas and for a short time. The political unity which the
Christian Church sought to bring about did not at any time merge
the Orthodox world with the Catholic. Neither did the political
unity which the papacy tried to bring about in the Catholic world
last for any length of time. So it was also in the Muslim world;
the political unity which existed at the beginning of its life was
not able to withstand the changes of circumstance for any length
of time. Even the Abbasid caliphate, at the height of its power
and glory, could not unite all the Muslims under its political
banner. Similarly, the lands ruled by this caliphate did not effectively preserve their political unity for very long. Nor was it long
after the founding of the caliphate that its control over some of
the provinces became symbolic rather than real; it could not prevent the secession of these provinces and their transformation into
independent political units. It deserves to be mentioned in this
connection that the spread of the Muslim religion in some areas
took place after the Muslim caliphate lost effective unity and
real power, so much so that in some countries Islam spread in a
manner independent of the political authority, at the hands of
missionary tradesmen, holy men, and dervishes. In short, the
Muslim world, within its present extensive limits, never at any
time formed a political unity. If, then, political unity could not
be realized in past centuries, when social life was simple and
political relations were primitive, when religious customs controlled every aspect of behavior and thought, it will not be possible to realize it in this century, when social life has become
150 complicated, political problems have become intractable, and

science and technology have liberated themselves from the control of tradition and religious beliefs.

I know that what I have stated here will displease many doctors of Islam; I know that the indications of history which I have set out above will have no influence over the beliefs of a great many of the men of religion, because they have been accustomed to discuss these matters without paying heed to historical facts or to the geographical picture; nor are they used to distinguishing between the meaning of religious brotherhood and the meaning of political ties. They have been accustomed to confuse the principles of Islamic brotherhood, in its moral sense, and the idea of Islamic unity, in its political sense. I think it useless to try to persuade these people of the falsity of their beliefs, but I think it necessary to ask them to remember what reason and logic require in this respect. Let them maintain their belief in the possibility of realizing Islamic unity, but let them at the same time agree to the necessity of furthering Arab unity, at least as one stage toward the realization of the Islamic unity in which they believe. In any event, let them not oppose the efforts which are being made to bring about Arab unity, on the pretext of serving the Islamic unity which they desire. I repeat here what I have written above: whoever opposes Arab unity, on the pretext of Muslim unity, contradicts the simplest requirements of reason and logic, and I unhesitatingly say that to contradict logic to this extent can be the result only of deceit or of deception. The deceit is that of some separatists who dislike the awakening of the Arab nation and try to arouse religious feeling against the idea of Arab unity, and the deception is that of the simple-minded, who incline to believe whatever is said to them in the name of religion, without realizing what hidden purposes might lurk behind the speeches. I therefore regard it as my duty to draw the attention of all the Muslim Arabs to this important matter and I ask them not to be deceived by the myths of the separatists on this chapter.

Perhaps the strangest and most misleading views that have been expressed regarding Arab unity and Islamic unity are the views of those who say that the idea of Arab unity was created to combat Islamic unity in order to isolate some Islamic countries, the better to exercise continuous power over them. I cannot imagine a view further removed from the realities of history and politics or more contradictory to the laws of reason and logic. The details 151

I have mentioned above concerning the relation of Muslim unity to Arab unity are sufficient, basically, to refute such allegations. Yet I think it advisable to add to these details some observations for further proof and clarity. It cannot be denied that the British, more than any other state, have humored and indulged the Arab movement. This is only because they are more practiced in politics and quicker to understand the psychology of nations and the realities of social life. Before anybody else they realized the hidden powers lying in the Arab idea, and thought it wise, therefore, to humor it somewhat, instead of directly opposing it. This was in order to preserve themselves against the harm they might sustain through it and to make it more advantageous to their interests.

We must understand that British policy is a practical policy, changing with circumstances and always making use of opportunities. We must not forget that it was Great Britain who, many times, saved the Ottoman state, then the depository of the Islamic caliphate, from Russian domination. She it was who halted Egyptian armies in the heart of Anatolia to save the seat of the Muslim caliphate from these victorious troops, and she it was who opposed the union of Egypt with Syria at the time of Muhammad Ali. Whoever, then, charges that the idea of Arab unity is a foreign plot utters a greater falsehood than any that has ever been uttered, and he is the victim of the greatest of deceptions. We must know full well that the idea of Arab unity is a natural idea. It has not been artificially started. It is a natural consequence of the existence of the Arab nation itself. It is a social force drawing its vitality from the life of the Arabic language, from the history of the Arab nation, and from the connectedness of the Arab countries. No one can logically pretend that it is the British who created the idea of Arab unity, unless he can prove that it is the British who have created the Arabic language, originating the history of the Arab nation and putting together the geography of the Arab countries. The idea of Arab unity is a natural concept springing from the depths of social nature and not from the artificial views which can be invented by individuals or by states. It remained latent, like many natural and social forces, for many centuries, as a result of many historical factors which cannot be analyzed here. But everything indicates that this period is now at an end, that the movement has come into the open and will manifest itself with ever-increasing power. It will, without any doubt, spread all over the Arab countries, to whom it will bring back their ancient glory and primeval youth; it will indeed bring back what is most fertile, most powerful, and highest in these countries. This ought to be the faith of the enlightened among the speakers of the *dad*.

Abd al-Rahman Azzam

13 The Arab League and World Unity[1]

Ladies and Gentlemen,

IT IS IMPOSSIBLE for us to discuss the [Arab] League, its purpose, and its aim toward world unity without considering a little history, because at the present, states are but a reflection, or a number of reflections, from their past. To realize the end toward which our new unity will lead we must understand as much as we can what our ancestors had in mind for hundreds of years, and what they worked for.

In their pre-Islamic past and before their great renaissance changed the face of history in the seventh century A.D., the Arabs constituted various tribes and clans in a state of anarchy. They nevertheless had many good qualities; there are numerous instances of their love of justice and bravery of which we will mention the *Confederacy of the Fudul*. Before the Muhammadan call, a merchant from Yemen cried out in Mecca complaining of the oppression of al-'As b. Wa'il, a leader in Quraish, who had not paid him for the goods he had bought from him. He said: "Oh, who will help the oppressed one far from his abode, his goods in the belly of Mecca and he at a great distance from home and help;" A group of men who, even in their pre-Islamic state, held justice sacred, rallied to his defense. The Banu Hashim, al-Muttalib, the Banu Zuhra b. Kilab, Asad b. Abd al-Uzza, and Taim b. Murra covenanted together and vowed to defend the oppressed, and come to their rescue.

Their covenant was called the Confederacy of the Fudul, and

---

[1] *Al-jami'a al-arabiyya wa'l-wahda al-alamiyya* (*The Arab League and World Unity*) (Cairo, 1946). This is an address given at the American University in Cairo, January 4, 1946.

154

Muhammad, then still a young man, was present at it. More than a quarter of a century later, when the great renaissance came about and Muhammad was master of the Peninsula, he said: "I have witnessed in the house of Abdullah b. Jud'an the Confederacy of the Fudul. If I were invited to take part in it during Islam I should do so. I would not exchange it for any number of fine camels. Now I have annulled it, for Islam lends more strength to its principles." To give help, then, to the oppressed is inherent in the nature of the Arab, both in the pre-Islamic and in the Islamic eras. We, the Arabs in the East and West, consider it our duty to help the oppressed, whether he be Muslim or Christian or Jew, or even an idolater. After fourteen hundred years, the Confederacy of the Fudul still retains its place in our affection and we gladly accept it. There is also the Pact of Khuza'a, between Khuza'a and Abd al-Muttalib, the Prophet's grandfather, which stipulated that they should always come to the help of each other. When Islam and the new renaissance came, Muhammad confirmed this pact but stipulated that he would come to Khuza'a's help only if they were oppressed, but not when they were oppressors. Khuza'a had not then become Muslim, but was still idolatrous. When the human race will hold sacred a principle such as this, then we will no doubt stride toward world unity.

Included among the bases which this universal Arab renaissance laid down was one that provided for international order; people did not understand it nor did they heed it until hundreds of years afterward: the League of Nations came into being, and now we have this other organization of the United Nations. The Arabs were hundreds of years earlier than other nations in their conception of an international organization and of universal principles based on human coöperation toward peace and freedom for all.

In the seventh century of the Christian era Muhammad made a covenant with the Jews and the idolaters. It may be considered as the basis for an international universal covenant among the religions, the communities, and the peoples of the world. Its essence would be freedom of belief and of the homeland, and coöperation toward this end. Muhammad's covenant I consider to be the first international agreement that aims at the realization of human unity and unites people in the preservation of their freedom, the freedom of their beliefs, and the freedom to propagate these beliefs. I call this covenant the Covenant of Yathrib, and I 155 consider it to be the basis of all present international treaties. This covenant, which I have said is based on freedom and its preservation for all, aims at democracy. The Arabs are by nature a democratic nation. But I regret to have to confess that the word "democracy," like the words "independence" and "freedom," has now acquired many meanings, and these different meanings are often contradictory. The democracy I have in mind, with which the Arabs are acquainted, means that men are free as individuals and as groups to determine and take care of their interests and their affairs. Men are equal, all being descended from Adam, and Adam is but of the dust. In their freedom men do not intend harm to others nor do they mean to rob them of their rights or to exercise power over them in any way or for any reason. They live within their own rights, masters of themselves and of their fate and of the kind of life they themselves desire. In this sense democracy has been realized by the Arabs from of old; it is inherent in their nature, and they do not have to simulate it nor to make a show of it. It is what they strive for today, and it is itself the aim of the Arab League, which wants nothing but this freedom for itself and peace for all.

Let me read you the Covenant of Yathrib to which I have referred: "In the name of God the Compassionate, the Merciful. This is a document from Muhammad the Prophet [governing the relations] between the believers and Muslims of Quraish and Yathrib, and those who have followed them and joined them and labored with them. They are one community, to the exclusion of all men. The Quraish emigrants, according to their present custom, shall pay the bloodwit within their number and shall redeem their prisoners with the kindness and the justice common among believers.

"The B. 'Auf, according to their present custom, shall pay the bloodwit they paid in heathenism; every section shall redeem its prisoners with the kindness and the justice common among believers."

He went on to mention each clan of the Helpers, and the members of each household who were parties to the treaty. He then referred to some of the Muslim's duties toward the Muslims which established the basis of unity of the Muhammadan state, and which made mutual assistance and brotherhood replace the

156

spirit of exclusiveness. He laid it down that anyone among the Jews who supported the Muslim community would be entitled to help and equality. This of course means that members of other religions who support Islam would have the same rights. Muhammad then proceeded to say: "The Jews shall contribute to the cost of war so long as they are fighting alongside the believers. The Jews of the B. 'Auf are one community with the believers (the Jews have their religion and the Muslims have theirs), their freedmen and their persons, except those who behave unjustly and sinfully, for these hurt but themselves and their families." He then enumerated those tribes of the Jews, their freedmen and their followers, who have rights and duties and who participated in the rights and duties of the covenant and went on to say: "The Jews must bear their expenses and the Muslims their expenses. Each must help the other against anyone who attacks the people of this document. They must seek mutual advice and consultation, and loyalty is consultation against treachery. A man is not liable for his ally's misdeeds. The wronged must be helped. The Jews must pay with the believers so long as war lasts. Yathrib shall be a sanctuary for the people of this document. A stranger under protection shall be as his host doing no harm and committing no crime. A woman shall only be given protection with the consent of her family. If any dispute or controversy likely to cause trouble should arise it must be referred to God and to Muhammad, the apostle of God. God accepts what is nearest to piety and goodness in this document. Quraish and their helpers shall not be given protection. The contracting parties are bound to help one another against any attack on Yathrib. If they are called to make peace and maintain it they must do so; and if they make a similar demand on the Muslims it must be carried out except in the case of a holy war. Everyone shall have his portion from the side to which he belongs; the Jews of al-Aus, their freedmen and themselves, have the same standing as the people of this document, in pure loyalty from the people of this document.

"Loyalty is a protection against treachery: He who acquires aught acquires it for himself. God approves of this document. This deed will not protect the unjust and the sinner. The man who goes forth to fight and the man who stays at home in the city is safe 157 unless he has been unjust and sinned. God is the protector of the good and God-fearing man." [2]

The text of this document is suited to the age in which it was made. The sense, however, is clear: it is possible for the Muslims and the followers of other religions to covenant together on the basis of freedom of belief and nonaggression. God will witness and guarantee this covenant. In other words, the pact issues from the core of belief and conscience.

The Arab nation made its appearance in the seventh century with a mission to found one nation. As the verse says, "Your nation is one nation and I am your God; therefore worship." This nation is divided into many parts. The first consists of the believers in the Muhammadan creed; these constitute one Muslim homeland without any boundaries, wherein they are co-citizens, equal in rights and duties, participating in one world-wide homeland where no Arab is superior to a non-Arab, except by reason of his piety or peaceableness. They did not want to make of their nationality a cause for eternal quarrels between themselves and other nations; they said that whoever enters this homeland and accepts their protection, even though not of their religion, will have the same rights and duties. This is how there grew inside the Muslim homeland nations and peoples of various origins and religions, equal in rights and duties. This was not all. Not only was there this vast homeland based on justice and the right to thought and freedom, but there was also, for the sake of world unity, the principle of treaty-making which considered all those who made treaties with the Arabs as their equals. They were all treated alike; permanent peace and the rights of neighborhood were guaranteed by treaty, and they would remain in their homes, secure from aggression. This treaty would be abrogated only in case of aggression by the non-Muslim party.

Should the Muslims wish to abrogate the treaty they do not proceed in the same manner as the Europeans and the others who abrogate treaties by surprise, and consider this a kind of capital to win benefits in war; the Muslims have to give a warning, and then the pact is denounced to the non-Muslim parties, after an opportunity is given to them to consider it among themselves and to discuss its renewal. Should they refuse, their countries become

---

[2] I have used the translation of the covenant as given by A. Guillaume, *The Life of Muhammad* (London, 1955). (S. G. H.)

the abode of war. The scholars have extensively discussed this ultimatum and its varieties. They said that it was necessary for the ruler of the non-Muslim party to be able to reach all the parts of his kingdom and acquaint them with its terms so that people would be clear that the state of peace was at an end. If things develop in such a manner that a state of war does exist, war for the Muslim, and I say for the Arab, is lawful only in order to repulse aggression. Should the enemy lean to peace, the Muslim community ought to accept peace, for as the verses say "Should they lean to peace then you do lean to it and put your trust in God," and "Should they wish to deceive you, your recourse is in God."

It is now clear to us that this is not as people do nowadays, for they do not stop fighting and they set themselves no bounds until they have destroyed the factories of their enemies, their institutes, and their houses, as they have done in Germany. As long as it is guided by the example of the just ancestors and their ideals, the Arab League cannot conceive of such a situation. The Arab League can then, by means of its spiritual heritage, aim toward world unity. The Arab is a man who is prepared to hold back at any time and who accepts peace whenever it is offered to him, without insisting on the complete defeat of his enemy, and with no arrogance on his own part. He does not exact tyrannical conditions such as are demanded by a state of mind weighted with materialism and cruelty, a state of mind which has nowadays overwhelmed humanity. For the Arab, all men are equal; they are descended from Adam, and Adam is but of dust. The principle in the Arab view is human coöperation. Men live by their opinions and ideas; this is their aim in earthly existence and their path to eternity. If they fight, then it is for their ideals and for nothing else, since God has forbidden war for the sake of increasing earthly benefits. As the verse says: "Do not say to whoever has offered you a peaceful salutation, You are not a believer; you would be after earthly gains. But with God there are many spoils."

Had postwar international relations been based on these generous ideals, war would not have engendered war; the peace concluded between Saudi Arabia and the Yemen is a noteworthy example, showing that the Arab still preserves much of this exalted ideal. The aims of life and of war for those great contemporary materialistic powers, and even for the small ones, are 159 different. Alas, their aim indeed is imperialism, domination, the desire to triumph, and the acquisition of raw materials and markets, whereas war for the Arabs is never lawful except in self-defense or in order to guarantee the freedom of propaganda for the faith. Their book says "A sanction is given to those who take up arms because they have suffered oppression. God is indeed well able to succor them, especially those who have been driven away from their homes unjustly, only because they say 'Our Lord is God.' And if God had not repelled some men by others, cloisters and churches and oratories and mosques in which the name of God is mentioned would have been destroyed."

Thus we see that the religion of the Arabs allows them to fight in self-defense and to protect the freedom of belief for Muslim and non-Muslim alike, for the mention of monasteries, churches, synagogues, and mosques among the places of worship for Jews, Christians, and others, as well as those which are for the worship of Muslims is the most remarkable thing that humanity can aim at for the sake of freedom of belief. The Muslim has to respect all religions and to defend them all alike. The ancient Arabian constitution does not make war lawful unless in self-defense or in defense of religion and worship for the Muslim or the non-Muslim, be he Christian or Jew or otherwise. The Arab or the Muslim may not make war a means for imperialism or for exploitation or for the conquests of strategic positions which would enable them to repeat the aggression and to make fresh preparations for war and to compel people to change their religions.

We Arabs have received from the renaissance of the seventh century a noble heritage to which we invite people to adhere today, not as a religion, because people are free to believe what they would; rather, we invite them to adhere to ideals, principles, and rules adopted by our forefathers which will serve well to realize international unity, perpetual peace, and human brotherhood among men. After this historical survey, let us go back and explain some of the principles on which the message of the Arabs in their new renaissance, in the shade of the League of Arab States, must rest, a message drawn from their history and their character:

First, the Arabs do not recognize racial or national differences and they do not admit them as a principle justifying the domination of one people over another in this world. As the verse says,

160 "We have made you [different] peoples and tribes that you may

know one other; the most pious among you has honor with God."
Men are therefore equal, no one being superior to another. The
Arab is not superior to the non-Arab, unless it be in his character
and personal qualities, and the white man is not to be distinguished above the black or the yellow; indeed, this Arab nation
comprises the black and the white within the limits of this vast
land which cherishes all its sons.

The second principle is the natural rights of man. We say that
man is the son of Adam. As the verse says, "You are all from
Adam, and Adam is but of dust." Every man is on a level with
another and equal to him in rights and duties. "Men are equal as
the teeth of a comb."

The third principle on which our message rests is, in essence,
that we do not recognize class distinctions. The poor and the rich
among us, the weak and the strong, are all equal and on the same
level within our social order. We therefore refuse this new phenomenon of the class war, and we have to provide for it a
fruitful remedy.

If, however, we were to continue this mode of living which
we follow now, with which we have been infected from the Western capitalistic nations, I say that through acceptance of this
sort of life, then our message will be empty and will become an
oppressive message, allowing exploitation of class by class. But we
do call to our true ideals and to our handsome heritage, which
allows the poor man, in spite of his poverty, to acquire the guarantee of the social organism as well as of the state, so that he may
obtain his share of education and life and be able to attain the
highest posts in the state through his merit and hard work.

The social organization which the ideals and the beliefs of our
forefathers require makes it necessary that we should take care
of the poor and protect them in their poverty, give security to the
sick in their sickness, and take care of them and their children
through all the stages of their lives, especially when they are
incapacitated or unemployed. Even in the stage of decadence of
our social organization, and before the invasion of materialistic
Western civilization, people used to take care of one another
within the family, the neighborhood, the village, or the quarter,
or the state. They used to believe firmly that they were brothers,
that their life in this world was but a transient one and that
they would not enjoy the blessings of eternity if they left the poor 161

in their misery while they indulged their own pleasures beside them. If we go back to these beginnings, we will find that when the state carries out its duties in accordance with our fundamental principles and with our intellectual and moral heritage, and whenever men take up their duties as their spiritual life requires them to do, then capitalism and the war between the classes resulting from capitalism will no longer exist.

If we had the freedom to choose between two evils—an extreme capitalism and runaway communism—we would say that our message is neither of these; the former makes one class happy whereas the latter cuts off the head of this same class and then engenders in time what it had not desired. We refuse to accept English and American capitalism, just as we refuse Russian communism. God has chosen us a middle nation to be witnesses to men, and I have no doubt that He desires to send us again as messengers to a world which shall be reformed through us, God willing. This is not the claim of a vain man but that of a believer. I believe that what goes on now in the world is but a preparation for a new message, and I am strongly hopeful in God, who has created us in the middle of this earth, and who has made us inherit the civilizations of the Pharaohs, the Babylonians, the Phoenicians, the Chaldeans, the Carthaginians, the Arameans, and the civilization of the later Arabs, and has given us for inheritance great religions brought forth through Moses, Jesus, and Muhammad, who has tried us long in order to cleanse and purify us. I believe in the message of this new nation, the nation of the future.

It is obvious that the great nations have failed in their messages. Here, for instance, is the British nation which, from a faraway island in the north of the globe, extends her domination over the world, from Hong Kong to the other end; her aim is to continue her domination and supremacy over the nations, be they white or yellow or black. And here is the new American nation on whom the world has pinned the greatest of hopes, revealing to us out of her distant new world the four freedoms and the Atlantic Pact, and then speedily following the example of her predecessors and aiming at other objects such as oil, markets, raw materials, and strategic positions. Will she gradually forget her principles and high ideals? I will admit, however, that I have not lost hope in her. I still say that her democracy has that which makes us hope that she will follow a course parallel to the message which we preach. As for the third great power, she began by preaching the succor of the poor and the protection of the weak. She started the class war, and may now dominate her two small neighbors, Iran and Turkey. She is following in the path of her predecessor, and the world will be engulfed in the quarrel between the powerful and the despotic.

Should you find me emotional or pessimistic tonight, or should you criticize my frankness in attacking the great powers, may I say that I cannot in any manner hide my feeling about the impending danger which threatens civilization as a result of the policies of these great powers. I find it my duty to be extremely frank and to implore you, O Arabs, to carry out your humanitarian mission. Yes, you are a nation scattered between the Occident and the Orient, but if you would understand your mission, refusing to be a plaything in the hands of those tyrants or to give in to an influence which may come from the north or from the south, and if you would call for peace and plead that men should live as brothers according to a human creed, so that races and individuals may become equal, and if you would struggle for this not one year, but ten and twenty, then you would be worthy of this mission, then you would save civilization and found it anew on a basis different from that of materialism and power politics. You are the heirs of religions and civilizations dating back to the dawn of history. Let forbearance and tolerance be your most prominent qualities, as they were the most noble qualities of your fathers before you.

If you were to ask me what this new Arab League is, I would say that it is the core round which I build these great hopes. In this world, everything starts from small beginnings, then grows and matures. All the evidence indicates that our union in the League will grow and become great. If in its present situation the League cannot undertake vast works, this is because her present organization is limited and laid down in the pact; even then this pact gives scope for coöperation. It is a pact which others may consider as an ideal, for in its shade we coöperate on the principle that all states are equal in rights. In our League we recognize neither big nor small states; Egypt, for instance, the biggest of these states, the most extensive, the richest in learning and in wealth, is in my view totally equal to her smallest sister, whether 163 it is Lebanon or Transjordan. We coöperate on this principle, and the United Nations might take us as an example. May the United Nations realize some day that in human coöperation there is neither big nor small. We coöperate to keep the peace among us and to make one another happy; yes, indeed, we coöperate to improve our economies, just as we coöperate to ameliorate our cultural and social conditions and to build, in time, our united social being.

As for the freedom and independence of the Arab peoples, this is a question of today and of tomorrow. The Arabs will not bear the domination of the imperialists, and ever since the founding of their League they have struggled to realize their freedom. The leaders of the Arabs, in their various regions, have never, whether in the pact of the League or in their announcements or in what they asked me to indicate, omitted to demand the withdrawal of foreign troops from their lands, or to insist that they should evacuate all the Arab areas. Those who say that the League has stood by Syria and the Lebanon because the League hates the French and wishes them ill, and that the League is silent about the evacuation of Egypt because that would anger the British who are the friends of the Arabs, I say that those who believe this believe in a lie and a falsehood. The Arab League defends the same ideal. Evacuation of Egypt, as well as evacuation of Syria, is the aim and the object. Moreover, the League will support the North African Arabs in their demand that the French withdraw from North Africa. It has, in fact, demanded the independence of Cyrenaica and Tripolitania, that is, their evacuation by the British. Nothing justifies the existence of this League, in the eyes of the Arabs, more than its frank stand in Arab matters. The League demands the evacuation of foreign troops from all Arab lands, starting with Egypt. Furthermore, there is the League's frank attitude toward world affairs; it must stand on the side of justice and freedom, whether the freedom in question is that of Indonesia or of vanquished Germany.

You will no doubt remember that the Arab League has in the last six months collided with the Jews. It was a violent collision with a weak and dispersed people who, of all peoples, most need our sympathy, for they are our persecuted cousins. All through history we were their brothers and protectors. The calamity of

164

Zionism has overtaken them, Zionism which the British at first supported with their bayonets, and the Americans with their money, so that Zionism may build a foreign, imperialistic state in an Arab land. The Zionists are a curse on the Jews themselves and, indeed, on us Arabs. We still extend to the Jews the hand of friendship, and we do not want to share in the crime of persecuting them. But what are we to do with a people who appeared in the midst of us with evil, and who make false claims, the claims of imperialism and domination? Here we are calling on the Jews of the world to repent and to remember that they have brothers in the East who would hate to increase the sum of their misery. We implore them to regain their senses and to make those among them who have erred return to the right path. This is the matter which has kept us busy these last six months. If you wish to know my opinion of the outcome, I say, confident in God and guided by the witness of current events, that in this matter we will win a victory which will not disperse the Jews as the Europeans dispersed them, for this is not in our nature nor in the nature of our fathers before us. They will realize, when they see our forbearance and the sanctity in which we hold the freedom of the individual and of the group, that we are their brothers, with whom they can live as our Christian brothers have done, and that they can reach in the common homeland of the Arabs the highest functions and positions.

Lastly, I hope I have not tired you and I beg to summarize for you the aims of this League in simple, easy language:

We, the Arabs, do not desire fighting and enmity among races, sects, or classes. He who has inhabited our lands, who has been brought up in our culture, and who prides in our honor is of us. We believe in outlawing war and that this world cannot experience a new war, for new wars would mean the fall of civilization. We therefore refuse to coöperate in starting wars, we also refuse to coöperate on the basis of imperialism, exploitation, domination, or conquest. We want brotherhood in this world, and we believe that the world is one land inhabited by men in order that they may be happy and coöperate with one another, the rich among them supporting the poor, and the strong the weak. We take part in the United Nations Organization so that we may coöperate in building up a new united, wholesome, and coöperative 165 world. Our call is sincere, before God, and our message is the message of love and fraternity. My last word to you is the immortal first word which 'Umar said to 'Amr, the conqueror of Egypt, after the defeat of two empires: "How is it that you have enslaved men when their mothers have borne them into the world free?"

Qustantin Zuraiq

14 Arab Nationalism and Religion[1]

[On the occasion of the anniversary of the birth of the noble
Arab Prophet]

IT IS NOT MY INTENTION in this address to discuss any
particular aspect of the life of the noble Arab Prophet, or to give
a detailed exposition of any part of the lofty teachings which were
revealed to him. This is rather an expression of life which the
memories of the past, the events of the present, and the hopes for
the future conjure up in me. It is an instinct and a feeling inspired in me by the anniversary of the exalted birth of Muhammad and by the spiritual message it holds for the sons of the Arab
nation at this critical stage in their life.

There has been lately much noise and much talk concerning
the relation between nationality and religion. This is not surprising.
Religion is one of the most important forces which we have inherited from the past, a past which many factors have worked together to anchor in our lives, to such an extent that most of its
aspects have been stamped with the peculiar stamp of religion.
This influence lasted for long centuries until, in recent times since
our contact with the West, new factors have arisen to weaken it or
to confine it to a particular side of our individual and social life.
These new factors have taken their place in the hearts of the
Arabs, in late years, and have encouraged the Arabs to seek a
new kind of life which guarantees for them freedom, happiness
and civilization. This national spirit increases its influence daily
and gathers new strength and extension. No wonder, then, that
there should be attraction and revulsion, union and disjunction,

[1] Al-wa'i al-qaumi (National Consciousness) (Beirut, 1949), pp. 109–118.
(S. G. H.)

between it and religion, sometimes one influencing the other and at another time engaging in a struggle which shakes the very roots of Arab life. It is also no wonder that today we should adopt toward these two titanic forces varying attitudes, partly because our souls are troubled concerning their significance and partly because of the friction and the clash between the two forces. Some of us link their nationality to a particular revealed religion, and for them communal feeling has the better of the national idea. Others make nationalism and religion radically contradictory and therefore advocate that religion and men of religion should be combated, in order that the structure of nationalism should be erected over their ruins. Between these two extremes there are shades of thinking and varieties of feeling which can be neither limited nor enumerated. All this is due to a lack of distinction between the religious spirit and communal fanaticism. True nationalism cannot in any way contradict true religion, for it is nothing in its essence but a spiritual movement which aims at resurrecting the inner forces of the nation and at realizing its intellectual and spiritual potentialities in order that the nation shall contribute its share to the culture and civilization of the world.

Nationalism, therefore, spiritual movement as it is, must converge toward religion and draw from it strength, life, sublimity, and excellence. Such is Arab nationalism in its true character: it does not in any way oppose or negate any religion, but it accepts all religions in order to draw from their sources the cups of purity and liberation, of strength and immortality. If nationalism does contradict anything, it is not the religious spirit but the destructive fanaticism which makes the communal tie stronger than the national tie and refuses to dissolve itself in the all-consuming crucible of the nation; for it is the fanaticism which often exploits innocent religious feeling for its own partisan ambitions and inclinations. This is the chronic disease of the land, and its authors are the enemies of Arab nationalism and the destroyers of its unity. True religion, however, which aims to develop the forces of the spirit, springs from the same source as nationalism, and they both go in the same direction, toward the same end. It is therefore incumbent on the Arab nationalists to go back to the sources of their religion in order to draw from them spiritual excellence and strength of soul, and to seek inspiration, among other things, from the histories of all their prophets so as to enrich their souls with the strength and the purity which overflow from these religions. They ought also to link what they obtain from these spiritual values with the nationalist idea for which they live, to the realization of which they devote themselves. Ought we not, then, while we are honoring the anniversary of the Prophet's birth, to turn our attention to the past and try to extract the moral which this anniversary holds for our present life, asking ourselves: What is the connection between the Prophet Muhammad and Arab nationalism, and what is his message for it?

The Prophet Muhammad is, in the first place, the Prophet of Islam; to him was revealed this honored religion, and through him it was spread to the four corners of the world. This religion has influenced every aspect of our Arab culture, for we cannot today understand our ancient Arab heritage, be it in philosophy or science or art, except after a deep study of the tenets and laws of the Muslim religion, and after reaching a correct understanding of its spirit and organization. This Arab heritage is part of our present culture; it is rather the foundation on which it stands. What is preached by some—namely, that we should throw away this ancient heritage and adopt the new Western culture—is indeed mistaken. The Arab heritage is part of us, whether we like it or not; moreover, it is that which distinguishes us among the nations. It has such creativeness, strength, and beauty that we are moved to treasure it and to exult in it before the world. This is why every Arab, no matter what his sect or community, who takes interest in his past culture and in its renaissance—and such an interest is at the head of those duties which his nationality imposes on him—should attempt to study Islam and to understand its reality; he should also sanctify the memory of the great Prophet to whom Islam was revealed.

In the second place, it is the Prophet Muhammad who unified the Arabs and mustered them together. He was sent to them when their divisions and quarrels were at the extreme: they were envious of one another, they squabbled among themselves and fought one another. There was no strong tie to bind them together and no banner to unify them and create amity among them. But he inspired them with his revivificatory spirit and suddenly these quarreling tribes became friends and these hostile masses drew nearer; suddenly they all formed one single whole, melted and refined in the crucible of faith, and thus overflowed the entire world, endowing it with strength and energy and spreading over it civilization and culture. Some may say that the religious bond at that time overshadowed the national bond, that Islam was stronger than Arabism. The answer is that nothing else was possible in the Middle Ages, whether in this Muslim East or in the Christian West. We do know that nationalism, in its true sense, is the offspring of the modern age and of the political, economic, and social forces which it has brought to birth. However, even in spite of this we still find a strong Arab feeling in the first age, when the Islamic religious emotion was still in full effervescence. The Muslims treated the Banu Taghlib and other Arab Christians quite differently from the way they treated non-Arab Christians; some Christian tribes took part in the early conquests and fought side by side with the Muslims. This Arab feeling grew in strength with the introduction of the foreigners and the growth of *shu'-ubiyya*; the Arabs became more united in order to fend off the attacks of the Persians, the Turks, and others. It is indeed true that these manifestations of national feeling among the Arabs are of little account when measured with the national feeling which has taken hold of the nations in the modern age. But if we bear in mind the circumstances of intellectual life in the Middle Ages, when religious sentiment overlaid everything, we find in these manifestations healthy seeds of Arab national life. These seeds continued to grow slowly and uncertainly, over the centuries, until the country wakened to the light of the modern age, when all at once the national bond became superior to every other; and this bond required that all should be equal, irrespective of the diversity of their religions and sects. When the Arabs today look back on the past, they find that the origin of their union and the seed of their amity was the work of the Arab leader Muhammad b. Abdullah.

In the third place, the prophet Muhammad is an example of the man of conviction. He appeared in Mecca and remained unhonored there a long time, putting up with all kinds of humiliation and persecution for the sake of his conviction; all the forces of society were made to bear, in order to turn him away from his creed, but he remained firm in his stand, strong in his belief, contemptuous of temptations and threats, and true to what he said to his uncle, Abu Talib: "By God! If they would put the

sun to my right and the moon to my left, so that I should abandon this matter, I would not do it until God should make it
manifest or I should perish for its sake." He remained thus until
God made him victorious over his enemies and made all the
people acknowledge him. This strong and burning conviction is
the foundation of the great Prophet's personality, and it is he
who gave his Companions the inspiration and transformed them
from simple people with narrow horizons and limited powers into
leaders and commanders who destroyed the thrones of despotic
nations and laid down the foundations of a new civilization.

Today, when personal whims and party struggles have swayed
us hither and thither, and when we have lifted up matter and
worldly dominations to the highest heaven and have trampled
down our spiritual values, we need more than ever, in our national struggle, to have leaders who may draw from the personality
of the Arab Prophet strength of conviction and firmness of belief. In this way they may engage, with courage and daring, in the
struggle for their principles, calmly facing persecution and scorn-
ing obstacles, that they may inspire in the breasts of those sons of
the Arab nation who are around them the spirit of sacrifice and
devotion, carrying them on to the straight path which leads to
the new life. This is the spiritual message contained in the anniversary of the Arabian Prophet's birth which is addressed to our
present national life. It is for this, in spite of their different
tendencies and their diverse religions and sects, that the Arab
nationalists must honor the memory of Muhammad b. Abdullah,
the Prophet of Islam, the unifier of the Arabs, the man of principle and conviction.

Abd al-Rahman al-Bazzaz

15 Islam and Arab Nationalism[1]

BEFORE I BEGIN, I had better explain the significance of
the title of this talk and limit its scope somewhat, because the
title's unqualified generality might give the impression that I
wish to examine thoroughly and in detail the "Principles of
Islam" and the "National Idea." This, however important, cannot be treated in one lecture, but deserves rather a special study.
All I aim at this evening is to define the relation of Arab nationalism, insofar as it is a "belief and a movement," to the Islamic
Shari'a, insofar as it is "a religion, a civilization, and a philosophy
of life"; in other words, my talk will try to elucidate the answer to
an important question, which I suspect has often occurred to
Arab intellectuals, and which has often confused them. The
question is: Is it possible for one of us to be a loyal nationalist
and a sincere Muslim, at one and the same time? Is there a fundamental contradiction between Arab nationalism, in its precise
scientific sense, and true Muslim feeling? And does the acceptance
of the one entail the rejection of the other? . . . Allow me to
simplify the question a little and to say: Does a contradiction or
opposition lie in our saying, "This man is a nationalist Muslim,"
or "This man is a Muslim nationalist," as when we say "This man
is an atheist believer," or "He is a religious atheist," or when we
join opposites, as "This man is a communist fascist," or "He is
a democratic dictator"? Or, if we wanted to use the terms of the
ancients, is there in our saying, "This is a nationalist Muslim,"
an incompatibility such as exists in saying, "This is a Jabari
Qadari," or "He is a Shi'a Kharejite"?

[1] The translation of. al-Islam wa'l-qaumiyya al-arabiyya (Baghdad, 1952),
by S. G. Haim, first appeared in Die Welt des Islams, n.s., III, Nr. 3–4
172 (Leiden, 1954). (S. G. H.)

I think the apparent contradiction between Islam and Arab nationalism which is still present in the minds of many people is, in the first place, due to misunderstanding, misrepresentation, and misinterpretation, involving both Islam and Arab nationalism.

The misunderstanding of Islam is due to the wrong significance attributed to the word "religion." We are influenced here—as a result of the intellectual imperialism under which a group of us still labor—by the Western concepts which restrict religion within narrow limits not extending beyond worship, ritual, and the spiritual beliefs, which govern a man in his behavior, in relation to his God and to his brother man, in his capacity of an individual independent of society. Islam does not admit this narrow view of religion, but opposes it and the purpose it serves to the utmost. Many people still believe that Islam is similar to Christianity or Buddhism, and consists in devotional beliefs and exercises, ethical rules and no more. But, in fact, Islam, in its precise sense, is a social order, a philosophy of life, a system of economic principles, a rule of government, in addition to its being a religious creed in the narrow Western sense. Some of the Western thinkers have come to realize the wide difference between the comprehensive nature of Islam and the limited nature of Christianity; Christianity pays more attention to the individual, as such, and to his spiritual purity, than to the individual as part of a whole and to his relation to this whole. This was inevitable because of the difference in the nature of the two religions, their circumstances, and the periods in which they were revealed. Christ was a member of the Israelite society which, under the authority of the Roman state, was devoid of any active share in the existing political organization. But the Prophet—Peace be on Him—was a leader and a statesman, as much as he was a social reformer and a religious teacher. Bertrand Russell, the contemporary philosopher, is one of those Western thinkers who have realized the difference between the two religions. He referred to it in his book *Education and the Social Order.* He considers Islam a political religion, or a socially directed religion, which pervades the life of the individual and the society completely; on the other hand, he regards Christianity and Buddhism as the religions of "individuals," or nonpolitical religions. Those who still consider Islam and understand it in a restricted sense, saying its significance derives from that of Christianity, make a 173 glaring mistake in the appreciation of its nature. Because Islam is a political religion, as Russell says, it does not therefore necessarily contradict Arab nationalism, unless their political aims differ. But this is unthinkable, as we shall see later.

Just as Islam has been misunderstood, so has Arab nationalism. The reason for this may be that some think that nationalism can be built only upon racial appeal or racial chauvinism, and that it would therefore be contrary to the universal nature of Islam. The exaggeration of some nationalists has undoubtedly been one of the important reasons for this misunderstanding; and no doubt what some Umayyad governors, princes, and walis have done in their enthusiastic tribal chauvinism and their racial propaganda was contrary to the nature of Islam. But the Arab nationalism in which we believe, and for which we call, is based, as our national pact stipulates, not on racial appeal but on linguistic, historical, cultural, and spiritual ties, and on fundamental vital interests. In this respect, too, there is no contradiction between Arab nationalism and Islam. Many young people have greatly misunderstood Arab nationalism. They know something of the history of the West, of its national revivals, and have found there obvious signs of contradiction between Christianity and these national movements; this is, of course, natural in Western societies. The Church, which used to claim great spiritual power over all the Christians, looked askance on all political movements which aimed at shaking off ecclesiastical authority. In other words, European society gave allegiance to two fundamental authorities, the spiritual authority of the Pope and the temporal authority of the Emperor.

This dualism, although it has come to us in some stages of our slow social evolution, is not known in true Islam, where it is not admitted. On the contrary, the unity of creed has led to the unity of life, and the unity of life has made the caliph of the Muslims the leader in prayer, the leader of the army, and the political head at the same time. The opposition of German or Italian nationalism to Christianity, for instance, does not therefore necessarily mean that Arab nationalism should be opposed to Islam. It befits us to remember here the great difference between the relation of Christianity to the West, and the relation of Islam to the Arabs. Christianity is a religion introduced to the West. It arose out of the spirituality of the East, and is in complete opposition to the nature of the Teutonic tribes in Germany and the Celtic in France; that is why the German or the French nationalist finds great difficulty in reconciling it with the elements of the nationality which he cherishes, and realizes that Christianity has not found it possible to penetrate to the roots of Germanic and Celtic life. The opposite is true of Islam and its influence over Arab society and the Arab nation, as we shall explain in some measure.

By misrepresentation I mean that surprising and imaginary picture by which many thinkers and writers, both Muslim and other, have represented Islam, in the past and in the present. They made Islam lose its content and its vitality, which pervades every aspect of life, and they have gradually transformed it into abstract general principles and ideals having but the faintest relation to actual life. Some writers have also made an effort to break the tie between Islam and Arab life which allowed Islam its first and most generous scope. This misrepresentation increased when some historians and men of letters intentionally presented the history of the Arab nation in a misleading way; and for a variety of reasons, with which this lecture cannot deal, the non-Arab Muslims, many of whom were *shu'ubis* who envied the Arabs their honorable achievement in the cause of Islam, strove to present the history of the Arab nation in a false light. A number of Arab historians such as Ibn Khaldun have themselves slipped; he called the Arabs by many an iniquitous name, and has committed injustice against them in many of his conclusions, and in many instances he only meant the bedouins, not the settled Arabs, as Sati' al-Husri has pointed out in his valuable study of the *Prolegomena* of Ibn Khaldun. It is natural that political events should have played their part in the elaboration of this mistaken view; when the political power of the Arabs waned and the non-Arabs penetrated into the administration and the government they were inclined to belittle the role of the Arabs and to give the picture of Islam a cosmopolitan character, and they also tended to suppress its connection with the Arabs as much as possible. Many of the Abbasid princes and ministers of the period exaggerated in this respect, just as some of the Umayyad rulers had exaggerated in the opposite direction. I do not want to review here the history of the Abbasid state in order to show the influence of the foreigners and of the clients through- 175 out its existence, from the time when propaganda for it started, when it appeared as a power on the stage of life, and until it perished. And I do not want to talk long about the petty dynasties, most of which were non-Arab, and their influence on the spirit of *shuʿubiyya*. Moreover, the fact that most of the Arabs remained under the Ottoman government for many centuries has helped very much to spread the mistaken view that Arab nationalism and Islam are in contradiction, because the awakening of any national feeling would expose the Ottoman caliphate to danger in its very foundations. That is also why the only Arab country which did not obey completely the rule of the Ottomans, and was always the scene of revolts which inflicted serious losses on the Turks, was the Yemen, the bulk of whose people were Zaidis, who believe that the caliphate belongs to Quraish and within Quraish to the Hashemite House, and within that house to the descendants of Zaid ibn Ali. The Ottoman caliphate was therefore illegal in the eyes of the Zaidis, as it contradicted the absolute principles of Islam itself.

By misinterpretation I mean, in the first place, the misinterpretation of some Koranic verses relating to the preaching of Islam. Islam, although it is a universal religion suitable for all peoples and has in fact been disseminated among many nations and races, is undoubtedly a religion revealed first to the Arabs themselves. In this sense, it is their own special religion. The Prophet is from them, the Koran is in their language; Islam retained many of their previous customs, adopting and polishing the best of them. In expressing this opinion, we are not speaking out of an uncontrollable national feeling, nor from emotion, nor do we speak heedlessly; we base ourselves on the wisdom of the Koran itself, on the true laws of the Prophet, and on the actions of the early caliphs of Islam who represent it best. It is these which represent true Islam, not the false and obscure concepts which have gradually become common in the Islamic world, and which the Muslims have followed as the power of the foreigners grew and they became the leaders in both the political and the intellectual sphere.

The Koranic verses which support this view are many, but I select the following from them:

In surat *Ibrahim* (XIV) verse 4, the Koran says: "We have never sent a messenger save with the language of his people."

The Arab messenger, then, has been sent to his people in their own Arabic tongue. Surat *al-Zakhraf* (XLIII) verse 24[2] reads: "It is indeed a reminder for you and for your people, and you shall be questioned," only means that the Koran is a reminder for the Prophet and for his people, the Arabs, who will be responsible if they transgress it. In surat *al-Baqara* (II) verse 143: "We have thus made you a middle nation that you may witness against mankind and that the Prophet may witness against you." There is no doubt that it is the Prophet's people who are being addressed; verse 2 of surat *Yusuf* (XII) is in the same vein: "We have revealed it an Arabic Koran that you may be wise." Those who are to understand are none other than those who know the sense of the Koran and understand it, and naturally they are the Arabs. Verse 58 of surat *al-Dukhkhan* (XLIV) is also to the same effect: "We have made it easy in thy language only that they be warned"; and verse 2 of surat *al-Jum'a* (LXII) says, "He it is who sent to the unlettered a Messenger from among themselves to recite to them his verses, to give them grace, and to teach them the Scriptures and Wisdom . . ."; also verse 128 of surat *al-Tauba* (IX): "There has come to you a Messenger one of yourselves, to whom all that you have suffered is important," and verse 66 of surat *al-An'am* (VI), "Your people have denied it, but it is the truth."

These gracious verses and many others, both Meccan and Medinese, confirm that Islam is the religion of the Arabs before being a universal religion. This does not contradict other verses, such as verse 107 of surat *al-Anbiya'* (XXI): "We have sent thee only in mercy for mankind," because it is proved historically that the sending of the Prophet to the Arabs revived the Arab nation in its entirety and resurrected it. This resurrection was, at the time, beneficial to all the inhabited universe. The Arabs were the propagators of Islam and the saviors of the world from the reigning oppression and from the absolute ignorance which was then supreme; they were, as Gustave Lebon said, the most merciful conquerors that the world has known.

There is more to support this view in the Tradition. Al-Bukhari and Muslim report Ibn Umar's saying about the Prophet: "Power will remain in Quraish so long as two of them still exist." There

---

[2] Verse 44 is meant. (S. G. H.)

is also the Tradition, "The Imams are from Quraish," and the Tradition attributed to Salman al-Farisi, who said, "The Prophet said to me: 'O Salman, do not hate me and part with your religion'; I said: 'O Prophet of God, how can I hate you, seeing that it is through you that God directed us?' He said: 'If you hate the Arabs, you hate me.'" The actions of the Muslims of the early period confirm indeed the Arab nature of Islam. The caliph Umar hesitated greatly before conquering the parts outside the Arabian Peninsula and the Fertile Crescent; he agreed to accept a double amount of the *zakat* from the famous Arab Christian tribe when they refused to pay *jizya*, which they considered a sign of humiliation, and many of the Christian tribes took part and helped in the conquests. Moreover the Muslims accepted the *jizya* from the followers of other religions among other races outside the Arab Peninsula, but in the Peninsula itself these were given the choice between Islam or evacuation. It appears from all this that the Arabs and their country have a special place in Islam. An indication of the favored position given to the Arabs in Islam and to Islamic jurisprudence may be gathered from the fact that some jurists have gone so far as to question whether, other things being equal, a foreigner was good enough to take an Arab woman in marriage. I can state that many principles which have become part of Islam are ancient Arab customs which Islam polished, and to which it gave a new stamp. The respect paid to the Kaaba and the pilgrimage thereto are old Arab customs; this is true also of many of the devotional practices and rules of the pilgrimage. Another proof of the Arab character of Islam lies in the veneration for Friday, which the Arabs used to call "The Day of Arabism," and, as the Tradition mentions, in setting it aside as a day of festivity and rejoicing. Many Arab concepts survive in the laws of inheritance and obligation, especially in the provisions giving the kin-group a claim on the inheritance and in the attention given to the claims of kinship.

We may also include under the heading misinterpretation that unjust description of the condition of the Arabs at the time of the Prophet's birth and of his message. The biographers and their followers are, to a great extent, responsible for this. They thought that the more they dwelt on the bad conditions amongst the Arabs before Islam, the more they would exalt the greatness of the Prophet—Peace be on Him. That is why there was no iniquity, or license, disorder, tyranny, or cruelty, that was not imputed to the Arabs. And the worst of all this was that they imagined the condition of all the Arabs, at all times, to have been the same as their condition at the time of the Prophet's Message—Peace be on Him—as though the Arabs, earlier, did not have states and civilizations, as though they did not have a language, or a poetry, or a literature, or concepts of life. I cannot, in this lecture, answer all the allegations which contradict the Koran itself, but I refer all those who are interested in this question to the valuable book of Muhammad Izzat Darwaza, *The Times of the Prophet and His Environment before the Message.* He gives a true description of that age, basing himself on the Koran, and he attacks the *shu'ubiyya* and the Orientalists who have followed its tradition, and puts the matter straight again.

The correct scientific explanation of the emergence of the Arabs in the first period of Islam is that it was one of the waves out of the Arabian Peninsula, although it was the most venerable of these waves and the most illustrious in the history of the Arabs themselves and in the history of the whole of mankind. There is no contradiction at all between our sincere Muslim feeling and our holding precious the ancient Arab civilizations of the Yemen, such as the civilization of the Ma'inites, the Himyarites, and the Sabaeans, or the civilization of the Amalekites and of the Nabataeans, and the Arab civilizations which preceded these, the civilizations of the Assyrians and of the Babylonians. Islam abandoned only what was bad in our customs and what was false in our laws and traditions. Islam holds, as the noble Hadith has it, that men are metals like gold and silver, those among them who were the best in the Jahiliyya remain the best in Islam. It would not have been possible for the Arabs to achieve such a revival and accomplish such tremendous actions, in war, politics, legislation, literature, art, sociology, and the other aspects of life, in such a short time, if their metal had not been pure and their abilities latent in them from long ago, their nature creative and their spirit strong and true. There could not shine among the Arabs, in one or two generations, men like Abu Bakr, Umar, Ali, Ibn Ubaida, Sa'd, Khalid, Ibn Abbas, Abu Durr, and Ibn Mas'ud, or women like Khadija, Fatima, A'isha, Asma, al-Khansa, and many other men and women of genius of that age, 179 had the Arabs not inherited an ancient and continuous civilization and had they not been prepared by their instinct to create and build and renovate. The fact that the Prophet Muhammad was Arab was not a matter of chance; a genius, he belonged to a nation of great abilities and qualities. But the ancient *shu'ubis,* as Abd al-Latif Sharara said in his *The Spirit of Arabism,* have solved this problem by denying the Arabs all quality, and by refusing to recognize any beneficent action of theirs in the affairs of humanity. They confined their interest, their consideration, and their appreciation to the Prophet in a forced manner and separated him from others before him, from his contemporaries and his compatriots, converting him into a universal being snatched from his land and sky, freed from his history and people. They pictured him as a prosperous plant growing in an empty desert, no one having helped him, and himself not indebted to anyone's help. Consequently, they pretend that there is no sense in talking of Muhammad as an Arab or a foreigner.

If we leave history aside and if we examine the language and the literature, we find that the Arabic language had reached, before Islam, a degree of progress, and literature, a degree of maturity, impossible to find in a primitive and artless community. . . . The Orientalist Nöldeke says: "We may be surprised by the richness of the ancient Arabic vocabulary when we remember how simple was the business of Arab life," and he goes on to say: "Arabic is not only rich in its vocabulary, but also in its grammar and conjugations." A language is the mirror of the intellectual life of a people and the measure of the progress of a society. It is a sign of the advance of Arab society that Arabic had attained this degree of comprehensiveness and of complexity; and indeed the Koran is witness to the greatness of the Arabs in the arts of speech and in their appreciation of fluency and eloquence. This only obtains in a society which is intellectually advanced; that is why nomadism, which was prevalent among the Arabs, was not a sign of primitiveness, as nomadism would be in other nations. The Arab, even the bedouin, is the resultant of old civilizations; the roughness and the discomfort of his external life has been imposed on him by nature. His mentality, qualities, and literature reveal great social progress.

It is clear from all this that the Arabs are the backbone of Islam. They were the first to be addressed in the verses of Revela-

tion; they were the *Muhajirin* and the *Ansar*; their swords conquered countries and lands, and on the whole they are as Umar
has described them in a saying of his: "Do not attack the Arabs
and humiliate them for they are the essence of Islam." If we
may take an instance from contemporary history, we can say that
the position of the Arabs in Islam is like that of the Russians in
the communist order, with the obvious difference between the
spiritual appeal of Islam and the material principles of communism. Moreover, you have to remember that the Prophet of Islam
was an Arab of the most respected Arab tribe, and that the constitution of Islam was revealed in a pure Arabic language. But
the preacher of communism was a German Jew, and the scripture
of communism, *Das Kapital*, appeared in German. I cannot understand how the preachers of cosmopolitanism in this country
can hold sacred the Russian homeland and be proud of the ancestors of the Russians to whom they are not related, objecting
all the time to the Muslim Arabs glorifying their own ancestors
and exalting their own heroes.

After this clear exposition of the intellectual problems and the
factors that contribute to the mistaken belief that there is a contradiction between the principles of Islam and Arab nationalism,
it befits us to define the meaning of nationalism, more particularly of Arab nationalism and of its assumptions, and to look
into these assumptions in order to see which are accepted by Islam and which, if any, are rejected.

Nationalism is a political and social idea which aims, in the
first place, to unify each group of mankind and to make it obey
one political order. The factors and the assumptions of nationalism are varied, and we do not intend to analyze them in this
lecture. But we can assert that modern nationalism is based on
language, history, literature, customs, and qualities. On the whole,
the ties that bind individuals together and make them into a
nation are both intellectual and material. If we examine these
assumptions carefully and inquire into the position of Islam toward each of them, we find a great similarity, and sometimes
complete agreement, between what Arab nationalism teaches and
what is affirmed by Islam. Language, then, is the primary tenet
of our national creed; it is the soul of our Arab nation and the
primary aspect of its life. The nation that loses its language is
destined to disappear and perish. It is the good fortune of the 181

Arabs that their language is not only a national duty but also a religious one, and the influence of Islam on its propagation and preservation is very great. The German Orientalist Johann Fück says in his book *Arabiya:* "No event in the history of the Arabs was more important for their future destiny than the rise of Islam. In that age, more than thirteen hundred years ago, when Muhammad recited the Koran to his compatriots in a pure Arabic tongue, a strong connection was established between his language and the new religion, and it boded great results for the future of this language." Moreover, as we have explained above, the Arabs had a glorious history before Islam, and their history is even more glorious and of greater moment after Islam; the Muslim Arab, when he exalts his heroes, partakes of two emotions, that of the pious Muslim and that of the proud nationalist.

In fact, the most glorious pages of Muslim history are the pages of Arab Muslim history, as the Western historians themselves admit. Lothrop Stoddard, author of *The New World of Islam,* has spoken to this effect, and Gustave Lebon, author of *The Civilization of the Arabs,* has made it explicit. Lebon says: "One difference is apparent to us among the nations which were of great intelligence, like the Arabs, and the degenerate nations like the barbarians of the Middle Ages who destroyed the Roman state, and the ancestors of the Turks and Mongols whose flood engulfed the state of Muhammad. The Arabs have created, from the beginning, after using the civilizations of the Greeks, the Romans, and the Persians, a new civilization superior to the civilizations which came before it. The brains of the barbarians were unable to understand the meaning of the civilization which they conquered, and they were merely imitative at the beginning. They did not develop it until their minds became polished, and they came, long after, to understand its significance." This independent French thinker regretted that the Arabs had not conquered Europe and said: "If Musa b. Nusair had been able to conquer Europe, he would have made it Muslim and would have saved it from the darkness of the Middle Ages which, thanks to the Arabs, Spain did not know."

I wonder, therefore, if there is any contradiction of the Muslim creed in exalting this history, or even pre-Islamic history. There is nothing to prevent the sincere Muslim and loyal Arab from holding precious the brilliant pages of the history of the Arabs.

Did not the Prophet—Peace be on Him—remember the *Fudul* pact in which all the clans of Quraish took part in pre-Islamic time in order to succor the oppressed and obtain his rights for him? He said: "How much it would please me to have taken an active part in a pact which I witnessed in the house of Ibn Jud'an. If I had been invited to it in Islam, I would have accepted."

As for Arabic literature which is the result of Arab feeling and emotion all through the ages, its greatest and most venerable parts came from Islam, and indeed, the Koran itself, in addition to being a book of direction, is the most awesome example of the elevated prose which the Arab, irrespective of his religion, exalts. How I wish the youth especially would read a small original book, *Descriptive Technique in the Koran,* by Sayyid Qutb to see the artistic beauty of the style of the Koran. Who can belittle the influence of the Koran on Arabic literature? As for pre-Islamic poetry, and especially descriptive and wisdom verse, there is in most of it nothing which contradicts the spirit of Islam.

The fourth element in Arab nationalism consists of "the good Arab customs and qualities." Here, undoubtedly, there is similarity, not to say complete identity, between the ethical ideal of Arab nationalism and that prescribed by Islam. Let us take a verse from the noble Koran which defines righteousness, the most honored of Muslim qualities, and let us see how much Arab nationalism admits it: "It is not righteousness that you turn your faces to the East or to the West. He is righteous who believes in God and in the Last Day, in the Angels and in the Book and the Prophets, and spends for love of Him, on his kin, on the orphans, the poor and the wayfarers, on those who beg, and for the ransoming of captives, and he who prays and pays the *zakat,* keeps his word when he has given it; those who are patient in misery and in affliction at the time of stress; they are the truthful and the God-fearing." Is there not in this noble verse a clear call for abnegation and sacrifice for the sake of others, who may be poor or enslaved and in need of help to regain their freedom. This verse also exhorts men to keep promises, to be patient in difficulties and calamities. And is chivalry, the sum of all Arab virtues, not the same as this? We do not pretend to say that all the pre-Islamic customs of the Arabs were good, but we maintain 183 that Islam has confirmed all that was best in Arab character. In our national call for exalting the Arab character, we mean those polished virtues which elevate man and make of him a being worthy of the description "polite."

Let us leave the Arab factors aside and examine nationalism as a political movement working to unite the Arabs and to give them self-government. The national movement is "democratic," "socialist," "popular," and "coöperative." Islam, although it did not lay down in detail the organization of government, requires consultation, and does, without any doubt, accept completely democratic organization. Its financial legislation and juristic principles are, in essence, socialist; Sayyid Qutb has succeeded in explaining this in his book *Social Justice in Islam.* It is enough to remember something of the life of the Prophet and of the caliphs, to realize the extent of the coöperative and the popular spirit of Islam. The position being such, the national government for which we call does not in any way contradict Islam.

But to say this is not to imply a call for Pan-Islamism. To say that Islam does not contradict the Arab national spirit is one thing, and to make propaganda for Pan-Islamism is another. Pan-Islamism, in its precise and true meaning, aims to form a comprehensive political organization which all the Muslims must obey. This organization, although it may be desired by all the pious Muslims, is not possible in practice, for many reasons—geographical, political, social—or, at least, it is not possible under the present conditions, even if we agreed to limit this union to the parts of the Muslim homeland which are contiguous. And even if we assumed that these parts could be united, then the unification of the parts which speak the same language, inherit the same literature, and have the same history, is more urgently needed and more worthy of consideration; it is not natural to expect the union of Iraq with Iran or Afghanistan, for instance, before Syria and Jordan are united. A view contrary to this is nonsense and deserves no answer. It follows, therefore, that the call to unite the Arabs—and this is the clearest and most important objective of Arab nationalism—is the practical step which must precede the call for Pan-Islamism. It is strange, however, to find that some of those who call themselves supporters of Pan-Islamism in the Arab countries are the most violent opponents of Pan-Arabism. If they would understand things as they are and would appreciate matters properly, if they did not follow mere emotion, they would admit that their call is misplaced, until the first aim of the Arab nationalists is fulfilled, namely the erection of a collective organization for the Arabs in Asia and Africa.

The conclusion is that no fundamental contradiction or clear opposition exists between Arab nationalism and Islam. The nearest analogy for the relation between them is that of the general to the particular. If we wanted to represent that relationship geometrically, we can imagine Islam and Arabism as two circles overlapping in the greater part of their surface, and in what remains outside the area that is common to the two circles the two are not in fundamental opposition to each other. This is a truth which we must realize, and it befits the Arabs to rejoice in this great good fortune, that their nationalism does not contradict their religion; the Muslim Turk, for instance, who wants to glory in his nationalism, finds an insoluble difficulty in reconciling this sentiment with his sincere religious feeling. His national feeling requires him to be proud of his language and to purify it of other foreign languages; this may drive him to belittle Arabic, which is the flowing source from which Turkish language and literature drew from the earliest days. And if he wants to exalt the glorious actions and the heroes of the past, this will drive him, in most cases, to feel that the Muslim Arabs were strangers to him and that they were, in spite of external appearances, his real colonizers, mentally, spiritually, and culturally; the nationalist Muslim Arab will not often encounter this kind of difficulty.

I do not know whether it is necessary for me to say that our call for Arab nationalism and for a comprehensive Arab being does not, under any circumstances, make us antagonistic to the non-Arab Muslims; for, as our national pact defines it, we consider the group of the Islamic peoples the nearest of all other groups to us; we see in this group a great force which we cherish, and we work to strengthen the ties with it and to coöperate with it. Our relation to the non-Arab Muslims who inhabit the Arab homeland is a brotherly one, for they are the brothers of the Arabs and have all the rights and all the duties of the Arabs. There is not in our nationalism a call to persecute any of the human races; on the contrary, there is no empty national arrogance nor blind racial chauvinism in it. When we take pride in our great actions and cherish our nationality, we want to inspire our nation to reach the place which it deserves among the peoples and the nations of the earth. This is a natural right, accepted by all religions, and recognized by the principles of justice. There is in it no feeling of superiority over others and no desire to oppress other races.

It also befits us to make it clear that there is nothing in this national call of ours which need exercise the non-Muslims among the Arabs or diminish their rights as good compatriots. Chauvinism, in all its aspects and forms, is incompatible with the nature of the Arabs; the non-Muslim Arabs used to enjoy all their rights under the shadow of the Arab state, from the earliest times, and the scope open to them was wide. The loyal nationalists among the Arab Christians realize this and know that Islam and the civilization which accompanied it are an indivisible part of our national heritage, and they must, as nationalists, cherish it as their brother Muslims cherish it.

Allow me, ladies and gentlemen, to conclude this lecture by reading to you these selected passages the meaning of which I hope you will consider seriously:

"True nationalism can, on no account, contradict true religion, because it is in essence no other than a spiritual movement which aims to resurrect the internal forces of the nation and to realize its spiritual and psychological abilities in order that the nation may do its share in the progress of the world and its civilization. . . . It is therefore the duty of every Arab, whatever his sect or his community, to interest himself in his past culture and his new renaissance. This interest is the first duty enjoined on him by his nationality. He must come forward to study Islam and understand its true nature and thus sanctify the memory of the great Prophet to whom Islam was revealed. . . ."

Do you know from whom this quotation is taken? From an Arab, a Christian, a cultured man; for these reasons his words constitute an authority for the nationalists, the Christians and the educated. These are the words of Qustantin Zuraiq, the Dean of the Syrian University and one of the leaders of modern Arab nationalism.

I realize indeed that this talk of mine and tens of other better

ones on this subject will not be enough to dispel all the common myths and mistakes about the meaning of Arab nationalism and Islam, and will not succeed in removing all the illusions which assume the existence of contradictions between the two. What those harmful pictures and wrong explanations, what past centuries have left, cannot be erased or effaced if we do not realize the three following matters:

First. We must free ourselves from the intellectual power of the West and its imported concepts, and we must think independently and with originality about our problems, affairs, and history. We must abandon false standards in intellectual and social matters, because the difference of the borrowed concepts and the variation in the factors and conditions will lead us to mistaken results and false judgments. We must become intellectually independent and consider things objectively; we must not borrow from the West, or when we do we must borrow and reject after a careful examination and a full and complete comparison.

Second. We must work earnestly and sincerely to present anew our nation's past and to write our history in a correct scientific manner, in order to eradicate these distorted pictures and to put a stop to these iniquitous judgments, to tear out those black pages which the pens of prejudiced intriguers have drawn. We must, in other words, clear our history from the false accusations of the *shu'ubiyya*, and from the stupidities of the ignorant ones—I shall not call them historians—and present our history in the way that the living nations present theirs, and confirm the civilized values and the beneficent contributions in knowledge, art, literature, jurisprudence, and the other aspects of intellectual life which we have given to mankind through the ages. Then will these distorted pictures and black phantoms concerning their nation's history which have clung to their minds be erased from the imagination of many of the young men and women of this generation. They will come to see that history as strong as strength can be, as clear as clarity itself, alive and full of rousing scenes, eternal heroisms, and general good.

Third. Last but not least, we must look to Islam, which we cherish so much and which we believe to be the reflection of the Arab soul and its spiritual source which does not exhaust itself. We must look at it as a whole, devoid of its communal and sectarian character, the Book of God and his Sunna flowing out of its clear and original sources, as our ancient ancestors used to understand it before some backward Muslims burdened it with what there remained in their subconscious of the influence of Zoroastrianism, of Buddhism, of the Israelite traditions, of Roman and Greek sophistry. We must receive it straight from its clear Arab environment, not mixed in an imaginary international environment, and not weighed down by the chains of symbolic Sufism or burdened by the dead hand of a petrified clergy.

Charles Malik

16 The Near East: The Search for Truth

I

BY THE NEAR EAST I mean the cradle of Western civilization. Take the fundamental generic components of that civilization and trace them back across the ages to their lands of
origin, and there you have the Near East. Thus if no fundamental
component can be shown to originate in a given country X, then
X is not part of the Near East. The concept therefore is neither
political, nor geopolitical, nor geographic, nor strategic: it is essentially cultural-genetic.

If a circle is drawn on the map with Beirut or Damascus or
Jerusalem as its center and with a radius of about nine hundred
miles, this circle will pretty nearly comprise the whole of the
Near East. It will include the following ten cities: Athens, Istanbul, Antioch, Beirut, Damascus, Baghdad, Jerusalem, Alexandria, Cairo and Mecca. Western civilization is an offshoot, in
diverse modes of relevance, of what was revealed, apprehended,
loved, suffered and enacted in these ten cities or in their hinterland.[2]

This cultural-genetic relatedness between the Near East and
the West has been the theme of wonder and reflection literally
for thousands of years. Nobody forgets his origins, and so the
Western World has never tired of brooding upon the great mystery of the eastern shores of the Mediterranean where it was

---

[1] From *Foreign Affairs*, 30 (Jan., 1952). (S. G. H.)
[2] The apparent exception of Rome is greatly mitigated by the fact that
the deepest things did not arise there; that what did arise there was actually
rooted in the Near East; and that the codification of Roman law was the
achievement of the eastern Mediterranean. Rome was faithful but not
original.

born. Is it a pure myth entirely devoid of any significance that
Europa was a lovely Phoenician princess who was carried off by
no less a god than mighty Zeus himself?

The fact that malevolence abounds in the world and may
misinterpret or misquote or distort what we say will not deter
us from facing our situation in the Near East squarely and honestly. There is abroad in the Near East today a new critical spirit.
It is dissatisfied with the given and is not afraid to voice its dissatisfaction. There is health and hope and freedom only in the
daring knowledge and confession of the truth, whatever risks that
may involve.

Our subject is not easy, not because of present complications,
but because in itself it raises the deepest issues. This study for
the most part only opens up horizons for thought, only sets up
sign-posts for further inquiry. Two lights alone guide us: truth
and love. In their company alone we propose to walk, and if we
stray from the right path it cannot be the fault of our lights,
but our own. It can only be because we have not loved enough
to deserve a fairer measure of the truth. But surely he who sets
his heart in all purity and love upon the vision of the truth may
hope that he will be granted a glimpse of it. It is this faith that
sustains us.

II

There are in the Near East today some twenty states and principalities. Greece, Turkey and Israel are the only non-Arab states.
Iran (Persia), another non-Arab state, does not fall properly
within the Near East according to our conception, although, being distinctly a borderline case, it presents a gradual transition
from the Near East to the Asiatic realms beyond. All the remaining Near Eastern states or principalities are Arab.[3] In the geographical area commonly known as the Fertile Crescent there

[3] The word "Arab" denotes neither a race nor a religion. For the most part
its connotation today is "Arabic-speaking." The overwhelming majority of
Arabic-speaking peoples (or Arabs) are Moslem, just as the overwhelming
majority of Moslems are non-Arab; so the two terms do not coincide. Although there are vast diversities of culture among them, the Arabs have certain general cultural traits in common. They also have common aspirations.
Whether all Arabic-speaking peoples constitute a single nation depends first
on the meaning of the term "constitute" and second on the "Arab" adapta-
tion of the European concept of "nation." All this of course is independent
of the question whether they *should* constitute a nation.

are the Republics of Syria and Lebanon, and the Kingdoms of Jordan and Iraq. In the Arabian Peninsula there are the Kingdoms of Saudi Arabia and Yemen, and the principalities of Muscat and Oman, Qatar, Kuwait, and Bahrein, as well as Trucial Oman and the Aden Colony and Protectorates. In North Africa there are Egypt and the Sudan. The other North African countries namely, Libya (which is scheduled to attain independence on January 1, 1952), Tunisia and Morocco (which are under French rule), Algeria (which is incorporated into France proper), and Spanish Morocco—although they are parts of the "Arab world," do not fall within the Near East. It is apparent, then, that the Near East is that unique region which connects the three continents of Europe, Asia and Africa.

Nine of the Near Eastern states (or ten if you include Iran) are members of the United Nations. Seven of the Near Eastern states form the League of Arab States, but only six of them are members of the United Nations. Turkey, Iraq and Afghanistan are loosely linked together by the practically obsolete Sa'adabad Pact of 1937. Turkey and Greece have been recommended for full membership in the North Atlantic Treaty Organization. Besides, several bilateral treaties link one or the other of the Near Eastern states either with another state in the same region or with some other members of the international community.

We shall exclude from the purview of our study the thematic treatment of Greece, Turkey and Iran. It is not difficult for the thoughtful reader to determine for himself how, where or to what extent the diverse parts of our inquiry apply to them.

Of all the countries of the Near East, Arab and non-Arab, the first to attain her modern form and structure was Egypt. The westernizing reforms of that great soldier-leader, Mohammed Ali, resulting in some modest industrialization and in an emergent middle class, antedate the reforms of Ataturk and Reza Shah by well over a century. If only Egypt's strategic importance were not what it is, and if as a result Mohammed Aii's ferment had worked itself out normally without inordinate interference from outside, it might be possible that Egypt today would present a different aspect, so far as social and economic advance was concerned, and be in a better position to play a more effective part in the maintenance of peace and security in the Near East.

Nevertheless, fate (which is here another name for the unalterable facts of geography, or better of geopolitics) would not have it this way, and the development of Egypt's sovereignty has been both slow and checkered: the product of a long process of insurrection and negotiation which even now is not entirely at an end. From the Napoleonic invasion of Egypt in 1798 until the British declaration of the Protectorate during World War I, the country had no respite from foreign invasion and occupation, or from rivalry and conflict of the Great Powers, particularly France, Britain and Ottoman Turkey. Nor were matters happier after the acknowledgment, by her rivals, of Britain's position of supremacy in Egypt, or even after the subsequent abolition of the Protectorate and the declaration of independence in 1922. Britain's unswerving insistence upon maintaining a foothold in Egypt caused subsequent negotiations for a treaty to fail on three successive occasions; and when, at last, the Treaty of 1936 was concluded, it continued to place obligations upon Egypt which Egypt is still struggling to remove. A readjustment of Britain's position in Egypt and in the Near East in general is clearly indicated (and has in fact already begun with respect to Palestine): the only question is as to its modality, as to the legacy of friendship or bitterness it might leave in its wake.

Politically Egypt leads in the Arab world. There is a significant Arabic literary movement in Egypt, and the Egyptian press dominates the Arab reading public everywhere. Egyptian universities draw students from all over the Moslem world, and there is an attempt to stamp out the curse of illiteracy.

The modern Sudan originally became known to the outside world through the invasion of it by Mohammed Ali's forces in 1820; and from then until the end of the century Egyptian forces supported by British troops were engaged in the pacification of the country. It was in 1899 that the Sudan was finally occupied in full. The Anglo-Egyptian Agreements of that year (January 19 and July 10) established the Condominium. These Agreements reflected on the whole the military aspect of Britain's participation in the administration of the Sudan, carefully circumventing the thorny issue of sovereignty by providing for the simultaneous use of the British and Egyptian flags and the dual process of appointment or removal of the Governor-General, in whom the supreme military and civil command of the Sudan was to be vested. Nor

were the provisions concerning the Sudan in the Anglo-Egyptian

Treaty of 1936 more final in nature than the Agreements of 1899 which they mainly reaffirmed.

Egypt's claims for the incorporation of the Sudan in some form under the Egyptian Crown are based on four facts: (a), the general community of culture between the Sudanese and Egyptian peoples (language, religion, race, general cultural patterns); (b), the general historical interactions between the two peoples, especially the role played by Egypt since the time of Mohammed Ali in the conquest and pacification of the region; (c), the desires of certain sections of the population (e.g. the Ashigga Party) to enjoy their autonomy under the Egyptian Crown; and (d), fundamental considerations of national welfare and security—for the Nile, which is the very existence of Egypt, passes *first* through the Sudan. This fourfold argument is precisely what is meant by the pregnant phrase, the unity of the Nile Valley, which is absolutely fundamental to Egyptian thought.

From the viewpoint of what is abiding and natural, there is no doubt that this unity of the Nile Valley must reassert itself sooner or later in closer living ties between Egypt and the Sudan. Again the only question is as to the modality of this relationship. If there is a modicum of fundamental confidence and trust (which raises profound questions concerning men and cultures), and if other fundamental issues are honestly faced, not only as between Britain and Egypt, but as between the whole Western world and the East, then a working formula embodying the essential interests and rights of all concerned can be found. Not to believe in this is to worship utter darkness: to despair of the power of man, coming back to himself with a purified heart, to rise above and reconcile conflicting interests. And the more one broods upon Britain, Egypt and the Sudan, in their positive relationship to one another, the more one grows in the conviction that their interests, for all their present clash, are nevertheless essentially reconcilable.

One question must be raised in passing. Any student of geopolitics knows that population problems are among the history determining issues, and will be so particularly during the coming decades. At the present rate of increase the population of Egypt will be doubled by the end of the century. How will this population pressure, in an already overpopulated country, be relieved? Where is Egypt's "living space" if it is not in North Africa and especially along the Nile? Long-term policy planners must ponder this question very deeply.

The two Kingdoms of the Arabian Peninsula, Saudi Arabia and Yemen, are slowly emerging from their original state of isolation, while the other principalities of the Peninsula remain more or less remote from the actual life of the region. The two sovereign Kingdoms are far yet from being full participants in the life of the Arab family of nations. They are indeed members of both the United Nations and the League of Arab States, but their contributions to the efforts of the former organization have been on the whole negligible. Nor is there much social interaction between them and the rest of the Arab world.

The Kingdom of Saudi Arabia does exercise some influence upon the political developments of the Arab States. It has been a moderating factor in many a tense situation. However, the absence of an enlightened and articulate public opinion, and of civil and political institutions commensurate with what obtains elsewhere in the Arab world, has restricted the impact of Saudi Arabia upon Arab affairs almost entirely to the governmental level; and even there its scope has been limited.

The Saudi Arabian monarch has played an important role in the first half of the twentieth century. There are so many inscrutable factors, both internal and external, in the situation that it is quite impossible to foretell what the fortunes of his kingdom will be in the coming decades. One thing is certain: the wealth accruing to the country from oil is bound sooner or later to induce significant changes in the otherwise changeless Peninsula.

The nationalist sentiment in Iraq, frustrated immediately after World War I, gave rise to the rebellion of 1920; and since then Britain has sought to meet piecemeal the Iraqi demands for full sovereignty, first through a period of probation under the Mandate, and subsequently through the declaration of independence and the conclusion of a series of treaties providing for certain military concessions. Here was another instance of the selfsame pattern of Anglo-Arab relations which prevailed since World War I: Britain devising formula after formula to reconcile her imperial interests with the shifting scene, a scene which would have been far more docile were it not for the tenacious attachment of the Arabs to their ideal of independence and for the internal relative weakening of Britain herself.

So strong has the nationalist sentiment in Iraq been for the last 30 years, and so preoccupied have the Iraqis been with the problem of independence, that there has been relatively little concern with the equally crucial problems of internal organization and social-economic reform. More so in Iraq perhaps than in the other Arab countries, nationalism pure and simple has been erected as a creed, a sole doctrine which dominates social thought and a single force which sways the public.

During the last three decades there has been on the average more than one cabinet change per year in Iraq. Three basic reasons explain this apparent political instability: the existence of powerful contending forces—racial, religious and social; the existence of what I might call a crisis of leadership in Iraq since the death of King Feisal; and the absence of an adequate socio-economic-ideological content in the nationalist movement, so that the support of the masses, in so far as it existed, was more based on sentimental than on objectively satisfying and enduring grounds.

I spoke of "apparent instability," for it will be apparent that the reigning Hashemite house has been the mainspring of stability in these decades. Nothing seems to be more firmly established in Iraq than this house and the love of the people for their boy monarch. Feisal II has every opportunity to prove one of the leading world figures during the second half of this century.

The story of the Hashemite Kingdom of Jordan is the story of the late King Abdullah. From the earliest stages of its history, when Transjordan, originally a part of the vilayet of Syria, was established as an Amirate and placed under the Mandate in 1922 and then recognized as an independent government under British tutelage in the following year; through the next 25 years of growth in self-government, during which period the succeeding stages of development were registered in successive treaties and agreements with Britain; up until the attainment of fuller independence, the transformation of the Amirate into a Monarchy, and the annexation of parts of Arab Palestine west of the river Jordan—during all this development the fortunes of the state revolved around the central figure of the Hashemite ruler.

The Amirate and the Kingdom owed their relative stability and limited progress to Abdullah's personal authority. His rule also spared the country (however good or bad this may have been) costly and periodic clashes with the dominating foreign power.

He practised perfectly the maxim that politics is the art of the possible. So intertwined were the fortunes of Jordan with the person of the slain King that it is unlikely that his place will be filled by a successor of the same caliber. But it is important to note that the vacuum created by Abdullah's assassination will probably be much more felt in the conduct of Jordan's foreign relations than in the internal administration of the country.

Syria and Lebanon alone of all the Arab Near East had to contend with French domination. The nationalist situation in Syria was from the beginning intense, owing to the important position of Damascus in Arab life and to the many frustrations suffered by Syria at the hands of the Allies. Greater Syria was dismembered, the southern and nothern parts being put under different administrations. Quarrels with the French never ended, and the policy of a national home for the Jews executed by the British administration in Palestine served at once to inflame Syrian nationalist feeling and to imbue it with a necessary anti-Western tinge. The nationalist movement came to look upon the West not as a friend, not as a liberator, but as a schemer and intriguer bent upon division, domination and the settlement, against the will of the native population, of countless Jews on Syrian soil.

The preoccupation of Syria during three decades with her national struggle for freedom and independence reflects itself today in the young republic, not so much in specifically anti-foreign sentiment as in the absence of dominant planning and strong leadership. It is difficult for the foreigner to appreciate the effect of these decades of resistance and struggle in which national emancipation seemed the only purpose for common endeavor. A whole generation has been schooled in the negative—if necessary— discipline of resistance, and it must take some time before the more positive virtues of responsibility, planning, statesmanship and strong government can perfect themselves.

Youthful leadership is today gradually finding itself. The three *coups* of 1949 did not cancel one another: they were more like three successive ripples emanating from one and the same impulse, an impulse partly arising from the Arab disaster in Palestine, partly from the inadequacy of the old leadership in face of the strenuous demands of the moment, partly from the urge of youth to replace this outworn leadership. No strong government has so far emerged from these events: nevertheless a new constitution has been enacted, and several moderate reforms have been introduced. Real endeavors have been made to improve the agricultural and other economic conditions of the country. Education and the army have shared the greater attention.

But the most promising fact in Syria today is the increasing activity of a few political parties which have more than the "creed of full independence" to commend them to public support. Perhaps more than anywhere else in the Arab world genuine political parties and social movements, with clear-cut platforms, social and idcological convictions, and effective organization, are gradually feeling their way towards the light. When positive, constructive plans are elaborated (and they are bound, I believe, to ensue sooner or later), and a strong leadership arises with an orientation towards the future and a grounding upon a creative conception of frccdom, thcn Syria, by rcason of her economic, human and spiritual possibilities, may play a fundamental role in Near Eastern and Arab affairs.

For about a century now the Lebanon has enjoyed some kind of autonomy. In the sixties of the last century six European Powers —France, Great Britain, Prussia, Austria, Russia and Italy—established in agreement with Ottoman Turkey an organic statute according to which Lebanon was to enjoy autonomy within the Ottoman Empire under a Christian governor to be nominated by the Porte and approved by the six Powers. Even during World War I this autonomy was at least nominally respected by the Ottoman Turks who did not draft the inhabitants of Lebanon into their army.

After World War I Lebanon was enlarged and placed under a League of Nations mandate, with France as the mandatory. The Republic of Lebanon was declared in 1926, but France remained the dominating power. The struggle for complete independence went on until in 1943 Parliament erased from the constitution every text in any way diminishing the independence of the country. Subsequent events confirmed this independent act.

The Lebanon has a positive vocation in the international field. It is not political. It is spiritual and intellectual. It consists in being true to the best and truest in East and West alike. This burden of mediation and understanding she is uniquely called to bear.

Some writers, whatever their motive, have depicted Israel as 197 destined to reconcile East and West. But how can one reconcile two things by being outside of them? The West is unthinkable apart from Christianity and the East apart from Islam. Israel is grounded neither in the one nor in the other. Lebanon—little and fragile as she is—is the only country, not only in existence today but perhaps throughout history, where East and West meet and mingle with each other on a footing of equality. The vigorous Moslem citizens of Lebanon bring in the integral contribution of the East, while the Christian citizens are in deepest spiritual and historical communion with the West. If this situation can endure, there is a wonderful possibility of creative confrontation.

The Lebanon could not be true to East and West alike unless she stood for existential freedom. In the end, this is alone her justification. This means freedom of thought, freedom of choice, freedom of being, freedom of becoming. Whoever is about to suffocate must be able to breath freely in the Lebanon. Here the possibility of access to the truth, the whole truth, must be absolutely real. Existential freedom interprets man as being subject only to the compulsion of truth. He is determined, but unlike the mob which is determined by every darkness and wind of doctrine, by the misguidance of every passing principality, his is the determination of truth.

Now the "middle term," the principle of mediation, is, according to Aristotle, the mark of reason. In this sense mediation *is* moderation. To be able to perform her moderating and mediating function between East and West, the Lebanon must be and feel secure in her existence. The narrow nationalist may grudge her her being; to the superficial aesthete she may be an embarrassment. But the Arab world, of which she is an integral part, and the West, in which she profoundly participates, must both see in a strong, self-respecting, peaceful, independent, free and secure Lebanon a blessing to everybody. Only the love of truth can really see this. Thus the secure existence of the Lebanon measures the degree of love abroad.

Everything that strengthens the Lebanon as thus conceived must be good. To swerve from her basic idea is to court disaster. Her basic idea is not political; on the contrary, her political existence is derivative. If she succumbs to the political temptation, to the manifestation of power, she will move from one defeat to another. The principle of international politics is power; but Lebanon's power is reason, truth, love, suffering, being.

Two things dominate the Arab mind in general: independence and unity. There is a deep-seated mystical element in both of these feelings. The only analogous situation I can think of is the radical sense of unity and independence which determined the history of the German peoples in recent decades. Independence springs from the Arab sense of difference from others, a sense that has been sharpened in recent centuries by the relative isolation of the Arabs from the rest of the world. Unity takes on many modalities: from the mild form of general community and consultation enshrined in the Arab League to the extreme form of complete political unification desired by certain nationalist movements, particularly in Iraq and Syria. But regardless of its modality, every Arab feels an immediate mystical unity with every other Arab. The elaboration of the ultimate causes and the real structure, limitation and promise of these two creative Arab persuasions is one of the most fascinating philosophical-cultural tasks to be undertaken by the loving and understanding mind.

The Arab League is an expression of the degree and modality of unity that prevails among the Arab States. However, the common aspiration for unity among most Arab intelligentsia (and to some extent among most Arab peoples) is greater than the actual unity among the Arab ruling circles. Thus there has been some popular dissatisfaction with the League on account of its failure to represent adequately, or even to promote, the existing unity among Arab peoples.

The League has been severely tried during the first years of its existence (it was founded in 1945). To take the single example of Palestine: the average Arab is not convinced that—notwithstanding "foreign interference" and Zionist preparedness—the Holy Land would have been lost to Israel had the Arab League been more adequate to meet its tasks. To ascribe every failure to the League itself is very sentimental; for the League cannot rise above the combined stature of its members.

The basic disunity from which the Arab League suffers is the result of several factors: the social and existential discontinuities in the Arab world itself, the dynastic rivalries, and the subterranean inter-Arab tensions, heightened by the focusing of world interest upon the Arab world. To these there has recently been added a more tangible and perhaps more serious factor of disunity: the physical existence of Israel on the only land-bridge which connects the northeastern and the western parts of the Arab world. The social, economic and strategic significance of this factor cannot be overestimated. The Arab League also suffers from the absence of daring, enlightened leadership. The crisis of leadership in the Arab world is as sharp in inter-Arab relations as in the purely national sphere.

But regardless of its political limitations, the Arab League can play a more active role in the economic, cultural and social life of the Arab world. There is ample room for the coördination of the energies of the various Arab countries in the socio-economic realm; nor is such inter-Arab coöperation as likely to be handicapped by the various internal and external factors of disunity as is the strictly political coöperation.

There will always be an Arab League, regardless of what guise it may take, or by what designation it may be known. For there will always be a measure of community among the Arabs which, particularly under the exacting conditions of present life, will call for appropriate expression and embodiment on the socio-political international level.

III

The rise of Israel is certainly a great historic event whose total consequences it is impossible now to foretell. But it is safe to affirm that as a result the Near East has now entered upon a new critical stage of development. The fate of the Near East is now intertwined with that of Israel.

The existence of Israel presents a real and serious challenge to Arab existence. It is a test of Arab patriotism, dynamism, wisdom and statesmanship. It constitutes a virtual touchstone of Arab capacities for self-preservation and self-determination. Both those Arabs who have been complacently contented with what has been termed "Arab renaissance" for the last 30 years, and those who have remained placidly indifferent to the fate of their countries, have been deeply shaken as a result of the recent events. There is abroad a grim sense of destiny.

There is today an internationally recognized state in the Near East called Israel. This new state quickly succeeded in becoming a member of the United Nations, while such older states as Italy or Ireland have not yet been able to join the world organization. Hundreds of thousands of Jews have been flocking into Israel, and the process of their absorption into the economy and community life of the new nation is in full swing. All this undoubtedly constitutes an historical achievement of the first magnitude.

Yet this achievement, great and real as it is, cannot by itself guarantee the future. To establish a state, or, for that matter, any institution, is one thing; to ensure its continued existence is entirely another. For no matter how difficult the act of establishment may be, I think it is clear that the effort at self-perpetuation will prove incomparably more exacting. Entirely different moral qualities are requisite for the accomplishment of that task. In the struggle for establishment you treat the others as alien forces, to be crushed or pushed back or at least prevented from encroaching upon you; your relation to them is external, summary, destructive, negative; under no circumstances can you allow internal, positive intercourse with them on a basis of equality. But in the struggle for enduring existence you must come to terms with them; you must take their existence positively into account; your idea must be softened and modulated and trimmed to accommodate their idea; you must enter into interacting relationship with them, based on mutual respect and trust. Whether the leadership and the ethos of Israel are adequate to the requirements of existence, of course only the future can disclose.

For it must not be forgotten that Israel is not yet at peace with her immediate world. Her Arab and Moslem environment has not yet recognized her. She has no dealings whatsoever with her surroundings. Besides this radical political and economic estrangement, there is a profound intellectual and spiritual chasm between Israel and the rest of the Near East. Two entirely different economies, two entirely different religions, two entirely different languages (at least two languages whose kinship is the outcome of distant origination from a third source and not immediate interaction, as e.g. between Arabic and Turkish or French and English), two entirely different mentalities, two entirely different cultures, two entirely different civilizations, face each other across this chasm. I do not know of a single other instance in the world where there is such radical existential discontinuity across national frontiers. The "ingathering" of the Oriental Jews may soften this discontinuity a bit, but not to the extent of making it at all comparable to the graded transition that obtains almost everywhere else in the world. Thus Israel is only geographically part of the Near East, and therefore her fundamental problem is not how to establish herself—a relatively easy matter, considering the world forces, both positive and negative, which aided her—but how to integrate herself, economically, politically, spiritually, in the life of the Near East; how to promote friendly, creative, sustained and sustaining, trustful, peaceful, internal relations with the Arab and Moslem worlds. Self-establishment by force is fairly easy—at least it is possible; but self-perpetuation by force is, in the nature of the case, absolutely impossible. At least history has not known an instance of a nation at permanent enmity with its immediate world.

I think the Zionist idea, reinforced by an organizational genius of the first order, and sharpened by the sufferings of the Jews in recent years, has proved itself exceedingly potent in summoning forth world-wide sympathy and support. Whether this same idea, in the next crucial phase of its development, is resourceful and resilient and humble enough to create genuine, internal relations of confidence and coöperation between itself and the Moslem-Arab world in the midst of which it has chosen to plant itself is altogether beyond my ken to prophesy or even to conjecture. But one thing can be said with certainty. If the present arrogance, defiance and ambition are to persist; and if Israel is to be again and again confirmed in her feeling that she is to be favored—just because the United States, owing to the position of the Jews in this country, to certain well-known peculiarities in the American political and social system, to widespread ignorance in the United States of real conditions in the Near East, and also to a certain genuine, well-meaning goodness of heart on the part of the American people will at the crucial moment always decisively side with Israel against her immediate world—then, I am afraid, there will never be peace in the Near East, and the United States cannot be altogether innocent of responsibility for that situation.

The fair account of the historical genesis of Israel, including the diverse factors that played a decisive role in this genesis, is yet to be written: and may not see the light of day before decades. Although I was a firsthand witness of and participant in the crucial events of 1947 and 1948 in the United Nations, it is not my intention to go into this matter here.[4] But on the profoundest possible plane a thoroughly grounded investigation (which I will touch upon in barest outline here) into the deep significance of Israel will have to inquire into four issues of prime importance. In this way, and from the nature of the case, as we shall see, Israel opens up vistas of thought that no other state can evoke.

The first fundamental issue is political. We have touched upon it already. It may be formulated thus: how a completely alien state that is suddenly thrust upon, and that is not wanted by, its immediate environment can survive, especially if this state has created for others the very problem (Arab refugees) it meant to solve for its own people. Here questions of diplomacy, strategy, external pressure, European and American interests, the psychological situation, the possibilities of explosion, and the balancing of the economic against the political, will all have to be responsibly discussed. I entitle this issue the political challenge of Israel.

The second fundamental inquiry may be formulated as follows: whether the concentration in one state of the factors at once of language, race and religion is not a challenge to the modern conception of the state, which is free of the necessary determination of any of these factors, and certainly of the three of them taken together. There is no other state in the world today—nor has there been for centuries—which is nationally characterized by a race, a language and a religion none of which nationally characterizes any other state. (I am aware of the recent disquisitions on the subject of race, but it can be shown that the conclusions therein reached, whatever their real scientific value, do not affect my present employment of the term which has—it can be fully demonstrated—a perfectly objective residual significance in the present discussion.) Israel as a state alone is Hebrew, Israel alone is Jewish, Israel alone is Judaic. No state is alone Moslem or Christian or Protestant or Catholic. No state is alone Aryan or Mongolian or Negro. And no state, except Israel and perhaps Ethiopia, has a national language of its own unconnected (in the sense of interaction) with any living language. This unique concentration of the three factors of race, language and religion is

---

[4] I mention in this connection, however, two recent books, *My Mission in Israel*, by James G. McDonald (New York: Simon and Schuster, 1951), and *The Forrestal Diaries*, edited by Walter Millis (New York: Viking, 1951), which are of special interest to the student of this subject.

thus a challenge to the modern conception of the state, and in any case is bound to generate a tremendous exclusiveness and intensity of feeling (issuing in the most radical form of nationalism) that must find an outlet in some dynamism with incalculable consequences. I may term this the philosophical challenge of Israel, because it relates to the very conception of the state.

Far deeper than anything economic or political or philosophical are the two theological challenges of Israel. The one stems from the Old Testament, the other from the New.

The Old Testament theological challenge has to deal with the great mystery of Ishmael and Isaac. Whoever broods with a pure and loving heart upon this mystery and contemplates in its light the present spiritual situation between Jews and Arabs in the Near East must experience a profound emotion of wonder. What we behold is something not purely immanent, not something just human or historical or economic or political: there is a significance splashing irresistibly and mysteriously upon us from the beyond. The Arabs call themselves the sons of Ishmael; but Abraham loved Ishmael, and Sarah's counsel that he cast out Ishmael and his mother was "very grievous" in Abraham's sight. (Gen. 21:11) There is a most necessary philosophico-theological inquiry to be undertaken, perhaps in several volumes, into this question: to show how, just as there is a great so-called "Jewish problem," so there is and there has been in an entirely different sense a profound "Arab problem." (Is it without significance that the United Nations ever since its foundation has been preoccupied with the Arabs as much as with any other people: problems of Syria, Lebanon, Palestine, Egypt, Libya, Morocco?) To dismiss the present conflict between the children of Isaac and the children of Ishmael, who are all children of Abraham, as just another ordinary politico-economic struggle, is to have no sense whatever for the awful and holy and ultimate in history. When history shall finally reveal its secret (of which we here and now already catch a real glimpse), the present confrontation between Isaac and Ishmael may turn out to be (the beautiful smile of the cynic is obvious at this point) one of the major keys unlocking that secret. The rise of Israel therefore presents a great challenge: that of the mystery of the two children of Abraham after the flesh.

The New Testament theological challenge may be formulated as follows: how is present-day Israel related on the one hand to the "old Israel" which, according to Christian theology, was once and for all dissolved by Christ, and on the other hand to the "new Israel," namely, the Church, which was founded by Christ? I believe no deeper question can be asked about Israel than this one, and here again we dimly perceive the distant vista of an important investigation yet to be attempted. The word "Israel" is mentioned 74 times in the New Testament. Is this fact (see especially Acts 13:23 and I Cor. 10:18) entirely unrelated to what exists in Palestine today? Christian theology has pondered most responsibly the mystery of "Israel" in relation to Christ. Are we to believe that its conclusions can have no bearing on present-day facts? Jerusalem is made a political center. But can the world ever forget the salvation wrought in Jerusalem? Zealots and politicians, whether Western, Jewish or Arab, would of course mock at these questions; but according to the truth, which is quite independent of all zeal and all politics, the challenge of love we are trying here to glimpse holds every determination in its hands, including above all that of Israel.

IV

In our study of the Near East we cannot stop with the political: we must press on to the deeper modes of human existence. Man does not exist only as ruler and ruled; man exists also as dealing with material nature and its forces, and as living with his fellow men. There is also man's own view of himself and of whoever is above this passing show. The last word about the Near East is not political: it must take full account of the material, social and spiritual problems besetting our existence. Therefore we turn now first to the examination of our economic and social situation: as to its realities, its possibilities and the prerequisites necessary to transform these possibilities into actual fact. In all this we cannot be humble enough, for only humility is proper to the truth.

All the countries of the Near East, and particularly the Arab countries, are economically and socially underdeveloped; in fact some of these territories are among the most underdeveloped in the world. On the other hand, in some sectors high levels of development have been reached. In this cradle of Western civilization the past rose to far greater levels of achievement than the present. The monuments of Arab architecture still standing intact and the remains of ancient Roman cities and of irrigation systems overrun by the desert are evidences of levels of prosperity and development from which these lands have fallen during the past millennium of decline and darkness. Thus we are not only behind others; we are behind ourselves. It follows that what was possible once is in some respects certainly possible again.

The measure of present underdevelopment and poverty can be seen from a comparison of the per capita incomes of the countries of the Near East with those of the advanced countries. The following figures of per capita incomes of the countries of the Near and Middle East are based on the latest estimates of the United Nations; those of the advanced countries of Europe and America are also compiled by the United Nations, but are based on reliable statistics of the countries themselves.

PER CAPITA INCOME IN DOLLARS

Arab Countries		Some Countries in America and Europe	
Lebanon	140		
Syria	100	United States	1,453
Egypt	100	Canada	870
Iraq	90	Switzerland	849
Saudi Arabia	60	United Kingdom	773
Yemen	40	Denmark	689
		France	482
Other Near and Middle East Countries		Czechoslovakia	371
		Argentina	346
Israel	389	Portugal	250
Greece	130	Italy	235
Turkey	125		
Iran	85		
Pakistan	51		

The estimates of per capita income in the Arab countries are perhaps lower than is actually the case, but they indicate the low standard of living of the peoples of these countries as compared with the advanced countries of Europe and America. The standard of living of the majority of the people in the Arab Near East is even lower than is indicated by figures of per capita incomes. Being averages, these figures do not reveal the true extent of poverty in the region. The inequality of wealth and income is such that the majority of the people live on a bare subsistence

level while a minority lives in luxury. Vigorous social consciousness and responsibility simply do not exist. It is perhaps safe to
estimate that 10 per cent of the population receive more than half
the national income and so live on a level comparable to that of
people in Western Europe, while the common people constituting
90 per cent of the population have an average income which is
only half the per capita income for the whole population.

The basic cause of the poverty of the countries of the Arab
Near East lies in the semi-feudal agrarian structure of their economy. This economy is predominantly agricultural, as shown by
the fact that over two-thirds of the population derive their livelihood directly or indirectly from the land. In spite of the considerable growth of manufacturing industry in recent decades, particularly in Egypt, Lebanon and Syria, the proportion of labour
employed in industry is still very low; in fact, all the indications
are that it has fallen with the growth of population and with the
decline of handicrafts and the shift to mechanized factory production. The backwardness of the agrarian structure limits agricultural productivity and so keeps down the living standard of the
majority of the people. To this basic cause of poverty must be
added a special cause in the case of Egypt, namely the pressure of
population on a limited area of cultivable land.

The semi-feudal structure in agriculture still predominates in
most Arab countries to a smaller or greater extent. It manifests
itself in the existence of large landholdings owned by a small
number of landlords who are mostly absentee owners and who
constitute a *rentier* class drawing comfortable incomes from the
land but taking little or no interest in its utilization. The extent
of large landholdings varies from one country to another. In
Egypt statistics of land ownership show that .4 per cent of the
landowners with holdings over 50 feddans each (one feddan is
approximately one acre) own 36.8 per cent of the total area, while
72.2 per cent of the owners with holdings of one feddan or less
own only 13.1 per cent of the area. In Syria it is estimated that
about half the land is owned by large landowners. In Iraq, where
this semi-feudal agrarian structure is superimposed on an old tribal
structure, the proportion is still higher.

Besides the class of absentee landlords, there is the class of poor
share-tenants and landless agricultural workers who cultivate the
land and constitute the great majority of the rural population.

The share-tenants, who are usually burdened with debts contracted at excessively high interest rates, have no incentive to improve the land. The difference between this semi-feudal share-tenancy and individual farm ownership is illustrated most vividly by the contrast in Lebanon between the mountain farmer who owns his land and the share-tenant of the plains. The mountaineer who won his title to the land scarcely a hundred years ago has transformed the barren and rocky mountain terrain into fruit orchards and vegetable gardens. He is literate, healthy, clean and progressive. His counterpart on the plains has done nothing to increase the productivity of the soil and remains in a state of poverty and degradation. The plight of the landless agricultural workers is even more pitiful than that of the share-tenants.

This semi-feudal agrarian structure is not only a basic obstacle to the development of agriculture in the Arab Near East but is also a limiting factor in the development of manufacturing industry. The low productivity and low purchasing power of the rural population, constituting a large majority of the people, limit the growth of manufacturing, which cannot develop large-scale low-cost production in the absence of a sufficiently large market.

The capital resources internally available for economic development are small, except in those Arab countries which receive substantial income from their oil resources. The governments are financially weak not only because of low national incomes but also because of the corruption and inefficiency of the taxation system. Their financial resources are generally insufficient to provide the basic social services needed by the people and to undertake projects of economic development. Expenditures on education are limited and consequently illiteracy remains high.

The growth of industry and trade in recent years, though still limited, has brought into being new social forces that are beginning to challenge the domination of the landlords. The industrial working class is organizing itself into unions and is beginning to have influence in public affairs. A new class of business and industrial enterprisers is rising and taking an increasing interest in economic and social development. The intellectuals are leading in new movements of national revival of much wider scope and greater depth than the old purely political struggle against foreign imperialist domination. But all these nascent social forces are still weak and without adequate leadership. The future therefore is docile in the extreme.

The possibilities of economic development in the Arab countries of the Near East are limited by a number of factors, the most important of which are natural resources, capital resources, labor efficiency and in some cases the growth of population.

Except for oil, the Arab countries are poor in natural resources. As far as is known there are no important coal and iron ore deposits. There are no non-ferrous metals worth mentioning. There are almost no forests. The most important resource is agricultural land which is of high fertility in most of the Arab countries. But the limiting factor in this case is water. The Arab territories receive little rainfall and are mostly desert and semi-desert. Nevertheless, large rivers such as the Nile, the Tigris and the Euphrates, as well as small rivers flowing from the mountains of Lebanon and Syria, provide considerable water resources for irrigation and hydroelectric power. Where irrigation is highly developed, as in Egypt, agriculture is highly productive. There are vast possibilities for irrigation development in Iraq and Syria which would enable them to support twice their present populations at an appreciably higher living standard. But a large investment of capital over a long period of years would be required for this purpose.

The oil resources of the Arab Near East are concentrated in the Persian Gulf area. Saudi Arabia, Kuwait and Iraq, and to a lesser degree Bahrein and Qatar, have very rich oil deposits which constitute about one-third of the world's known reserves. These countries are at present receiving considerable income from the concessionary companies exploiting these resources and are expected to receive more as production increases and higher royalties are agreed upon.

The second general limiting factor is capital. The capital resources that are currently available in the Arab countries or that may be mobilized in the future are small. The present rate of capital formation would enable economic development to keep up with population growth and, except in Egypt, to raise per capita incomes and standards of living at less than one per cent annually. The possibilities of an increased rate of capital formation are very limited except in the case of those countries with large oil revenues, namely Iraq, Saudi Arabia and Kuwait. It has been estimated by a United Nations group of experts that the countries of the Middle East, including the Arab countries, are saving on the average about 6 per cent of their national incomes and that they need to invest at the rate of 15 per cent of their national incomes in industry and agriculture in order to raise their per capita incomes annually by 2 per cent. This estimate is roughly applicable to the Arab countries. With increased income from oil and increased efforts in the mobilization of internal capital resources it would be possible to increase the rate of national savings to 10 per cent on the average. Capital from foreign countries will still be needed to the extent of 5 per cent of the national incomes of the Arab countries taken together, if their per capita incomes are to be raised by 2 per cent, annually. This would amount to an annual capital inflow of $175,000,000. An annual increase of 2 per cent in per capita income represents a fairly rapid rate of development and would result in an increase of 50 per cent in 20 years.

A third limiting factor is labor efficiency. A technically efficient and trained labor force in agriculture and industry is necessary for economic development. This means a greater degree of literacy, better education, improved public health services, increased technical training and a government extension service, for the improvement of agricultural techniques. The Point Four Program has a real and important contribution to make in this field. However, the introduction of new technology into agriculture, industry, public health and government administration is very difficult and complex. It cannot simply be imported from the West, but requires much cultural readjustment and assimilation.

The growth of population is a special limiting factor where, as in Egypt, the pressure of population on a limited area of cultivable land makes it difficult to increase per capita income and so raise standards of living. It is believed by some students of Egyptian economic development that in the last 50 years the standard of living of the majority of Egyptians has fallen because of the growth of population at a rate greater than the increase of national production.

The question is not whether it will be possible to promote the economic and social development of the Arab Near East in the next 50 years but whether it will be possible to achieve such a rapid rate of development as would not only keep pace with population growth but also raise living standards sufficiently to transform the life of the people from misery and despair to decency and hope. The question is further whether material conditions comparable to those obtaining elsewhere, such as in America, Europe, Russia or certain parts of Asia, can be developed in the Arab Near East so as to support a vigorous culture that will make a real positive dent upon the world.

To attempt an answer to these questions, one must at least consider certain prerequisites of rapid economic and social development in the Arab Near East. I would like to suggest four internal prerequisites and two of an external character.

The first internal prerequisite is land reform which would give the cultivator a stake in the land and transform the agrarian structure from its present state of stagnation and hopelessness to a state where free and progressive farmers acquire the incentives for raising the productivity of the soil and developing a new way of life in rural communities. The rural population constitutes the large majority of the people in Arab countries, and as long as they remain in their present degradation there is little hope for developing strong, prosperous, forward-looking and stable nations in the Arab Near East.

The second prerequisite is an efficient government administration. In the Arab countries, local private enterprise cannot be relied upon to undertake the tasks of rapid economic and social development because its resources and experience are limited. On the other hand, foreign private enterprise (even if interested) either will not be trusted because of past experience or will not be allowed to make the high profits which it would require in return for the risks of foreign investment. The conclusion is that government enterprise, or at least government participation and guidance, is necessary in many fields of development where neither local nor foreign private enterprise would be available or acceptable. It is therefore essential, if governments are to undertake programs and even specific projects of development, that government administration attain a high degree of efficiency.

The third prerequisite is wise, enlightened and strong national leadership. Without it no basic reforms can be carried out, efficiency in government administration cannot be ensured and maintained at a high level, capital cannot be mobilized and directed to the most productive fields of development, and the necessary efforts and sacrifices by the people will not be forth-coming.

Fourthly, one of the most important prerequisites of economic development in the Arab Near East is a social and economic order in which freedom and equality of opportunity are ensured to all members of the community; where special economic, social and political privilege has been eliminated; and where every person will receive the rewards of his own efforts and exertion. Rapid economic and social development consciously planned and directed requires for its success the participation of the people in a democratic national movement involving sacrifices and re-wards that are fairly distributed in an environment where free-dom, justice and responsibility abound.

These four prerequisites of land reform, efficiency in govern-ment administration, wise and strong national leadership, and an environment of freedom and equality of opportunity will enable the Arab countries to embark, each in its own territory, on a vigorous policy of economic and social development. To be fully successful, however, such a policy would require not only separate action, but also coöperation among all the Arab countries. Such economic coöperation is necessary in order to promote territorial division of labor, establish a wider market as a basis for indus-trialization and counter the economic threat of Israel.

One final requirement which is essential for the rapid economic development of the Arab Near East is foreign, and particularly United States, economic assistance. Foreign economic assistance in the form of technical aid, grants, and loans would be needed at least in the first ten years of a large-scale program of development in order to set the wheels in motion, to acquire badly needed capital equipment and to help make the basic capital investments in such fields as irrigation, hydroelectric power, communications and basic social services in public health, education, agricultural extension and rural credit. But even if foreign assistance is not available on the required scale, the Arab countries can and should make all the efforts and sacrifices necessary for shouldering the burdens required for their economic and social development.

V

In the present politico-ideological situation—with Communism eating into the body of the great Eurasian continent until only the fringes of that immense land mass remain outside its clutches, with even those fringes and the lands beyond considerably softened in diverse ways from within, with the Near East occupying the most strategic position in the world, and with the well-known Soviet-Russian aspirations in the direction of the Persian Gulf— the question of the relationship between the Near East on the one hand and the Communist and non-Communist worlds on the other is of the greatest importance.

The total impact of these two worlds upon the Near East today can best be gauged by the performance of a radical intellectual experiment. Truth reveals itself most clearly at the limit, and in the inner relationships between cultures and peoples war is one of the limits. Let us assume, then, for the purposes of this experiment, that war has broken out between the Communist and the non-Communist worlds. With this assumption, the experiment consists in answering seven questions for each Near Eastern country on a comparative tabulation sheet. The situation is so transparent that it is perfectly possible to reach truthful answers within a very small margin of error. The questions are:

1. What is the attitude of the government towards the war?

2. What is the attitude of the people, as distinct from the government, towards the war?

3. Whatever the answers to the previous two questions, what is the possibility of Communist sabotage and fifth column activity?

4. In case of a Communist invasion and the elimination of Western influence from the Near East, who in each country in question will really miss the West?

5. In case of the Sovietization of the Near East, what is the possibility of the rise of underground resistance movements?

6. In case the West succeeds in pushing back Communism from the Near East (some time limit here must be assumed, say five or ten years of Sovietization), what will be the attitude of the people to the returning West?

7. What tentative blueprints can be made of the shape of things to come after the Communist onslaught is swept back?

This experiment is purely hypothetical, but the questions raised are exceedingly critical. They touch the very heart of the situation. Nothing is likely to illuminate the student of these matters more profoundly than an honest, thorough, objective execution of this experiment. If the West wants to know where the Near East 213 stands, let it face up honestly to this experiment. Let it further summon its deepest genius to inquire at each stage why the results of the experiment are what they are. In all this the West must make four precise distinctions: what is proper for propaganda and expediency, namely for "kidding" people along in times of crisis; what is the real truth; what is the Near East's responsibility for this truth; and what is the West's responsibility for this truth.

VI

"Whither the Near East" is ultimately, for the most part, "whither Islam." This question raises the profoundest issues, which I shall try to face as truthfully as I can.

First it is important to note that the question concerns not only the Moslems, but the entire world. For Islam is a vigorous force in the world and therefore much depends on its developments. Just as the Moslems must inquire "whither this or that system or culture," including their own, so the non-Moslems must in this amazingly shrunk world ponder deeply and with absolute responsibility "whither Islam." Certainly the Near East cannot be understood apart from this problem. We have all become one another's neighbors, and no man can remain indifferent to where his neighbor is tending.

And for the Christians of the Near East it is obvious that this is a peculiarly crucial issue. The fate of Islam is in a certain sense their fate. For Islam is more than a religion: it is a total outlook. Thus for the Christians of the Near East, Moslem culture, whether Arab or Turkish or Persian, is in a deep sense their culture. They have always shouldered civic, economic, political and intellectual responsibility with their Moslem brethren. Therefore they cannot be too deeply interested in the development of their common heritage.

In varying degrees of metaphysical depth men have brooded on this issue: Toynbee has done so in England, as well as Gibb and his assistant Hourani; so has Massignon in France and so have Hocking and Hitti in the United States; and many others elsewhere. In the Near East, Taha Hussein in Egypt and Zurayk in Syria wrestled with it somewhat. But I do not expect the final word on this matter, on the plane of theory, to emerge before many years. We are at the earliest stages of a most important cultural-historical-existential investigation. In the nature of the case, the utmost that can be done now and for some time to come is to clear the ground, lay the foundations, indicate the vast scope of the problem, suggest the sort of questions that must be gone into, and define the moral and intellectual prerequisites for any inquiry that will really face and yield the truth. It is enough if the mind is whetted in absolute love and humor and seriousness to face the issue; for truth has a way always of revealing itself in time to the inquiring mind.

The following outline only raises issues. Its suggestion of "solutions" (an awful word) is meager. But the very raising of an issue is itself of the utmost importance. The proper facing, the adequate description, the real understanding, the living appreciation, the honest and full apprehension—in short, the *being*—of these issues is a matter of the distant future. Whether it will be a Toynbee or a Gibb or a Hourani or a Hussein who will finally wrestle with these great questions to their uttermost depths I do not know. One thing I know: that the *whole truth* of these matters is known somewhere, certainly in the quiet bosom of eternity, and that it takes only a purity of heart and a single and sustained determination of the will to find it.

1. Nothing is more important than to contemplate the desert and the mode of being proper to the desert, and to understand how this mode of being differs radically from that of the most temperate zones, such as Europe, where there are rain and snow and green mountains, where there are sharpness of transition and variety, and where nature is prolific with forms of life.

2. The "whither" we are seeking raises the prior question of the complete significance of the mentality of the *badu*, who are the inhabitants of the desert.

3. The existence and persistence throughout Arab history of overwhelming numbers of lower classes and the absence of the middle class. Hence the phenomenon of the masses and of the mob. To please them you must in the long run cater to their imagination and desires: you must become one of them. The all-absorbing, self-avenging, overwhelming phenomenon of the mob: in the end they dominate, not you.

4. Hence the great difficulty of being a leader, really leading and not in fact following. The ultimate tribulation of leadership

in the Moslem-Arab world: you must conform. In the light of this difficulty the achievement of Mohammed appears utterly superhuman.

5. Hence also the phenomenon of the court poet. To rule you must employ a rhetorician or a poet or be one yourself. The incredible magical power of the Arabic language to rouse and satisfy the masses. The "whither" we are seeking raises the entrancing question of the nature, mystery, significance and "whither" of the Arabic language.

6. In one great agony of his life, Ibn Rushd (Averroes) distinguished between that which is proper to the masses and that which is proper to the intimate circle. The tragic existential significance of this distinction. The *batiniyyah* (esoterism) that follows from this dualism must mean that not everything that is hid shall be revealed.

7. An inquiry into the discontinuities, gaps, divisions, interruptions (geographical, social and historical) in Arab society. The distinction between the unity of community and unity by reason of an identically inherited pattern. The "whither" we are seeking raises the question of the essence of community.

8. The bearing of this on the possibility in Islam of compromise and modification and on real awareness of others. Distinction between real change (appropriation, assimilation, inner adjustment) and apparent change (repeating, copying, "using").

9. The strength and the weakness of the immense mixing of races that has occurred in Islam. The geographical determinism of this phenomenon.

10. The ontological significance of the pull and the lure which the past exerts on the Arab. His prodigious memory and his vivid imagination. The dreams of reënaction of exactly what happened in the past. The "whither" we inquire into can never be determined without knowing the bearing of all this on decision, creation, freedom, indetermination, the will, the future, real change, the perception of the objective realities of the world.

11. The phenomenon in recent decades of "the Orientalist." How much good and how much harm has Orientalism done? Why a corresponding phenomenon of "the Occidentalist" did not arise?

12. The dearth of great works of reason, great *summas*. The important works of Moslem-Arab and Christian-Arab philosophers

and mystics did not transform life and literature: they influenced West more than East. Connectedness and unity of reason soon overwhelmed by imagination, language, fatigue. Breath of reason short. If reason is the creator of the world, is there any future, whether to Christianity or to Islam, without reason being properly enshrined in the hearts and minds of men?

13. If instinctive nature is given, can it nevertheless be controlled by reason? The order of the emotions.

14. The question of fatalism, for after all the "whither" may have no meaning at all.

15. The significance of the repudiation by Al-Ghazzalli of cause and effect. Cause and effect in Arab life and its bearing on the "whither."

16. No deeper confrontation occurred in Arab history than that between Al-Ghazzalli and Ibn Rushd in the two *tahafuts*. Here for the first time East met West internally within Islam. It has never happened since.

17. The Christian and Moslem doctrines of revelation (*al-wahi*).

18. The problem of the pluralization of history. Is there an absolute beginning? If not, where do we start? Is it possible to compare cultures on an absolute scale? No deeper question can be asked and therefore we cannot be too careful in answering it.

19. Now the "whither" means asking, questioning, wondering, reflecting on oneself, tearing one's clothes, beating upon one's breast, "where am I going?" This requires fundamental self-criticism. But so far striking absence of a strong line of reformers, critics, thinkers, prophets, rebels. There is room for a hundred Mohammed Abdou's: kindled by one another, building upon one another, absorbing and reflecting one another, criticizing, reinterpreting, creating, departing from one another, accepting profound spiritual responsibility. The "whither" is a function of the joy of free, grounded, responsible reflection and self-criticism.

20. Nature and destiny of man; the individual human soul; immortality; reason, nature, rebellion, vision, joy; freedom of thought, of being and of becoming.

21. There is an amazing ignorance of Christian literature, doctrine and life, despite the fact that Christ and His Mother are deeply revered by Islam. There isn't a single Moslem scholar in all history, so far as I know, who has written an authentic essay on Christianity; whereas Christian scholars, both Arab and non-

Arab, have written authoritative works on Islam, and on other religions too. Inquiry into the mystery of this estrangement. There will always be fear, uncertainty, embarrassment, uneasiness, lack of joy, lack of freedom, a predisposition to self-defense, until this intellectual and spiritual balance is redressed.

22. Islam explicitly grounds itself in the Judaic-Christian tradition and conceives itself as completing and sealing that tradition. There is room here for a responsible investigation into what it has adopted and what it has rejected from this tradition, and into the sort of Christianity Islam came in touch with. Since the Christian tradition persists independently of Islam, and in all likelihood is not going to be displaced, it is obvious "whither Islam" is inseparable from "whence Islam."

23. In this connection the infinite importance of the history of the seventh and eighth centuries, particularly in regard to the relationship then and afterwards between Islam and the Graeco-Roman-Christian-European synthesis.

24. Three central Christian doctrines are repudiated: the Incarnation, the Cross and the Church. Significance of this repudiation for the "whither." Suffering then is not of the essence, personal sin need not be atoned, the divine does not take the form of an actual total man. The fact of the Church raises the tremendous question of the difference between the Christian and the Moslem conceptions of history.

25. Contemplative existence in Islam and in Christianity. The recent growth of contemplative orders in the West. Inwardness, interiority, contemplation, pure vision, asceticism, in Islam.

26. An inquiry into the ontology of Moslem art.

27. An inquiry into the possibility of the separation of state and religion in Islam.

28. "Whither Islam" must depend in part on how much the Christian and Moslem worlds can in this materially and existentially interdependent world sit together and inquire, on the deepest possible plane, through their scholars and thinkers, in all patience, humility, love and openness, into the truth of Christianity and truth of Islam, and into their common spiritual and temporal problems. Nothing is more crucial for the future of Islam and indeed for the history of the world than to provide objective, political, social and existential conditions under which

this intellectual and spiritual getting together can fruitfully take place.

29. The growth in recent years of Western interest in Islam and the Moslem world. The phenomenon of institutes of Islamic and Near Eastern studies in the United States. No greater service can be done the cause of truth, understanding, peace and concord between East and West than the promotion of these institutes. Distinction, however, between dedication to truth alone and the utilization of historical, sociological and economic information for political and commercial purposes. Truth the only savior of the world.

30. There is room for 20 first-class universities in the Near East, where the disciplined mind can range over all subjects in absolute freedom, joy and responsibility. No greater service can be done the Moslem world and in the end the cause of understanding between East and West than the promotion of liberal education in the Near East where the humane tradition, both of Islam and of the West, can be vigorously brought to the fore, and where freedom of thought and inquiry and a complete trust in the life-giving power of the truth penetrate the atmosphere on every level of existence.

31. On the level of the universal, and therefore of truth, peace and understanding, the following five great achievements of the Moslem world in the ages of its greatest brilliance cannot be stressed enough: the humble receptivity of important thinkers and seekers to the truth of cultures outside their own; the great achievements of Arab science, especially in mathematics, physics, astronomy and medicine; certain brilliant achievements of Moslem theology (*al-kalam*); the wonderful line of Moslem-Arab philosophers; and perhaps on the deepest level the unbelievable spirituality of certain *sufis*. The "whither" we are seeking is in my opinion largely "whether" these five solid achievements can be rediscovered, reappropriated, reinterpreted, developed and perfected. If only Ibn Rushd and Jalal-al-Din Al-Rumi can be loved, understood and transcended!

32. The greatest single intellectual thing that can happen in the Arab world is a responsible movement for publishing in Arabic one or two hundred volumes of the world's finest classics, both from the Moslem-Arab and from the Western traditions.

33. An inquiry into dependence and independence: on every level—political, geopolitical, economic, cultural, historical, intellectual, spiritual. Meaning of justice and equality in an order of interdependence. The Aristotelian principle of the priority of actuality.

34. The complex relationship between the existentially strong and the existentially weak. The free obligations of the existentially strong.

35. The *Logos*, the Word, the intermediary between God and man in Christian and Moslem theologies. The significance of the rejection of the Trinity.

36. Is a Christian Arab possible? Is a Christian Arab culture possible?

37. Has there been sufficient love and concern for the Moslem-Arab world? Have sufficient tears of love been shed on its behalf?

38. Where are these things fully and responsibly discussed and faced: discussed not spectatorially, but with a view to the truth, and faced not inquisitively, but in absolute love? Can objective material and human conditions be developed whereby the mind will be able to articulate the truth of these questions in a manner that will live for a thousand years?

These are the topics that the question "whither Islam" seems to me to involve. It is very well for people to be "interested" in the Near East. It is very well to think in terms of independence and of economic and social advance. But politics and economics will lead absolutely nowhere until these deeper issues are faced. Well-meaning goodwill need not wonder why it does not always succeed: it must first open up these horizons and acquire an existential grounding in them. The degree of superficiality with respect to the Near East, both in the Near East and in the Western world, is simply astounding. It is an expression of the crisis of the West.

VII

The Western world is responsible for the situation in the Near East on every level of that situation. In the end this is an exemplification of the *Western* principle that "unto whomsoever much is given, of him shall be much required." Near Eastern existence is largely derivative from or a reaction against Western

existence. One can set up a one-to-one correspondence between

the problems and great crises through which Western civilization
has gone during the past centuries and the reflections these problems and crises induced in the life of the Near East. The Near
East mirrors, by deposit or by reaction, the problems of the world.
Whatever face the Arab East shows today is fundamentally a reflection of the face which the West has shown it; and whatever
weaknesses the Arab East exhibits are largely an expression of the
weaknesses of the West. In a deeper sense the problem of the
Near East is the problem of the West.

On the other hand there is a reflection of some of the virtues
of the West; the beginnings of a new administrative structure,
of social and health services, of an improvement in standards of
living, of great public works (e.g. in Egypt and Iraq) and of a
revival of learning (largely due to Western schools and books).
In all this we see reflections of the great dominating ideas of the
modern West: order, health, worldly happiness, science, social
consciousness.

On the other hand the Arab East shows another face: the existence of a million Arab refugees, deep divisions between the
various Arab states, estrangement between the Arabs and their
neighbors (hostility to Israel, suspicion of the Turks, indifference
to the Persians), the growth of tension between Judaism, Christianity and Islam, the lack of progress towards social justice (it
is not certain that social organization today is more just than
what it was before the coming of the West), and above all a
universal and profound hatred of the West (although this does
not prevent friendly personal relations and the desire to obtain
new and efficient tools of thought and action from the West).

To say that all of this is due simply and purely to the West
is of course nonsense. There is fundamental superficiality, negativity, unreality, darkness, distortion and error in the Near East
which made all this in the first place possible. Unless these de-
fects are brought to the surface and remedied there is no hope
for us. East and West can come together in peace only if they
repent together under transcendent judgment.

With these qualifications, of what can we accuse the West?

1. Lack of unity. The strife and rivalry of the Western Powers.
This led not only to the weakening of the West, but also to the
divisions and rivalries among the Near Eastern states. I do not
agree that Western lack of unity is a good thing for us, for I

221

refuse to believe that the West can only reach agreement upon our corpse.

2. Lack of responsibility. Failure to accept the fact in all honesty that they were responsible for shaking the whole life of the Near East. No long-term planning; day-to-day opportunism; hence no stable political life in the Near East. In particular, the instability due to the alternation in British policy between interference and noninterference: interference when a Western interest is at stake (e.g. oil and Suez), and refusal to do something—under the pretense that the states are independent—when what is involved is merely the welfare or interests of the peoples themselves. All this bespeaks halfheartedness in facing up to one's responsibilities.

3. Lack of sincerity. There has been from the beginning an element of hypocrisy in Western policy: Napoleon's claim to be the protector of Islam, the use of Christian missions for political ends, the use of minorities by all Powers, a façade of morality given to the mandate system when as a matter of moral principles to justify their own actions and the ignoring of them when they were inconvenient, and so forth.

4. Lack of understanding of the deeper issues at stake. In particular, failure to understand that all political problems in the Near East are interwoven with religion, so that a true attitude to those problems can rest only upon a basis of true doctrine, and a false attitude to them will have disastrous effects upon the whole relationship between the great religions. The West did not offer the highest goods of its positive tradition, but the false gods of modern Western civilization: nationalism, materialism, Communism. Thus the Near East has been given the choice between embracing the falsehoods of Europe and falling back upon its own inadequate past.

5. Lack of love. Strategy, commerce, exploitation, securing an imperial route: these were why the West for the most part came to the Near East, not because it loved us. Add to this the immense racial arrogance of modern Europe. The West has not been true to itself, and therefore it could not have been true to us.

This sad, privative face is of course not the authentic face of the West. But it has called forth in the East its exact unhappy image. One can show that if there is lack of unity, lack of responsibility, lack of sincerity, lack of understanding and lack of love in the Near East, the Near East caught on these things largely from the West. The disturbing rise of fanaticism in the Near East in recent years is a reaction to the thoughtlessness and superficiality of the West. When you are not loved, what is there to prevent you from hating yourself and the world? There is no escape from the fundamental metaphysical principle that actuality is in every way prior to potentiality, and that the latter takes on the form of the former.

In all this we are really touching upon the great present crisis in Western culture. We are saying when that culture mends its own spiritual fences, all will be well with the Near East, and not with the Near East alone. We are saying it is not a simple thing to be the heir of the Graeco-Roman-Christian-European synthesis and not to be true to its deepest visions. One can take the ten greatest spirits in that synthesis and have them judge the performance of the Western world in relation to the Near East. The deep problem of the Near East then must await the spiritual recovery of the West. And he does not know the truth who thinks that the West does not have in its own tradition the means and power wherewith it can once again be true to itself.

VIII

Those who live and die in the Near East (and in certain parts of it more than others), namely, those who suffer our existence from within, are granted the opportunity—which very few of them seize—of beholding something eternal, of seeing right before their eyes the deepest problems of humanity almost in shimmering physical embodiment. Elsewhere these problems certainly exist, but they are usually *resolved* one way or the other, rightly or wrongly, or else they are judiciously covered up. But with us they remain in eternal suspension, as though there must be one place in the world to remind us all of the essential problematic character of human existence, of the utter folly of "resting in peace" when we have cleverly covered up our problems or supposed that we have "solved" them.

The great moments of the Near East are the judges of the world. The Near East is of course today utterly unworthy of them. But it is these moments alone, properly understood, that can bind East and West together, in judgment and in truth.

What is the ultimate trouble with the world today? It is the loss of the dimension of transcendence, the fact that the world hugs itself in happy self-sufficiency; it is—to use the concept of a certain modern philosophy—the belief that the world is self-creative. But the one message deposited by the Near East in the whole of its history is the absolute negation of this belief. There is an original transcendent order, full of meaning and power, open to the faithful and pure: an order creating, judging, disturbing, healing, forgiving. The Western world today is disturbed by the challenge of Communism. But this is nothing; for Communism will pass away, and so will "heaven and earth," but the vision and world of the Near East will never pass away. In fact, Communism with its radical immanentism is a challenge only because the transcendental challenge of the Near East has long ago overcome the West and will never let it go. Only as the West comes to the cradle of its civilization, recognizing in all responsibility, truth and love the relics of its origins; and only as the Near East regains a glimpse of its own lost transcendent visions, casting aside all doubt, negativity and childishness and clasping hands with all those who first drank from the well of its life: only as these two movements reach for and meet each other can peace and righteousness come, not only to the Near East, but to the whole world.

Abd al-Latif Sharara

17 The Idea of Nationalism[1]

WHEN A FEELING is real and its reality resides in its leading to action, it may no longer be considered an illusion, but is
to be taken as a realistic event, just like any other; it acquires
an objective quality on which it is possible to build. When, for
example, I feel that I am an Arab, I am not laboring under an
illusion, even though I may have been brought up in Mexico
or Spain or India, because such a feeling cannot arise out of a
mistake, and is not a fancy in the mind; it is, rather, a complex
of mysterious facts of which I am ignorant. But my lack of knowledge does not make reality an illusion any more than its mysterious quality makes me into a Mexican, a Spaniard, or an Indian.

We deduce from this that whenever anybody "feels" a certain
nationality (qaumiyya) with a true feeling, such feeling is an
indication of his true national personality.

Such feeling is the basis on which the idea of nationalism has
been established among every nation (umma) in the world.

Man considered as a personality, however, is not the same as
an animal or a plant. An animal or a plant is tied to the region
in which it grows and takes on the characteristic of the land from
which it springs, whereas a sane man—not an abnormal or a
deviant or a disturbed person—is linked, in the first place, to the
spiritual unit out of which he grows, that is, to his nation pri-
marily; because man is mind, or soul, or spirit—call him what
you will—more than he is body. He is distinguished from all
other species of animals by his mind and his spiritual and moral
characteristics. For this reason, national feeling requires mental

---

[1] Fi'l-qaumiyya al-arabiyya (On Arab Nationalism) (Beirut, 1957), pp. 10–
16. (S. G. H.)

225

and spiritual excellence, and national life cannot be realized until civic feeling has become highly manifest in the consciousness of the individual.

As for the regional sentiment (*atifa iqlimiyya*) which binds man to a particular spot or a particular region of the earth, it is a survival of animality in him; and every man, whoever he is, is an animal who must necessarily be reared in a region or locality with geographical limits and distinctive natural landmarks. By reason of his origin, man loves the earth which has nourished him and the skies which have sheltered him, the people who have cherished his infancy, who have been the companions of his youth, and whose environment formed his mentality.

But this regional sentiment is not an ultimate human truth, because man is not bound to the earth like a plant, that is, in a way that does not admit of the separation of a man from his soil, even though he springs from it and to it he returns.

The ultimate truth which distinguishes man from animals and plants is that he loves his region only because of the existence therein of men who are similar to him in respect of a genuine spirit which expresses itself in a particular language, with particular customs and particular ways of thought and action. This is what the Arab poet has made clear in a most eloquent verse when he said:

It is not the dwelling places which have stolen my heart
But the love of those who have dwelt in the dwelling places.

This genuine spirit and all the manifestations which give expression to it, such as language, the identity of feelings, hopes, memories, aims, and aspirations, is what the Arabs have been used to call by the word *umma* and the Westerners by the word *nation.*

The nation is a human, not a geographical reality. It is not a thought which we invent or a poetical fancy which occurs to the minds and is bounded by vocables or 'by material limits, and lastly, it is not a philosophical theory which we reach by research, speculation, the interpretation of history, or the explanation of the past from a special point of view. The nation either is a nation, or else it is nothing. As an idea, it can never exist, as some would have it, on a peninsula between being and nothingness.

If the cause of the nation were dependent on a mode of thinking or on a regional sentiment, or on the peculiarities of a particular spot or locality, then it would have been possible to create many nations out of a single one.

Take any one of the nations of this age. Take France, for instance, and you will find that the people of the north (Flanders) are different from the people of the south (the Midi), just as the Arabs of the north (the Hijaz and Najd) are different from the people of the south (the Yemen and Hadramaut), or as the people of Jabal Amil (southern Lebanon) are different from the people of Akar (northern Lebanon) in many respects such as religious beliefs, character, traditions, accents. So that if it occurred to the people of the Midi to form a nation, they would not be lacking in characteristics which may easily be described as a nationality, geographic boundaries, regional accent, and so forth.

It would be possible, on this faulty basis, to create many nations in the Lebanon, such as the Amili nation, the Akari nation, the Kasrawani nation, the Mitni nation, the Shoufi nation. This requires no more than to use words for something other than what they mean, to make realities of our fanciful thoughts, and facts out of our individual personal interests.

If the problem could be solved by the erection of frontiers; by a variation in accents; by the emergence of wishes; by the existence of secondary, trivial differences in habits, traditions, and creeds; and by mental concentration on a narrow regional sentiment, it is to be observed that these factors are to be found in every village, in every town, in every nation, and there is no point in deep philosophizing for the sake of denying them.

When the reality of the nation is being affirmed, it is necessary to use criteria for the use of words, and to clarify concepts. There are four words which people confuse prodigiously whenever they talk of nationalities. These are: nation (*umma*), fatherland (*watan*), people (*sha'b*), and state (*daula*). They frequently use the word "state" when they mean "nation;" and talk of "fatherland" to signify "people" or else speak of "people" when they intend the "nation," without distinction between the meaning of these vocables, or precise realization of what they denote, or a firm grounding in the differences between the respective concepts.

Nationalism (*qaumiyya*) as an idea is related, in the first   227 place, to the concept of the nation and is not concerned with the other words except in a secondary, albeit essential, way.

The fatherland is the soil and the climate in which live a group of people. The people is that group of men who live in one land, who have the same historical origin, and have the same political order. The state is that political organization which a people sets up in a fatherland, and which always derives its name from the particular political order in existence and from the name of the fatherland in which it is found, such as the Lebanese Republic, the Kingdom of Iraq, or the Principality of Kuwait.

The nation, however, is a wider conception than the state, greater than the people, and more meaningful than the fatherland.

It is not necessary for a nation to have one state or one fatherland, or to be composed of one people; but it must have its own language, its own history, its own ideals, its own shared aspirations, its own shared memories, and its own particular natural links which bind its members in two respects, the moral and the economic.

If a group of men have their own language, a common history, common ideals, and are linked together by the same memories and the same aspirations for the future, the same economic and cultural interests, then such a group is a nation, no matter how many and various are its fatherlands, states, and peoples.

Nationalism is that emotion and common interest, combined in one feeling and one idea within the members of the nation.

Such is the Arab point of view on the nation and nationalism which any inquirer, whatever his creed, may elicit when he studies Arab history, interrogates the popular movements in the generality of the Arab countries, when he goes deep in his understanding of the Arabic language, and notices what words denote and the way in which they are used by the *homo arabicus* in every time and place.

Gamal Abdel Nasser

18 The Philosophy of the Revolution[1]

THE THREE CIRCLES

WE SHOULD first of all agree upon one thing before we proceed further with this discourse, and that is to define the boundaries of place as far as we are concerned. If I were told that our place is the capital we live in I beg to differ. If I were told that our place is limited by the political boundaries of our country I also do not agree. If our problem, as a whole, is confined within our capital or inside our political boundaries, it will be easy. We would lock ourselves in, close all the doors, and live in an ivory tower away as much as possible from the world, its complications, its wars and crises. All these crash through the gates of our country and leave their effects upon us, though we have nothing to do with them.

But the era of isolation is now gone. Gone also are the days when barbed wires marked the frontiers separating and isolating countries, and every country must look beyond its frontiers to find out where the currents that affected it spring, how it should live with others. . . . It has become imperative that every country should look around itself to find out its position and its environment and decide what it can do, what its vital sphere is, and where the scene of its activity and what its positive role could be in this troubled world.

As I often sit in my study and think quietly of this subject I ask myself, "What is our positive role in this troubled world and where is the scene in which we can play that role?"

[1] *Falsafat al-thaura* (*The Philosophy of the Revolution*) (Cairo, n.d.), pp. 53–56, 71–73, of the English version put out by the publishers of the original Arabic text. (S. G. H.)

I survey our conditions and find out we are in a group of circles which should be the theater of our activity and in which we try to move as much as we can.

Fate does not play jokes. Events are not produced haphazardly. Existence cannot come out of nothing.

We cannot look stupidly at a map of the world, not realizing our place therein and the role determined to us by that place. Neither can we ignore that there is an Arab circle surrounding us and that this circle is as much a part of us as we are a part of it, that our history has been mixed with it and that its interests are linked with ours. These are actual facts and not mere words.

Can we ignore that there is a continent of Africa in which fate has placed us and which is destined today to witness a terrible struggle on its future? This struggle will affect us whether we want or not.

Can we ignore that there is a Muslim world with which we are tied by bonds which are not only forged by religious faith but also tightened by the facts of history? I said once that fate plays no jokes. It is not in vain that our country lies to the southwest of Asia, close to the Arab world, whose life is intermingled with ours. It is not in vain that our country lies to the northeast of Africa, a position from which it gives upon the dark continent wherein rages today the most violent struggle between white colonizers and black natives for the possession of its inexhaustible resources. It is not in vain that Islamic civilization and Islamic heritage, which the Mongols ravaged in their conquest of the old Islamic capitals, retreated, and sought refuge in Egypt, where they found shelter and safety as a result of the counterattack with which Egypt repelled the invasion of these Tartars at Ein Galout.

All these are fundamental facts, whose roots lie deeply in our life; whatever we do, we cannot forget them or run away from them.

I see no reason why, as I sit alone in my study with my thoughts wandering away, I should recall, at this stage of my thinking, a well-known story by the Italian poet Luigi Pirandelli [*sic*] which he called, "Six Personalities in Search of Actors" [*sic*].

230   The annals of history are full of heroes who carved for them-

selves great and heroic roles and played them on momentous occasions on the stage. History is also charged with great heroic roles which do not find actors to play them on the stage. I do not know why I always imagine that in this region in which we live there is a role wandering aimlessly about seeking an actor to play it. I do not know why this role, tired of roaming about in this vast region which extends to every place around us, should at last settle down, weary and worn out, on our frontiers beckoning us to move, to dress up for it, and to perform it, since there is nobody else who can do so.

Here I hasten to point out that this role is not a leading role. It is one of interplay of reactions and experiments with all these factors aiming at exploding this terrific energy latent in every sphere around us and at the creation, in this region, of a tremendous power capable of lifting this region up and making it play its positive role in the construction of the future of humanity.

There is no doubt that the Arab circle is the most important and the most closely connected with us. Its history merges with ours. We have suffered the same hardships and lived the same crises, and when we fell prostrate under the spikes of the horses of conquerors they lay with us.

THE ISLAMIC CIRCLE

The third circle now remains, the circle that goes beyond continents and oceans and to which I referred as the circle of our brethren in faith who turn with us, whatever part of the world they are in, toward the same kibla in Mecca and whose pious lips whisper reverently the same prayers.

My faith in the positive efficacy which can be the outcome of further strengthening the Islamic bonds with all other Muslims became deeper when I went to the Saudi Kingdom with the Egyptian mission who went there to offer condolences on the occasion of its late King.

As I stood in front of the Kaaba and felt my sentiments wandering with every part of the world where Islam had extended I found myself exclaiming, "Our idea of the pilgrimage should change. Going to the Kaaba should never be a passport to heaven, after a lengthy life. Neither should it be a simple effort to buy 231 indulgences after an eventful life. The pilgrimage should be a great political power. The press of the world should resort to and follow its news, not as a series of rituals and traditions which are done to amuse and entertain readers, but as a regular political congress wherein the leaders of Muslim states, their public men, their pioneers in every field of knowledge, their writers, their leading industrialists, merchants, and youth draw up in this universal Islamic parliament the main lines of policy for their countries and their coöperation together until they meet again. They should meet reverently, strong, free from greed but active, submissive to the Lord, but powerful against their difficulties and their enemies, dreaming of a new life, firm believers that they have a place under the sun which they should occupy for life."

I recall I expressed some of these sentiments to His Majesty King Saoud. He said to me, "This is the real wisdom of the pilgrimage." Verily I cannot visualize a higher wisdom.

When my mind traveled to the 80 million Muslims in Indonesia, the 50 million in China, and the several other millions in Malaya, Siam, Burma, and the 100 million in Pakistan, the 100 million or more in the Middle East, and the 40 million in Russia as well as the other millions in the distant parts of the world, when I visualize these millions united in one faith I have a great consciousness of the tremendous potentialities that coöperation amongst them all can achieve: a coöperation that does not deprive them of their loyalty to their countries but which guarantees for them and their brethren a limitless power.

I now revert to the wandering role that seeks an actor to perform it. Such is the role, such are its features, and such is its stage.

We, and only we, are impelled by our environment and are capable of performing this role.

19 *Constitution*

FUNDAMENTAL PRINCIPLES

First Principle: Unity and Freedom of the Arab Nation

THE ARABS form one nation. This nation has the natural right to live in a single state and to be free to direct its own destiny.

The Party of the Arab Ba'th therefore believes that:

1) The Arab fatherland constitutes an indivisible political and economic unity. No Arab country can live apart from the others.

2) The Arab nation constitutes a cultural unity. Any differences existing among its sons are accidental and unimportant. They will all disappear with the awakening of the Arab consciousness.

3) The Arab fatherland belongs to the Arabs. They alone have the right to administer its affairs, to dispose of its wealth, and to direct its destinies.

Second Principle: Personality of the Arab Nation

The Arab nation is characterized by virtues which are the result of its successive rebirths. These virtues are characterized by vitality and creativeness and by an ability for transformation and renewal. Its renewal is always linked to growth in personal freedom, and harmony between its evolution and the national interest.

The Party of the Arab Ba'th therefore believes that:

1) Freedom of speech, freedom of assembly, freedom of belief,

---

[1] From a French version made by the Bureau Arabe de Presse et de Publicité, Damascus, 1951. The Arab Ba'th is officially described as "A national, popular, revolutionary movement fighting for Arab Unity, Freedom, and Socialism." (S. G. H.)

233

as well as artistic freedom, are sacred. No authority can diminish them.

2) The value of the citizens is measured—once all opportunities have been given them—by the action they take to further the progress and prosperity of the Arab nation, without regard to any other criterion.

Third Principle: The Mission of the Arab Nation

The Arab nation has an eternal mission. This mission reveals itself in ever new and related forms through the different stages of history. It aims at the renewal of human values, at the quickening of human progress, at increasing harmony and mutual help among the nations.

The Party of the Arab Ba'th therefore believes that:

1) Colonialism and all that goes with it is a criminal enterprise. The Arabs must fight it with all possible means, just as they must take it on themselves to help, according to their physical and moral abilities, all peoples fighting for their freedom.

2) Humanity constitutes a whole, the interests of which are solidary and the values and civilization of which are common to all. The Arabs are enriched by world civilization and enrich it in their turn. They stretch a fraternal hand to other nations and collaborate with them for the establishment of just institutions which will ensure for all the peoples prosperity and peace, as well as moral and spiritual advance.

GENERAL PRINCIPLES

Article 1 The Party of the "Arab Ba'th" is a universal Arab Party. It has branches in all the Arab countries. It does not concern itself with regional politics except in relation to the higher interests of the Arab cause.

Article 2 The headquarters of the party is for the time being located in Damascus. It can be transferred to any other Arab city if the national interest should require it.

Article 3 The Party of the Arab Ba'th is a national party. It believes that nationalism is a living and eternal reality. It believes that the feeling of national awakening which intimately unites the individual to his nation is a sacred feeling. This feeling has

234

within itself a potential of creative power; it binds itself to sacrifice, it seeks the exercise of responsibilities, and it directs the individual personality in a concrete and active manner.

The national idea to which the party appeals is the will of the Arab people to free themselves and to unite. It demands that the opportunity be given to it to realize in history its Arab personality, and to collaborate with all the nations in all the fields which will ensure the march of humanity toward welfare and progress.

Article 4 The Party of the Arab Ba'th is a socialist party. It believes that socialism is a necessity which emanates from the depth of Arab nationalism itself. Socialism constitutes, in fact, the ideal social order which will allow the Arab people to realize its possibilities and to enable its genius to flourish, and which will ensure for the nation constant progress in its material and moral output. It makes possible a trustful brotherhood among its members.

Article 5 The Party of the Arab Ba'th is a popular party. It believes that sovereignty is the property of the people, who alone is the source of all authority. It believes that the value of the state is the outcome of the will of the masses from which it issues and that this value is sacred only to the extent that the masses have exercised their choice freely. That is why, in the accomplishment of its mission, the party relies on the people with whom it seeks to establish intricate contact, the spiritual, moral, material, and physical level of whom it is trying to raise, in order that the people may become conscious of its personality and that it may become able to exercise its right in private and public life.

Article 6 The Party of the Arab Ba'th is revolutionary. It believes that its main objectives for the realization of the renaissance of Arab nationalism or for the establishment of socialism cannot be achieved except by means of revolution and struggle. To rely on slow evolution and to be satisfied with a partial and superficial reform is to threaten these aims and to conduce to their failure and their loss.

This is why the party decides in favor of:

1) The struggle against foreign colonialism, in order to liberate the Arab fatherland completely and finally.

2) The struggle to gather all the Arabs in a single independent state.

3) The overthrow of the present faulty structure, an overthrow

which will include all the sectors of intellectual, economic, social, and political life.

Article 7 The Arab fatherland is that part of the globe inhabited by the Arab nation which stretches from the Taurus Mountain, the Pocht-i-Kouh Mountains, the Gulf of Basra, the Arab Ocean, the Ethiopian Mountains, the Sahara, the Atlantic Ocean, and the Mediterranean.

Article 8 The official language of the state, as well as that of all the citizens, is Arabic. It alone is recognized in correspondence and in teaching.

Article 9 The emblem of the Arab state is that of the Arab revolution begun in 1916 to liberate and unify the Arab nation.

Article 10 An Arab is he whose language is Arabic, who has lived on Arab soil, or who, after having been assimilated to Arab life, has faith in his belonging to the Arab nation.

Article 11 To be excluded from the Arab fatherland: whoever has fought for or has belonged to a factious anti-Arab association, whoever has lent himself inside the Arab fatherland to colonial ends.

Article 12 The Arab woman enjoys all the rights of citizenship. The party struggles to raise up woman's level in order to make her fit to exercise these rights.

Article 13 The party strives to give all the citizens the same opportunities in the field of schooling and livelihood in order that, in the various aspects of human activity, everyone should be equally able to show his real abilities and to develop them to the maximum.

THE WAY: INTERNAL POLICY OF THE PARTY

Article 14 The regime of the Arab state will be a constitutional parliamentary regime. Executive power is responsible before the legislative, which is directly elected by the people.

Article 15 The national tie is the only tie that may exist in the Arab state. It ensures harmony among all the citizens by melting them in the crucible of a single nation and counteracts all religious, communal, tribal, racial, or regional factions.

Article 16 The administrative system of the Arab state is a system of decentralization.

Constitution of the Arab Ba'th Party

Article 17 The party strives to make popular feeling universal and to make the power of the people a living reality in the life of the individual. It undertakes to give the state a constitution guaranteeing to all Arab citizens absolute equality before the law, the right to express their opinions in absolute freedom, and a true choice of their representatives, thus ensuring for them a free life within the framework of the law.

Article 18 A single code of laws is to be established freely for the whole of the Arab nation. This code will be in conformity with the spirit of the times and will take into account the past experiences of the Arab nation.

Article 19 The judicial power will be independent. It will be free from interference by other powers and enjoy total immunity.

Article 20 The rights of citizenship are granted in their totality to every citizen living on Arab soil who is devoted to the Arab fatherland and who has no connection with any factious association.

Article 21 Military service is compulsory in the Arab fatherland.

FOREIGN POLICY OF THE PARTY

Article 22 The foreign policy of the Arab state will be guided by the interests of Arab nationalism and of the eternal mission of the Arabs which seeks to establish in coöperation with other nations a free, harmonious, and secure world, continuously advancing in progress.

Article 23 The Arabs will struggle with all their power to destroy the foundations of colonialism and of foreign occupation and to suppress all foreign political or economic influence in their country.

Article 24 Since the Arab people is the sole source of power, all treaties, pacts, and documents concluded by governments which detract from the total sovereignty of the Arabs will be abrogated.

Article 25 Arab foreign policy seeks to give a true picture of the will of the Arabs to live in freedom, and of their sincere desire to see all other nations enjoy the same liberty.

ECONOMIC POLICY OF THE PARTY

Article 26 The Party of the Arab Ba'th is a socialist party. It believes that the economic wealth of the fatherland belongs to the nation.

Article 27 The present distribution of wealth in the Arab fatherland is unjust. Therefore a review and a just redistribution will become necessary.

Article 28 The equality of all the citizens is founded on human values. This is why the party forbids the exploitation of the work of others.

Article 29 Public utilities, extensive natural resources, big industry, and the means of transport are the property of the nation. The state will manage them directly and will abolish private companies and foreign concessions.

Article 30 Ownership of agricultural land will be so limited as to be in proportion to the means of the proprietor to exploit all his lands without exploitation of the efforts of others. This will be under the control of the state and in conformity with its over-all economic plan.

Article 31 Small industrial ownership will be so limited as to be related to the standard of living of the citizens of the state as a whole.

Article 32 Workers will participate in the management of their factory. In addition to their wages—fixed by the state—they will receive a proportion of the profits, also fixed by the state.

Article 33 Ownership of immovable property is allowed to all the citizens so long as they do not exploit it to the harm of others, and so long as the state ensures for all citizens a minimum of immovable property.

Article 34 Property and inheritance are two natural rights. They are protected within the limits of the national interest.

Article 35 Usurious loans are prohibited between citizens. One state bank is to be founded to issue currency, which the national output will back. This bank will finance the vital agricultural and industrial plans of the nation.

Article 36 The state will control directly internal and external trade in order to abolish the exploitation of the consumer by the producer. The state will protect them both, as it will protect the national output against the competition of foreign foods and will ensure equilibrium between exports and imports.

Article 37 General planning, inspired by the most modern economic ideas, will be organized so that the Arab fatherland will be industrialized, national production developed, new outlets opened for it, and the industrial economy of each region directed according to its potential and to the raw material it contains.

SOCIAL POLICY OF THE PARTY

Article 38 Family, Procreation, Marriage.

§1) The family is the basic cell of the nation. It is for the state to protect, to develop, and to help it.

§2) Procreation is a trust given in the first place to the family, and then to the state. Both must ensure its increase, and look to the health and education of the descendants.

§3) Marriage is a national duty. The state must encourage it, facilitate it, and control it.

Article 39 Public Health. The state will build, at its expense, institutions of preventive medicine, dispensaries, and hospitals which will meet the needs of all citizens, for whom the state ensures free medical treatment.

Article 40 Labor.

§1) Labor is an obligation for all those who are capable of it. It is for the state to ensure that work is available to every citizen, whether intellectual or manual.

§2) The employer must ensure at the least a decent standard of living for his employee.

§3) The state sees to the maintenance of all persons incapable of work.

§4) Just laws will be promulgated to limit the workman's daily hours of work, to give him the right to paid weekly and annual holidays, to protect his rights, to ensure social security for him in old age, and to indemnify him for any cessation of work, whether partial or total.

§5) Free workmen's and peasants' unions will be established and encouraged, so that they may constitute an instrument efficient in the defense of their rights, in raising their standard of living, in developing their abilities, in increasing the opportunities offered to them, in creating among them a spirit of solidarity, and in representing them in joint works councils.

§6) Joint works councils will be created in which the state and the unions of workmen and peasants will be represented. These councils will have power to decide the issues arising among the unions, the works managers, and the representatives of the state.

Article 41 Culture and Society.

§1) The party seeks to develop a general national culture for the whole Arab fatherland which shall be Arab, liberal, progressive, extensive, profound, and humanist; it attempts to disseminate it in all sections of the population.

§2) The state is responsible for the protection of the liberty of speech, of publication, of assembly, of protest, and of the press, within the limits of the higher Arab national interest. It is for the state to facilitate all the means and the modalities which tend to realize this liberty.

§3) Intellectual work is one of the most sacred kinds. It is the state's concern to protect and encourage intellectuals and scientists.

§4) Within the limits of the Arab national idea, every freedom will be given for the foundation of clubs, associations, parties, youth groupings, and tourist organizations, as well as for obtaining profit from the cinema, radio, television, and all the other facilities of modern civilization in order to spread generally the national culture, and to contribute to the entertainment of the people.

Article 42 Separation of the classes and differentiation among them are abolished. The separation of the classes is the consequence of a faulty social order. Therefore, the party carries on its struggle among the laboring and oppressed classes of society so that such separation and differentiation will come to an end and the citizens will recover the whole of their human dignity and will be enabled to live in the shadow of a just social order in which nothing will distinguish one citizen from another except intellectual capacity and manual skill.

Article 43 Nomadism. Nomadism is a primitive social state. It decreases the national output and makes an important part of the nation a paralyzed member and an obstacle to its development and progress. The party struggles for the sedentarization of nomads by the grant of lands to them, for the abolition of tribal customs, and for the application to the nomads of the laws of the state.

POLICY OF THE PARTY IN EDUCATION AND TEACHING

The educational policy of the party aims at the creation of a new Arab generation which believes in the unity of the nation, and in the eternity of its mission. This policy, based on scientific reasoning, will be freed from the shackles of superstitions and reactionary traditions; it will be imbued with the spirit of optimism, of struggle, and of solidarity among all citizens in the carrying out of a total Arab revolution, and in the cause of human progress.

Therefore the party decides as follows:

Article 44 A national Arab stamp will mark all the aspects of intellectual, economic, political, architectural, and artistic life. The party establishes once again the links of the Arab nation with its glorious history and urges it toward a future even more glorious and more exemplary.

Article 45 Teaching is one of the exclusive functions of the state. Therefore, all foreign and private educational institutions are abolished.

Article 46 Education at all stages shall be free for all citizens. Primary and secondary education shall be compulsory.

Article 47 Professional schools with the most modern equipment shall be established, where education shall be free.

Article 48 Teaching careers and all that relates to education are set aside for Arab citizens. An exception to this rule is made in the instance of higher education.

AMENDMENT OF THE CONSTITUTION

Single Article The fundamental and general principles of the Constitution cannot be amended. Other articles may, however, be amended, provided that two-thirds of the General Council of the party agree thereto, on a motion put by the Executive Council, or by a quarter of the members of the General Council, or by ten members of the Party Organization.

Michel Aflaq

20 Nationalism and Revolution

Nationalism Is Love before Everything Else.[1]

I FEAR that nationalism might fall, among us, to the level of mere intellectual knowledge and verbal discussion, and thus lose affective power and warmth of feeling. Often I hear students asking for a definition of the nationalism for which we call! Is it racialism founded on blood, or a spiritual quality drawn from history and a common culture, and does it banish religion or make a place for it?!

It seems as though their belief in nationalism depends on the extent to which its definition is true and has power to convince, in spite of the fact that faith must precede knowledge and mocks at definitions, and that, indeed, it is faith that leads to knowledge and lights its way.

The nationalism for which we call is love before everything else. It is the very same feeling that binds the individual to his family, because the fatherland is only a large household, and the nation a large family. Nationalism, like every kind of love, fills the heart with joy and spreads hope in the soul; he who feels it would wish to share with all people this joy which raises him above narrow egoism, draws him nearer to goodness and perfection. Such a joy is therefore beyond human will and as far removed from hatred as possible, because he who feels its sanctity is led at the same time to venerate it in all people. It is, then, the best way to a true humanity. And as love is always found linked to sacrifice, so is nationalism. Sacrifice for the sake of nationalism leads to heroism, for he who sacrifices everything

---

[1] *Fi sabil al-ba'th* (*Toward the Ba'th*) (Beirut, 1959), pp. 29–30. This essay is dated 1940. (S. G. H.)

for his people, in defense of its past glory and future welfare, is more elevated in spirit and richer in his life than he who makes a sacrifice for the sake of one person.

He who loves does not seek reasons for his love. If asked to explain it, he cannot account for it clearly. He who cannot love except for some clear reason shows that love has either weakened or died within him.

How, then, can some young men allow themselves to require those incontrovertible arguments which would convince them that their love for their own Arab nationality ought to have the better of their love for the Russians, for example, or ought to be preferred to any partiality they may have for a particular sect or tribe or region? How can they allow themselves to ask whether the Arabs have virtues worthy of being loved? He who does not love his nation unless it is free from blemishes does not know real love. In my view, the only question which young men ought to ask themselves and their teachers is the following: Since we love our nation, with all its good and bad points, how can we transform this love into useful service, and in what manner?

Love, O young man, before everything. Love comes first and the definition follows. If love is the soil in which your nationalism is nourished, then there is no scope for different views on how it ought to be defined and delimited. Nationalism is racial in the sense that we hold sacred this Arab race which has, since the earliest historical epochs, carried within itself a vitality and a nobility which have enabled it to go on renewing and perfecting itself, taking advantage of triumphs and defeats alike. Nationalism is spiritual and all-embracing, in the sense that it opens its arms to and spreads its wings over all those who have shared with the Arabs their history and have lived in the environment of their language and culture for generations, so that they have become Arab in thought and feeling. There is no fear that nationalism will clash with religion, for, like religion, it flows from the heart and issues from the will of God; they walk arm in arm, supporting each other, especially when religion represents the genius of the nationality and is in harmony with its nature.

Aspects of Revolution[2]

I will not in this address deal completely and compendiously with the subject, but would prefer, rather, to consider some implications of the idea of revolution on which the Arab Ba'th is based.

Brethren: Let us free ourselves from traditional views, from the repetition of customary phrases and abstract words, and let us try to rise a little above the contingent problems of the day. Let us try to do all this in order to draw nearer to the truth concerning our one great problem, to the living and great truth of our cause, as it seeks true life, and as it finds its way by itself, by its own effort, in confidence and faith.

What is revolution? Shall we stop at political definitions? Shall our understanding be limited to political programs, and the schemes and suggestions they contain for organizing public life in its different aspects? Or are we to understand by revolution something truer and deeper? By revolution we understand that true awakening which it is no longer possible to deny or to doubt, the awakening of the Arab spirit at a decisive stage in human history. The reality of the revolution lies in this awakening, the awakening of the spirit which had been weighed down by stationary and vitiated conditions which, for a long time, prevented it from rising and radiating its influence. This spirit at last senses great danger, fateful danger, and rises up decisively.

This awakening, and its progress, cannot but be in a direction contrary to the conditions which have prevented its manifestation, have weighed it down, and have distorted its development, progress in a direction contrary to that of the existing conditions, of the vitiated, sickly, and artificial conditions. This opposition to the current is in order that what remains of the true spirit should awake, wherever it is found, come together, and coalesce. It is necessary to embark on such a progress, which is in contradiction to matter, which begins to live with every step it takes, which awakens and arouses attention, which revitalizes hidden or sleeping powers and restores to them seriousness, lucidity, the feeling of their independence, their value, and their influence. *Revolution, then, before being a political and social program, is that prime*

---

[2] *Ibid.*, pp. 145–150. This is the text of an address given at the Homs branch of the Arab Ba'th Party in February, 1950. (S. G. H.)

propelling power, that powerful psychic current, that mandatory struggle, without which the reawakening of the nation is not to be understood. This is what we understand by revolution.

We do not then fight existing conditions merely because they are vitiated; rather, we fight them because we are compelled to fight, because we cannot but fight. The nation must discover in itself what remains of its true power, and we must extract from its depth the treasures of hidden vitality. We struggle and fight against the artificial vitiated political and social conditions, not only to remove and change them but so that the nation may recover its unity in this struggle also. The nation has denied its being as a result of its long sleep, and as a result of the distortion which it has undergone. It no longer knows itself, its parts no longer know one another, it has become mightily divided, and its parts and members have been scattered. It has sunk to a low level, being imprisoned in selfishness, in petty interests, in the habit of immobility and unadventurousness. At this level, no unity can be created in the nation, no focusing of that warmth necessary for acquaintance and friendship among the millions of Arabs. Fervor is then necessary, turmoil and movement at a high level are necessary, hardships to be overcome are necessary, a long march in which intellect and morality interpenetrate is necessary, trial and error and the correction of error are necessary. In this way, we may know one another and resume our relations, so that the nation may be unified in the path of struggle and hardships.

This is as far as the nation, taken as an entity, is concerned. As far as its individual members are concerned, revolution, which we have defined as opposition to the current, will alone reconstitute the Arab personality and will place on each individual the responsibility of his actions. It will liberate the intellect and make it independent, and make morality earnest and responsible; it will release the source of faith in the soul, because such a long and strenuous march does not find faith superfluous. On the contrary, its flesh and blood originate from so spiritual a source.

Revolution, then, is a path, a path leading to the desired aim, to the healthy society which we seek. It is, however, not one of many paths, but indeed the only one. For this reason, even if present conditions were done away with, by some miracle, the nation which we desire and the aims which we seek will not be, and we will not be able to build the society we desire. The nation we seek, the society we want to build, depends on us, on our efforts, on our rectitude, on our awareness. It cannot descend from heaven; it cannot come in a mechanical fashion; it inheres in our intellect and morality. This path, therefore, is mandatory on us.

To oppose the current is, in our condition, the only criterion which distinguishes between truth and falsehood, between earnestness and make-believe. When we find ourselves ready to oppose the current, then will words, deeds, programs, and everything else become secondary, and the only tangible existing thing on which we can rely will be that we can find some who are ready to assume the responsibility and to go in a direction contrary to the existing situation in the Arab countries. Then, gradually, will come into existence and germinate the necessary virtues necessary to continue on this road and to build anew at the end of it. *Revolution is the opposition of truth to the existing situation,* because the nation has a truth in spite of its backwardness and mutilation, and this truth proclaims itself, however masterful the existing conditions. *Revolution is this proclamation, this assertion of the existence of truth. Revolution is the opposition of the future to the present,* because our aims, drawn from our depths and from our soul, have shone forth and have sped on to outdistance us, in order to beckon us on and to speed us on toward themselves; this is the future. Revolution, then, is the opposition of this future, which is the truth of ourselves and our aims, to the counterfeit present, to the present which is alien to our truth.

Brethren: the past is a real thing, and well established in the life of the nation. It would be in vain, it would show error and sterility of thought, to deny this eternal truth. We mean by the past that period of time when the Arab soul was realizing itself. What can we mean by the future, and what can this future be which beckons us on and drives us to struggle, if not that period of time in which our true soul is realized?

Our past, then, understood in this pure and true sense, we have stationed in the vanguard, a light to show us the way. We have not left it behind in order that we may bemoan the period when it existed and call upon it to help us while, passively immobile, we await its coming and expect it to descend to our present level. This is not the past. The past, considered as the reality of the Arab spirit, as the self-realizing reality of the Arab spirit, cannot come, cannot come back and come down and descend; rather, we must march toward it, onward in a progressive spirit. We must ascend to it, raise ourselves up to its level. We must walk a difficult and tiring road until we can grow in ourselves the virtues, the talents, and the capacities which will make us fit to understand it, to intermix and join up with it.

The progressive march, then, the ascendant march on the road of the revolution, is the only possible means for us to join up with our past, and this joining up cannot but be an ascent. It cannot be a descent or a degeneration; it cannot be immobility or persistence in immobility and passivity.

Side by side with this view of the past which places it in a distant future to evoke our energies in order to ascend and reach up to it after a struggle, and to deserve it nobly, there is the other view which reflects the black, ugly, heavy shadows of the present on that past. This, in consequence, is understood as a clinging to the present and an obstinate stand for preserving it and for sinking deeper into its faults and vices. How, then, can such a past provide spiritual release, an inventive intellect, upright and independent behavior, or a living and overflowing faith?

To hold on to existing conditions, to preserve them, to defend these conditions which threaten the Arabs with extinction; such is the past, it is [also] the present, the vitiated reality, the selfishness, and the servitude to material interests. As for the true past, it is our yearning for it which leads us to strive and work, to struggle and ascend. This is the free, spiritual, healthy past which the Arabs had. Such a past was an epoch in which the spirit was realized; that is, it was, itself, a revolution in which the intellect attained freedom and independence and youthfulness of feeling for life and the world; it innovated, organized, and was in harmony with the laws of life and nature. The human personality realized in it freedom, individuality, earnestness, and responsibility, and went on to engage in free actions, to take up heroic stands, to transcend the limits of egoism, to harmonize with the general will and with the whole. Then the spirit reached its pure source and was filled with fertility and renewal; it knew its eternal destiny and was filled with faith.

Our past was a revolution, and we will never reach its level or meet with it except through revolution. The new revolution, then, is a march, full of sharp awareness and of faith, toward those heights where contradictions are resolved and opposites are united, 247 *where the past meets the future and the nation is reconciled to itself in its creativity and in the accomplishment of its mission.*

They ask us, Brethren, what do you mean by the mission, *the eternal Arab mission?* The Arab mission does not consist in words which we proclaim, it does not consist in principles to be incorporated in programs, it does not constitute matter for legislation. All these are dead, counterfeit things, because between us and the time when we may legislate out of the inspiration of our spirit and mission, there is a long distance and a high barrier. What, then, is this mission today?

It is our life itself, *it is to agree to experience this life with a deep and true experience, great and massive in proportion to the greatness of the Arab nation, in proportion to the depth of suffering undergone by the Arabs, in proportion to the great dangers which threaten its continued existence. This living and true experience will bring us back to ourselves, to our living realities; it will make us shoulder our responsibilities and will set us on the true path* in order that we may fight these diseases and these obstacles, these counterfeit conditions, in order to fight social injustice, class exploitation, and the eras of selfishness, bribery, and exploitation, in order to combat tyranny, the falsification of the popular will, and the insults to the dignity of the Arab as a citizen and a man; *for the sake of a free society in which every Arab will regain consciousness of himself, of his existence, his dignity, his thinking, and his responsibilities.* The experience in which our struggle takes place is that of the Arab nation dismembered into different countries and statelets, artificial and counterfeit; we struggle until we can reunite these scattered members, until we may reach a wholesome and natural state in which no severed member can speak in the name of all, until we can get rid of this strange and anomalous state. Then will it be possible for the Arabs to unite, for their spirit to be upstanding, their ideas clear, their morality upright; then will there be scope for their minds to create, for they will have become that wholesome natural entity, one nation. This wholesome and true experience, struggling against the existing conditions until we return to the right state, such is the Arab mission. A mission is what one part of the humanity presents to the whole of humanity. Nothing narrow or selfish may be called a mission; a mission has to have comprehensive, eternal, human significance. You may inquire what this mission will be like in

248

tackling our problems. I would say to you that when the Arabs embark on this experience—and in reality they have already embarked on it, and will not go back—then such an experience will not only solve their problems, but they will emerge from it with a deep human experience which will create in them a personality instinct with the sufferings of human life, the knowledge of its secrets, the cure for its ills, and they will then present to the world and to humanity the fruit of this eternally memorable experience.

Bibliography

I—WESTERN PUBLICATIONS

Adams, C. C. *Islam and Modernism in Egypt.* London, 1933.
Antonius, G. *The Arab Awakening.* London, 1938.
Azoury, Negib. *Le Réveil de la Nation Arabe dans l'Asie Turque en Présence des Intérêts et des Rivalités des Puissances Étrangères, de la Curie Romaine et du Patriarcat Oecuménique.* Paris, 1905.
Binder, L. "Radical Reform Nationalism in Syria and Egypt," *The Muslim World,* XLIX (1959), nos. 2, 3.
Colombe, M. "L'Egypte et les Origines du Nationalisme Arabe," *L'Afrique et l'Asie,* no. 14 (1951).
"Documents sur les origines de la Ligue des Etats Arabes," *Orient,* no. 14 (1960), pp. 177–216.
G. "Textes Historiques sur le Réveil Arabe au Hedjaz," *Revue du Monde Musulman,* XLVI, XLVII (1921); L (1922), LVII (1924).
Haim, S. G. "The Arab Awakening—A Source for the Historian?" *Die Welt des Islams,* n.s., II (1953).
———. "Alfieri and al-Kawakibi," *Oriente Moderno,* XXXIV (1954).
———. "Blunt and al-Kawakibi," *Oriente Moderno,* XXXV (1955).
———. "Intorno all'Origine della Teoria del Panarabismo," *Oriente Moderno,* XXXVI (1956).
———. "Islam and the Theory of Arab Nationalism," in *The Middle East in Transition,* ed. W. Z. Laqueur. London, 1958.
Hartmann, R. "Islam und Nationalismus," *Abhandlungen der Deutschen Akademie der Wissenschaften zu Berlin, Jahrgang 1945–46.* Philosophisch-historische Klasse, nr. 5. Berlin, 1948.
Hendessi, Mehdi. "Pages peu connues de Djamal al-Din al-Afghani," *Orient,* no. 6 (1958).
Jovelet, L. "L'Évolution Sociale et Politique des 'Pays Arabes' (1930–1933)," *Revue des Études Islamiques,* VII (1933).
Jung, E. *La Révolte Arabe (1906–1924).* Paris, 1924, 1925. 2 vols.
Kedourie, E. *England and the Middle East—The Destruction of the Ottoman Empire 1914–1921.* London, 1956.

Bibliography

————. "Panarabism and British Policy," in *The Middle East in Transition*, ed. W. Z. Laqueur. London, 1958.

————. "Religion and Politics—The Diaries of Khalil Sakakini," *St. Antony's Papers*, No. IV (1958).

Khairallah, K. T. *Le Problème du Levant. "Les Régions Arabes Libérées" Syrie-Irak-Liban. Lettre ouverte a la Société des Nations.* Paris, 1919.

Lewis, Bernard. *The Emergence of Modern Turkey.* London, 1961.

Malik, C. "The Near East: The Search for Truth," *Foreign Affairs*, 30 (Jan., 1952).

Montagne, R. "L'Union Arabe," in *Politique Etrangère*. Paris, 1946.

Nune, E. "L'Idea dell'Unità Araba in Recenti Debattiti della Stampa del Vicino Oriente," *Oriente Moderno*, XVIII (1938).

Nuseibeh, H. Z. *The Ideas of Arab Nationalism.* Ithaca, 1956.

Rabbath, E. *Unité Syrienne et Devenir Arabe.* Paris, 1937.

Rossi, E. *Documenti sull'Origine e gli Sviluppi della Questioni Araba 1875–1944.* Rome, 1944.

————. "Una Traduzione Turca dell'Opera della Tirrannide di V. Alfieri Probabilmente Conosciuta da al-Kawakibi," *Oriente Moderno*, XXXIV (1954).

Smith, W. Cantwell. *Islam in Modern History.* Princeton, 1957.

Snouck Hurgronje, C. "L'Islam et le Problème des Races," *Revue du Monde Musulman*, L (1922).

Steppat, F. "Islam und Nationalismus bei Mustafa Kamil," *Die Welt des Islams*, n.s., IV (1956).

Zeine, Z. N. *Arab-Turkish Relations and the Emergence of Arab Nationalism.* Beirut, 1958.

Ziadeh, N. A. "Recent Arabic Literature on Arabism," *The Middle East Journal*, 6 (1952).

Zurayk, C. K. (Qustantin Zuraiq). "The Essence of Arab Civilization," *The Middle East Journal*, 3 (1949).

II—PUBLICATIONS IN ARABIC

Abd al-Aziz al-Duri. "Mustaqbal al-alam al-arabi" ("The Future of the Arab World"), *al-Abhath* (Beirut), V (1952). A comment by N. Ziadeh follows immediately after the article.

————. *al-Judhur al-tarikhiyya li'l-qaumiyya al-arabiyya (The Historical Origins of Arab Nationalism).* Beirut, 1960.

Abd al-Latif Sharara, *F'il-qaumiyya al-arabiyya (On Arab Nationalism).* Beirut, 1957.

Abd al-Rahman Azzam. *Al-Jami'a al-arabiyya wa'l-wahda al-alamiyya (The Arab League and World Unity).* Cairo, 1946.

————. "al-Wahda al-arabiyya" ("Arab Unity"), *al-Hilal* (Cairo, Sept.-Oct., 1943).

Bibliography

Abd al-Rahman al-Bazzaz. *Al-Islam wa'l-qaumiyya al-arabiyya* (*Islam and Arab Nationalism*). Baghdad, 1952.

——. *Min ruh al-islam* (*From the Spirit of Islam*). Baghdad, 1959.

Abd al-Rahman al-Kawakibi. *Tabai' al-istibdad* (*The Characteristics of Tyranny*). Cairo, n.d.

——. *Umm al-qura*. Cairo, 1931.

Abdullah al-Alayili. *Dustur al-arab al-qaumi* (*The National Constitution of the Arabs*). 1st ed. Beirut, 1941.

Ahmad Qadri. *Mukhakkirati an al-thaura al-arabiyya al-kubra* (*My Memoirs of the Great Arab Revolt*). Damascus, 1956.

Ali Fahmi Kamil. *Mustafa Kamil Pasha fi arba' wa thalathin rabi'* (*Thirty-four Years of Mustafa Kamil's Life*), Cairo, 1908–1911. 9 vols.

——. *Rasa'il misriyya faransiyya* (*Franco-Egyptian Letters*). Cairo, 1909. Letters from Mustafa Kamil to Mme. Juliette Adam. The volume contains both an Arabic and an English version of the letters.

Ali Nasir al-Din. *Qadiyyat al-arab* (*The Cause of the Arabs*). Beirut, 1946.

Amin Sa'id. *al-Thaura al-arabiyya al-kubra* (*The Great Arab Revolt*). Cairo, 1934.

Anis Fraiha. "Mafhum al-dimuqratiyya inda'l-arab" ("The Concept of Democracy among the Arabs"), *al-Abhath*, IV (1951).

Anis al-Maqdisi. *al-'Awamil al-fa'ala fi'l-adab al-arabi al-hadith* (*Vital Forces in Modern Arabic Literature*). Cairo, 1939.

Anis Sayigh. *al-Fikra al-arabiyya fi Misr* (*The Arab Idea in Egypt*). Beirut, 1959.

Arab League. *Jam'iyat al-duwal al-arabiyya—mithaquha wa nubdha tarikhiyya anha* (*The League of Arab States—Its Charter together with a Short Historical Account*). Cairo, 1947.

Arab League, Cultural Department of. *al-Alam al-arabi* (*The Arab World*), ed. Ahmad Amin. Vol. I. Cairo, 1949.

al-Arab wa'l-Islam fi'l-asr al-hadith (*Arabs and Islam in the Modern Age*). Special issue of *al-Hilal*. (Cairo, April, 1939).

Faisal I, King of Iraq. *Faisal ibn al-Husain fi aqwalihi wa khitabihi* (*Faisal ibn al-Husain in His Sayings and Speeches*). Baghdad, 1945.

Gamal Abdel Nasser. See Jamal Abd al-Nasir.

al-Hizb al-suri al-qaumi al-ijtima'i (usually trans. as Parti Populaire Syrien). *Ila al-nayuraj'iyyin al-urubiyyin* (*To the Arabizing Neo-Reactionaries*). Beirut, 1949.

Jamal Abd al-Nasir (Gamal Abdel-Nasser). *Falsafat al-thaura* (*The Philosophy of the Revolution*). Cairo, 1952. This book is translated into many Western languages; a current English translation is the one published in New York: Economica Books, 1959.

Jamal al-Din al-Afghani. *al-Urwa al-wuthqa* (*The Indissoluble Link*). 3d ed. Beirut, 1933.

Michel Aflaq. *Dhikra al-rasul al-arabi* (*The Anniversary of the Birth of*

Bibliography

the Arabian Prophet). 2d ed. Damascus, 1943. Also included in Fi sabil al-ba'th, Beirut, 1959.
————. Fi sabil al-ba'th (Toward the Ba'th). 3d ed. Damascus, 1954. Contains some material not included in the larger volume of the same title published in Beirut in 1959.
————. Fi sabil al-ba'th (Toward the Ba'th). Beirut, 1959.
Muhammad Jamil Baihum, al-Uruba wa'l-shu'ubiyyat al-haditha (Arabism and Modern shu'ubiyyas). Beirut, 1958.
Muhammad al-Makhzumi. Khatirat Jamal al-Din al-Afghani (The Opinions of Jamal al-Din al-Afghani). Beirut, 1931.
Muhammad Rashid Rida. "Madaniyyat al-arab" ("The Civilization of the Arabs"), al-Manar, III (Cairo, 1900), 289–294, 319–322, 385–391, 409–414, 529–533.
————. "al-Mas'ala al-arabiyya" ("The Arab Question"), al-Manar, XX (1917), 33–47.
————. "al-Turk wa'l-arab" ("The Turks and the Arabs"), al-Manar, III (Cairo, 1900), 169–172, 193–198.
Muhibb al-Din al-Khatib. al-Muntaqa min muhadarat jam'iyyat al-muslimin (Selections from the Lectures of the Young Men's Muslim Association). Cairo, 1930–1931. 2 vols.
Musa al-Alami. Ibrat filastin (The Lesson of Palestine). Beirut, 1949.
Mu'tamar al-tullab al-arab fi uruppa (Conference of the Arab Students in Europe, held in Brussels, Dec. 27–29, 1938). al-Qaumiyya al-arabiyya—haqiqatuha—ahdafuha—wasa'iluha (Arab Nationalism—The Truth about It—Its Aims—Its Means). Beirut, n.d.
Mu'tamar al-tullab al-arab fi London fi 1946 (Conference of the Arab Students in London held in 1946). Report. Beirut, n.d.
Nabih Amin Faris. "al-Arab fi'l-qarn al-ishrin" ("The Arabs in the Twentieth Century"), al-Abhath, IV (1951).
————. Ghuyum arabiyya (Arab Clouds). Beirut, 1950.
————. "Ghuyum fi sama' al-arab" ("Clouds in the Arab Sky"), al-Abhath, I (1948).
Nadi al-ba'th al-arabi (The Club of the Arab Ba'th). al-Mithaq al-qaumi al-arabi (The Arab National Pact). Baghdad, 1951.
Niqula Ziyada (N. A. Ziadeh). al-Uruba fi mizan al-qaumiyya (Arabism in the Balance of Nationalism). Beirut, 1950.
Qadri Hafiz Tuqan. Ba'd al-nakba (After the Disaster). Beirut, 1950.
Qustantin Zuraiq (C. K. Zurayk). "al-Hidara al-arabiyya" ("Arab Civilization"), al-Abhath, II (1949).
————. al-Wa'i al-qaumi (National Consciousness). Beirut, 1949.
————. "Wajibat al mufakkir al-arabi fi'l-waqt al-hadir" ("The Duties of the Arab Thinker Today"), al-Abhath, I (1948).
Rafiq al-Azm. Majmu'at athar Rafiq Bey al-Azm (Literary Remains of Rafiq Bey al-Azm). Cairo, 1926. 2 vols. Preface by Muhammad Rashid Rida.
Ra'if al-Khuri. Ma'alim al-wa'i al-qaumi (Characteristics of National Consciousness). Beirut, 1941.
254 Salah al-Din al-Baitar & Michel Aflaq. al-Qaumiyya al-arabiyya wa

mauqafuha min al-shuyu'iyya (*Arab Nationalism and Its Attitude toward Communism*). Damascus, 1944.

Sami al-Khuri. *Radd 'ala Sati' al-Husri* (*Reply to Sati' al-Husri*). Beirut, 1956.

Sami Shawkat. *Hadhihi ahdafuna* (*These Are Our Aims*). Baghdad, 1939.

Sati' al-Husri. *Ara' wa ahadith fi'l-qaumiyya al-arabiyya* (*Views and Addresses on Arab Nationalism*). Cairo, 1951.

———. *Ara' wa ahadith fi'l-wataniyya wa'l-qaumiyya* (*Views and Addresses on Patriotism and Nationalism*). Cairo, 1944.

———. *Difa' 'an al-uruba* (*Defense of Arabism*). Beirut, 1956.

———. *Ma hiya al-qaumiyya* (*What Is Nationalism?*). Beirut, 1959.

———. *Muhadarat fi nushu' al-fikra al-qaumiyya* (*Lectures on the Origins of the Nationalist Idea*). Cairo, 1951.

———. *Safahat mina'l-madi al-qarib* (*Pages from the Recent Past*). Beirut, 1948.

———. *al-Uruba awwalan* (*Arabism First*). Beirut, 1955.

———. *al-Uruba bain du'atiha wa mu'aridiha* (*Arabism between its Protagonists and Opponents*). Beirut, 1957.

Shakib Arslan. *al-Wahda al-arabiyya* (*Arab Unity*). Damascus, 1937.

Sulaiman Faidi. *Fi ghamrat al-nidal* (*In the Midst of the Struggle*). Baghdad, 1952.

Taha Husain. "al-Udaba' hum bunat al-qaumiyya al-arabiyya" ("Writers Are the Builders of Arab Nationalism"), *al-Adab* (Beirut, Jan., 1958).